Experimentation in Software Engineering

T0192036

Claes Wohlin • Per Runeson
Martin Höst • Magnus C. Ohlsson
Björn Regnell • Anders Wesslén

Experimentation in Software Engineering

 Springer

Claes Wohlin
School of Computing
Blekinge Institute of Technology
Karlskrona, Sweden

Per Runeson
Department of Computer Science
Lund University
Lund, Sweden

Martin Höst
Department of Computer Science
Lund University
Lund, Sweden

Magnus C. Ohlsson
System Verification Sweden AB
Malmö, Sweden

Björn Regnell
Department of Computer Science
Lund University
Lund, Sweden

Anders Wesslén
ST-Ericsson AB
Lund, Sweden

ISBN 978-3-642-43226-2   ISBN 978-3-642-29044-2 (eBook)
DOI 10.1007/978-3-642-29044-2
Springer Heidelberg New York Dordrecht London

ACM Codes: D.2

Foreword

Experimentation is fundamental to any scientific and engineering endeavor.

Understanding a discipline involves building models of the various elements of the discipline, e.g., the objects in the domain, the processes used to manipulate those objects, the relationship between the processes and the objects. Evolving domain knowledge implies the evolution of those models by testing them via experiments of various forms. Analyzing the results of the experiment involves learning, the encapsulation of knowledge and the ability to change and refine our models over time. Therefore, our understanding of a discipline evolves over time.

This is the paradigm that has been used in many fields, e.g., physics, medicine, manufacturing. These fields evolved as disciplines when they began applying the cycle of model building, experimenting, and learning. Each field began with recording observations and evolved to manipulating the model variables and studying the effects of changes in those variables. The fields differ in their nature, what constitutes the basic objects of the field, the properties of those objects, the properties of the system that contain them, the relationship of the objects to the system, and the culture of the discipline. These differences affect how the models are built and how experimentation gets done.

Like other science and engineering disciplines, software engineering requires the cycle of model building, experimentation, and learning. The study of software engineering is a laboratory science. The players in the discipline are the researchers and the practitioners. The researcher's role is to understand the nature of the object (products), the processes that create and manipulate them, and the relationship between the two in the context of the system. The practitioner's role is to build 'improved' systems, using the knowledge available to date. These roles are symbiotic. The researcher needs laboratories to study the problems faced by practitioners and develop and evolve solutions based upon experimentation. The practitioner needs to understand how to build better systems and the researcher can provide models to help.

In developing models and experimenting, both the researcher and the practitioner need to understand the nature of the discipline of software engineering. All software is not the same: there are a large number of variables that cause differences and their effects need to be understood. Like medicine where the variation in human genetics and medical history is often a major factor in the development of the models and the interpretation of the experiment's results, software engineering deals with differing contexts that affect the input and the results. In software engineering the technologies are mostly human intensive rather than automated. Like manufacturing the major problem is understanding and improving the relationship between processes and the products they create. But unlike manufacturing, the process in software engineering is development not production. So we cannot collect data from exact repetitions of the same process. We have to build our models at a higher level of abstraction but still take care to identify the context variables.

Currently, there is an insufficient set of models that allow us to reason about the discipline, a lack of recognition of the limits of technologies for certain contexts, and insufficient analysis and experimentation going on but this latter situation is improving as evidenced by this textbook.

This book is a landmark in allowing us to train both the researcher and practitioner in software engineering experimentation. It is a major contribution to the field. The authors have accumulated an incredible collection of knowledge and packaged it in an excellent way, providing a process for scoping, planning, running, analyzing and interpreting, and packaging experiments. They cover all necessary topics from threats to validity to statistical procedures.

It is well written and covers a wide range of information necessary for performing experiments in software engineering. When I began doing experiments, I had to find various sources of information, almost always from other disciplines, and adapt them to my needs as best I could. If I had this book to help me, it would have saved me an enormous amount of time and effort and my experiments would probably have been better.

Professor Victor R. Basili

Foreword

I am honored to be asked to write a foreword for this revision of the authors' book with the same title that was published in 2000. I have used the original edition since its publication as a teacher and a researcher. Students in my courses at Colorado State University, Washington State University, University of Denver, and Universitaet Wuerzburg have used the book over the years. Some were full-time employees at major companies working on graduate degrees in Systems Engineering, others full-time Masters and Ph.D. students. The book worked well for them. Besides the treatment of experimental software engineering methods, they liked its conciseness. I am delighted to see that the revised version is as compact and easy to work with as the first.

The additions and modifications in this revised version very nicely reflect the maturation of the field of empirical software engineering since the book was originally published: the increased importance of replication and synthesis of experiments, and the need of academics and professionals to successfully transfer new technology based on convincing quantitative evidence. Another important improvement concerns the expanded treatment of ethical issues in software engineering experimentation. Especially since no formal code of ethics exists in this field, it is vitally important that students are made aware of such issues and have access to guidelines how to deal with them.

The original edition of this book emphasized experiments. In industry, however, case studies tend to be more common to evaluate technology, software engineering processes, or artifacts. Hence the addition of a chapter on case studies is much needed and welcomed. So is the chapter on systematic literature reviews.

Having taught a popular quantitative software engineering course with the original edition for a dozen years, this revised version with its additions and updates provides many of the materials I have added separately over the years. Even better, it does so without losing the original edition's compactness and conciseness. I, for one, am thrilled with this revised version and will continue to use it as a text in my courses and a resource for my student researchers.

Professor Anneliese Amschler Andrews

Foreword from Original Edition

It is my belief that software engineers not only need to know software engineering methods and processes, but that they also should know how to assess them. Consequently, I have taught principles of experimentation and empirical studies as part of the software engineering curriculum. Until now, this meant selecting a text from another discipline, usually psychology, and augmenting it with journal or conference papers that provide students with software engineering examples of experiments and empirical studies.

This book fills an important gap in the software engineering literature: it provides a concise, comprehensive look at an important aspect of software engineering: experimental analysis of how well software engineering methods, methodologies, and processes work. Since all of these change so rapidly in our field, it is important to know how to evaluate new ones. This book teaches how to go about doing this and thus is valuable not only for the software engineering student, but also for the practicing software engineering professional who will be able to

- Evaluate software engineering techniques.
- Determine the value (or lack thereof) of claims made about a software engineering method or process in published studies.

Finally, this book serves as a valuable resource for the software engineering researcher.

Professor Anneliese Amschler Andrews (formerly von Mayrhauser)

Preface

Have you ever had a need to evaluate software engineering methods or techniques against each other? This book presents experimentation as one way of evaluating new methods and techniques in software engineering. Experiments are valuable tools for all software engineers who are involved in evaluating and choosing between different methods, techniques, languages and tools.

It may be that you are a software practitioner, who wants to evaluate methods and techniques before introducing them into your organization. You may also be a researcher, who wants to evaluate new research results against something existing, in order to get a scientific foundation for your new ideas. You may be a teacher, who believes that knowledge of empirical studies in software engineering is essential to your students. Finally, you may be a student in software engineering who wants to learn some methods to turn software engineering into a scientific discipline and to obtain quantitative data when comparing different methods and techniques. This book provides guidelines and examples of how you should proceed to succeed in your mission.

Software Engineering and Science

The term "software engineering" was coined in 1968, and the area is still maturing. Software engineering has over the years been driven by technology development and advocacy research. The latter referring to that we have invented and introduced new methods and techniques over the years based on marketing and conviction rather than scientific results. To some extent, it is understandable with the pace the information society has established itself during the last couple of decades. It is, however, not acceptable in the long run if we want to have control of the software we develop. Control comes from being able to evaluate new methods, techniques, languages and tools before using them. Moreover, this would help us turn software engineering into a scientific discipline. Before looking at the issues we must address to turn software engineering into science, let us look at the way science is viewed in other areas.

In "Fermat's Last Theorem" by Dr. Simon Singh, [160], science is discussed. The essence of the discussion can be summarized as follows. In science, physical phenomena are addressed by putting forward hypotheses. The phenomenon is observed and if the observations are in line with the hypothesis, this becomes evidence for the hypothesis. The intention is also that the hypothesis should enable prediction of other phenomena. Experiments are important to test the hypothesis and in particular the predictive ability of the hypothesis. If the new experiments support the hypothesis, then we have more evidence in favor of the hypothesis. As the evidence grows and becomes strong, the hypothesis can be accepted as a scientific theory.

The summary is basically aiming at hypothesis testing through empirical research. This may not be the way most research is conducted in software engineering today. However, the need to evaluate and validate new research proposals by conducting empirical studies is acknowledged to a higher degree today than 10 years ago. Empirical studies include surveys, experiments and case studies. Thus, the objective of this book is to introduce and promote the use of empirical studies in software engineering with a particular emphasis on experimentation.

Purpose

The purpose of the book is to introduce students, teachers, researchers, and practitioners to experimentation and empirical evaluation with a focus on software engineering. The objective is in particular to provide guidelines of how to perform experiments to evaluate methods, techniques and tools in software engineering, although short introductions are provided also for other empirical approaches. The introduction into experimentation is provided through a process perspective. The focus is on the steps that we have to go through to perform an experiment. The process can be generalized to other types of empirical studies, but the main focus here is on experiments and quasi-experiments.

The motivation for the book comes from the need of support we experienced when turning our software engineering research more experimental. Several books are available which either treat the subject in very general terms or focus on some specific part of experimentation; most of them focusing on the statistical methods in experimentation. These are important, but there is a lack of books elaborating on experimentation from a process perspective. Moreover, there are few books addressing experimentation in software engineering in particular, and actually no book at all when the original edition of this book was published.

Scope

The scope of the book is primarily experiments in software engineering as a means for evaluating methods, techniques etc. The book provides some information regarding empirical studies in general, including case studies, systematic literature reviews and surveys. The intention is to provide a brief understanding of these strategies and in particular to relate them to experimentation.

The chapters of the book cover different steps to go through to perform experiments in software engineering. Moreover, examples of empirical studies related to software engineering are provided throughout the book. It is of particular importance to illustrate for software engineers that empirical studies and experimentation can be practiced successfully in software engineering. Two examples of experiments are included in the book. These are introduced to illustrate the experiment process and to exemplify how software engineering experiments can be reported. The intention is that these studies should work as good examples and sources of inspiration for further empirical work in software engineering. The book is mainly focused on experiments, but it should be remembered that other strategies are also available, for example, case studies and surveys. In other words, we do not have to resort to advocacy research and marketing without quantitative data when research strategies as, for example, experiments are available.

Target Audience

The target audience of the book can be divided into four categories.

Students may use the book as an introduction to experimentation in software engineering with a particular focus on evaluation. The book is suitable as a course book in undergraduate or graduate studies where the need for empirical studies in software engineering is stressed. Exercises and project assignments are included in the book to combine the more theoretical material with some practical aspects.

Teachers may use the book in their classes if they believe in the need of making software engineering more empirical. The book is suitable as an introduction to the area. It should be fairly self-contained, although an introductory course in statistics is recommended.

Researchers may use the book to learn more about how to conduct empirical studies and use them as one important ingredient in their research. Moreover, the objective is that it should be fruitful to come back to the book and use it as a checklist when performing empirical research.

Practitioners may use the book as a "cookbook" when evaluating some new methods or techniques before introducing them into their organization. Practitioners are expected to learn how to use empirical studies in their daily work when changing, for example, the development process in the organization they are working.

Outline

The book is divided into three main parts. The outline of the book is summarized in Table 1, which also shows a mapping to the original edition of this book. The first part provides a general introduction to the area of empirical studies in Chap. 1. It puts empirical studies in general and experiments in particular into a software engineering context. In Chap. 2, empirical strategies (surveys, case studies and experiments) are discussed in general and the context of empirical studies is elaborated, in particular from a software engineering perspective. Chapter 3 provides a brief introduction to measurement theory and practice. In Chap. 4 we provide an overview of how to conduct systematic literature reviews, to synthesize findings from several empirical studies. Chapter 5 gives an overview of the case studies as a related type of empirical studies. In Chap. 6, the focus is set on experimentation by introducing general experiment process.

Part II has one chapter for each experiment step. Chapter 7 discusses how set the scope for an experiment, and Chap. 8 focuses on the planning phase. Operation of the experiment is discussed in Chaps. 9 and 10 presents some methods for analyzing and interpreting the results. Chapter 11 discusses presentation and packaging of the experiment.

Part III contains two example experiments. In Chap. 12, an example is presented where the main objective is to illustrate the experiment process, and the example in Chap. 13 is used to illustrate how an experiment in software engineering may be reported in a paper.

Some exercises and data are presented in Appendix A. Finally, the book displays some statistical tables in Appendix B. The tables are primarily included to provide support for some of the examples in the book. More comprehensive tables are available in most statistics books.

Exercises

The exercises are divided into four categories, the first presented at the end of each chapter in Parts I and II of the book (Chaps. 1–11), and the other three in Appendix A:

Understanding. Five questions capturing the most important points are provided at the end of each chapter. The objective is to ensure that the reader has understood the most important concepts.

Training. These exercises provide an opportunity to practice experimentation. The exercises are particularly targeted towards analyzing data and answering questions in relation to an experiment.

Reviewing. This exercise is aimed at the examples of experiments presented in Chaps. 12–13. The objective is to give an opportunity to review some presented experiments. After having read several experiments presented in the literature, it is

Table 1 Structure of the book

Subject	Revised version	Original edition	Major updates
Part I. Background			
Introduction	1	1	
Empirical Strategies	2	2	New sections on replication, synthesis, technology transfer and ethics
Measurement	3	3	New section on measurement in practice
Systematic Literature Reviews	4	10[a]	New chapter
Case Studies	5		New chapter
Experiment Process	6	4	
Part II. Steps in the Experiment Process			New running example
Scoping	7	5[b]	Adapted terminology
Planning	8	6	
Operation	9	7	
Analysis and Interpretation	10	8	
Presentation and Package	11	9	Major revision
Part III. Example Experiments			
Experiment Process Illustration	12	11	
Are the Perspectives Really Different?	13		New chapter
Appendices			
Exercises	A	13	Understanding exercises moved to each chapter
Statistical Tables	B	A	

[a] Entitled Survey, and with a different scope
[b] Entitled Definition

clear that most experiments suffer from some problems. This is mostly due to the inherit problems of performing experimentation in software engineering. Instead of promoting criticism of work by others, we have provided some examples of studies that we have conducted ourselves. They are, in our opinion, representative of the type of experiments that are published in the literature. This includes that they have their strengths and weaknesses.

Assignments. The objective of these exercises is to illustrate how experiments can be used in evaluation. These assignments are examples of studies that can be carried out within a course, either at a university or in industry. They are deliberately aimed at problems that can be addressed by fairly simple experiments. The assignments can either be done after reading the book or one of the assignments can be carried out as the book is read. The latter provides an opportunity to practice while reading the chapters. As an alternative, we would like to recommend teachers to formulate an assignment, within their area of expertise, that can be used throughout the book to exemplify the concepts presented in each chapter.

Acknowledgements

This book is based on "Experimentation in Software Engineering: An Introduction", which was published in year 2000. This new version is both a revision and an extension of the former book. We have revised parts of the book, but also added new material, for example, concerning systematic literature reviews and case study research.

A book is almost never just an achievement by the authors. Support and help from several persons including families, friends, colleagues, international researchers in the field and funding organizations are often prerequisite for a new book. This book is certainly no exception. In particular, we would like to express our sincere gratitude to the readers of "Experimentation in Software Engineering: An Introduction". Your use of the book has been a great source of inspiration and a motivation to publish the current version. In particular, we would like to thank Mr. Alan Kelon Oliveira de Moraes, Universidade Federal de Pernambuco, Brazil for sending the email that actually triggered the revision of the book. Furthermore, we would like to thank the following individuals for having contributed to the book.

First, we would like to thank the first main external user of the book Prof. Giuseppe Visaggio, University of Bari in Italy for adopting a draft of this book in one of his courses, and for providing valuable feedback. We would also like to express our gratitude to Prof. Anneliese Andrews, Denver University, USA and Dr. Khaled El Emam, University of Ottawa, Canada for encouraging us to publish the book in the first place and for valuable comments. We also would like to thank Dr. Lionel Briand, University of Luxembourg, Luxembourg; Dr. Christian Bunse, University of Mannheim, Germany and Dr. John Daly formerly at Fraunhofer Institute for Experimental Software Engineering, Kaiserslautern, Germany for providing the data for the example on object-oriented design. Our thanks also to Dr. Thomas Thelin for allowing us to include an experiment he did together with two of the authors of the book.

Early drafts of the book was used and evaluated internally within the Software Engineering Research Group at Lund University. Thus, we would like to thank the members of the group for providing feedback on different drafts of the book. In particular, we would like to thank Dr. Lars Bratthall for taking the time to review the manuscript very thoroughly and providing valuable comments. We would also like to acknowledge the anonymous reviewers for their contribution to the book.

For the current version of the book, we have received valuable input and improvement proposals, and hence we would like to thank the following individuals for their valuable input: Prof. Anneliese Andrews, Denver University, USA; Prof. David Budgen, Durham University, UK; Prof. Barbara Kitchenham, Keele University, UK; Prof. Dieter Rombach and Moinul Islam, University of Kaiserslautern, Germany; Prof. Jürgen Börstler, Dr. Samuel Fricker and Dr. Richard Torkar, Blekinge Institute of Technology, Sweden. Thanks also to Mr. Jesper Runeson for work on the LATEXtransformation of the book.

In addition to the above individuals, we would also like to thank all members of ISERN (International Software Engineering Research Network) for interesting and enlightening discussion regarding empirical software engineering research in general.

For the chapter on case studies, we are grateful for the feedback to the checklists from the ISERN members and attendants of the International Advanced School of Empirical Software Engineering in September 2007. A special thank to Dr. Kim Weyns and Dr. Andreas Jedlitschka for their review of an early draft of the chapter.

Numerous research projects at Lund University and Blekinge Institute of Technology have over the years contributed to the book. Different grants have funded research projects where empirical studies have been a cornerstone, and hence helped shape our experience that we have tried to document through the book. This book is to some extent a result of all these research projects.

Prof. Claes Wohlin,
Prof. Per Runeson,
Prof. Martin Höst,
Dr. Magnus C. Ohlsson,
Prof. Björn Regnell, and
Dr. Anders Wesslén

Contents

Part II   Steps in the Experiment Process

Part I
Background

Chapter 1
Introduction

The information technology revolution has meant, among other things, that software has become a part of more and more products. Software is found in products ranging from toasters to space shuttles. This means that a vast amount of software has been and is being developed. Software development is by no means easy; it is a highly creative process. The rapid growth of the area has also meant that numerous software projects have run into problems in terms of missing functionality, cost overruns, missed deadlines and poor quality. These problems or challenges were identified already in the 1960s, and in 1968 the term "software engineering" was coined with the intention of creating an engineering discipline that focused on the development of software-intensive systems.

Software engineering is formally defined by IEEE [84] as *"software engineering means application of a systematic, disciplined, quantifiable approach to development, operation and maintenance of software"*. Software engineering in general is presented and discussed in books as, for example, by Sommerville [163], and Pfleeger and Atlee [134]. The objective here is to present how empirical studies and experiments in particular fit into a software engineering context. Three aspects in the definition above are of particular importance here. First, it implies a software process through pointing at different life cycle phases; secondly, it stresses the need for a systematic and disciplined approach; finally, it highlights the importance of quantification. The use of empirical studies is related to all three of them. The software engineering context is further discussed in Sect. 1.1. The need to turn software engineering more scientific and how empirical studies play an important role in this is discussed in Sect. 1.2.

1.1 Software Engineering Context

A software process model is used to describe the steps to take and the activities to perform when developing software. Examples of software process models are the waterfall model, incremental development, evolutionary development, the spiral

C. Wohlin et al., *Experimentation in Software Engineering*,
DOI 10.1007/978-3-642-29044-2_1, © Springer-Verlag Berlin Heidelberg 2012

Fig. 1.1 An illustration of
the software process

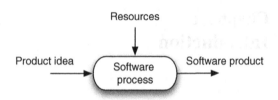

model and different agile approaches to software development. These and other
models are discussed in the general software engineering literature. A simplistic
view of the software process is shown in Fig. 1.1. It should be noted that the process
is crucial whether we work with development of a new product or maintenance of
an existing product.

In Fig. 1.1, an idea and resources, primarily in the form of people, are inputs to
the software process, and the people develop a software product going through the
different steps and performing the different activities in the software process.

The development of software products is many times a complex task. Software
projects may run over a long period of time and involve many people (even if using
agile methods), due to the complexity of the software products that are developed.
This implies that the software process often also becomes very complex. It consists
of many different activities and many documents are written before the final product
can be delivered. The complexity of the software process means that it is difficult to
optimize it or even find a good enough process. Thus, it is important for companies
to strive to improve their way of making business if they intend to stay competitive.
This means that most companies are continuously trying to improve their software
process in order to improve the products, lower the cost and so forth. The software
process stresses the need for a systematic and disciplined approach to working.
Being agile is not an exception, there is still a need to have structured approach
although agile methods stress the need to not document too much and emphasize
the need to have running code continuously instead of "only" at the end of a large
project. A systematic and disciplined approach is also needed when improving the
software process, and hence a way to improve process is needed.

An example of an improvement process tailored for software development is the
Quality Improvement Paradigm (QIP), defined by Basili [7]. It consists of several
steps to support a systematic and disciplined approach to improvement. The QIP is
presented briefly in Sect. 2.9.2. A more general improvement process is the well-
known Plan/Do/Study/Act cycle [23, 42]. The improvement processes include two
activities, although the same terminology is not always used, that we would like to
highlight:

- Assessment of the software process.
- Evaluation of a software process improvement proposal.

The assessment is conducted to identify suitable areas for improvement. Several
models exist for assessing the software process. The most well known is probably the Capability Maturity Model (CMM) from Software Engineering Institute

at Carnegie-Mellon University, USA [33, 130]. The assessment models help in pinpointing where improvements are needed. CMM has five maturity levels with so called key process areas on each level. It is recommended that companies focus on improvement areas according to their maturity level.

Assuming that it is possible to identify areas for improvement through some form of assessment, the next step is to determine how these areas of improvement may be addressed to cope with the identified problems. For example, if too many defects are found in system testing, it may be possible to improve earlier testing, inspections or even specific parts in the development, for example, software design. The objective is that the assessment of the current situation and knowledge about the state-of-the-art should result in that concrete process improvement proposals can be identified. When the improvement proposals have been identified, it is necessary to determine which to introduce, if any. It is often not possible just to change the existing software process without having more information about the actual effect of the improvement proposal. In other words, it is necessary to evaluate the proposals before making any major changes.

One problem that arises is that a process improvement proposal is very hard to evaluate without direct human involvement. For a product, it is possible to first build a prototype to evaluate whether it is something to work further with. For a process, it is not possible to build a prototype. It is possible to make simulations and compare different processes, but it should be remembered that this is still an evaluation that is based on a model. The only real evaluation of a process or process improvement proposal is to have people using it, since the process is just a description until it is used by people. Empirical studies are crucial to the evaluation of processes and human-based activities. It is also beneficial to use empirical studies when there is a need to evaluate the use of software products or tools. Experimentation provides a systematic, disciplined, quantifiable and controlled way of evaluating human-based activities. This is one of the main reasons why empirical research is common in social and behavioral sciences, see for example Robson [144].

In addition, empirical studies and experiments in particular are also important for researchers in software engineering. New methods, techniques, languages and tools should not just be suggested, published and marketed. It is crucial to evaluate new inventions and proposals in comparison with existing ones. Experimentation provides this opportunity, and should be used accordingly. In other words, we should use the methods and strategies available when conducting research in software engineering. This is further discussed next.

1.2 Science and Software Engineering

Software engineering is a cross-disciplinary subject. It stretches from technical issues such as databases and operating systems, through language issues, for example, syntax and semantics, to social issues and psychology. Software development is human-intensive; we are, at least today, unable to manufacture new software. It is a discipline based on creativity and the ingenuity of the people working in the field. Nevertheless, we should, when studying and doing research in software engineering, aim at treating it as a scientific discipline. This implies using scientific methods for doing research and when making decisions regarding changes in the way we develop software.

In order to perform scientific research in software engineering, we have to understand the methods that are available to us, their limitations and when they can be applied. Software engineering stems from the technical community. Thus, it is natural to look at the methods used for research in, for example, hardware design and coding theory, but based on the nature of software engineering we should look at other disciplines too. Glass summarized four research methods in the field of software engineering [62]. They were initially presented in a software engineering context by Basili [9]. The methods are:

Scientific   The world is observed and a model is built based on the observation, for example, a simulation model.

Engineering   The current solutions are studied and changes are proposed, and then evaluated.

Empirical   A model is proposed and evaluated through empirical studies, for example, case studies or experiments.

Analytical   A formal theory is proposed and then compared with empirical observations.

The engineering method and the empirical method can be seen as variations of the scientific method [9].

Traditionally, the analytical method is used in the more formal areas of electrical engineering and computer science, e.g. electromagnetic theory and algorithms. The scientific method is used in applied areas, such as simulating a telecommunication network in order to evaluate its performance. It should, however, be noted that simulation as such is not only applied in the scientific method. Simulation may be used as a means for conducting an experiment as well. The engineering method is probably dominating in industry.

The empirical studies have traditionally been used in social sciences and psychology, where we are unable to state any laws of nature, as in physics.[1] In social sciences and psychology, they are concerned with human behavior. The important observation, in this context, is hence that software engineering is very much governed by human behavior through the people developing software. Thus, we cannot expect to find any formal rules or laws in software engineering except perhaps when focusing on specific technical aspects. The focus of this book is on applying and using empirical studies in software engineering. The objective is in particular to emphasize the underlying process when performing empirical studies in general and experimentation in particular. An experiment process is presented,

---

[1]Lehman [110] referred to laws of software evolution, but this notion has not been widespread in subsequent work on theory, see further Sect. 2.7.

which highlights the basic steps to perform experiments, provides guidelines of what to do and exemplifies the steps using software engineering examples.

It must be noted that it is not claimed that the analytical, scientific and engineering methods are inappropriate for software engineering. They are necessary for software engineering as well, for example, we may build mathematical models for software reliability growth [116]. Moreover, the research methods are not orthogonal, and hence it may, for example, be appropriate to conduct an empirical study within, for example, the engineering method. The important point is that we should make better use of the methods available within empirical research. They are frequently used in other disciplines, for example, behavioral sciences, and the nature of software engineering has much in common with disciplines outside the technical parts of engineering.

The very first experiments in software engineering were conducted in the late 1960s by Grant and Sackmann [69] about on- and off-line work in testing, according to Zendler [182]. In the 1970s, a few pioneers conducted experiments on structured programming [115], flowcharting [151] and software testing [126]. The need for systematic experimentation in software engineering was emphasized in the middle of the 1980s by Basili et al. [15]. Other articles stressing the need for empiricism in software engineering have since been published, see for example work by Basili, Fenton, Glass, Kitchenham, Pfleeger, Pickard, Potts and Tichy [9,57,62,97,140,169]. The lack of empirical evidence in software engineering research is stressed by Tichy et al. [170], Zelowitz and Wallace [181] and Glass et al. [63]. The latter publications indicate that the research in software engineering is still too much of advocacy research [140]. A more scientific approach to software engineering is needed. The focus of this book is on software engineering and the application and use of empirical studies, in particular experimentation, in software engineering. The number of published experiments in software engineering has increased, and a substantial number of experiments has been published, as reviewed by Sjøberg et al. [161].

Empirical strategies in software engineering include:

- Setting up formal experiments,
- Studying real projects in industry, i.e. performing a case study, and
- Performing surveys through, for example, interviews.

These strategies are described in some more detail in Chaps. 2 and 5 before focusing the rest of this book on experimentation. A more general introduction to these research strategies is presented by, for example, Robson [144]. Case studies in general are elaborated by Yin [180] and case studies specifically in software engineering are elaborated by Runeson et al. [146]. The research strategies are neither completely orthogonal nor competing. They provide a convenient classification, but some studies may be viewed as combinations of them or somewhere between two of them. Thus, there are both similarities and differences between the strategies.

The main reason to use experimentation in software engineering is to enable understanding and identification of relationships between different factors, or variables. A number of preconceived ideas exist, but are they true? Does object-orientation improve reuse? Are inspections cost-effective? Should we have inspection meetings or is it sufficient to hand-in the remarks to a moderator? This type of questions can be investigated in order to improve our understanding of software engineering. Improved understanding is the basis for changing and improving the way we work, hence empirical studies in general and experimentation in particular are important.

The introduction to the area is based on the introduction of a process for experimentation. The basic steps in the process can be used for other types of empirical studies too. The focus is, however, on providing guidelines and support for performing experiments in software engineering. Furthermore, it should be noted that 'true' experiments, i.e. experiments with full randomization, are difficult to perform in software engineering. Software engineering experiments are often quasi-experiments, i.e. experiment in which it, for example, has not been possible to assign participants in the experiments to groups by random [37]. Quasi-experiments are important, and they can provide valuable results. The process presented in this book is aimed at both 'true' experiments and quasi-experiments. The latter is particularly supported by a thorough discussion of threats to experiments.

Thus, the intention of this book is to provide an introduction to empirical studies and experimentation, in order to highlight the opportunities and benefits of doing experiments in the field of software engineering. The empirical research method can, and should be used more in software engineering. The arguments against empirical studies in software engineering are refuted by Tichy et al. [169]. Hopefully, this practical guide to experimentation in software engineering facilitates the use of empirical studies and experimentation both within software engineering research and practice.

1.3 Exercises

1.1. Why can experiments be viewed as prototyping for process changes?

1.2. How can experiments be used in improvement activities?

1.3. Why are empirical studies important in software engineering?

1.4. When is the empirical research method best suited in software engineering in comparison with the scientific, engineering and analytic methods respectively?

1.5. Which three strategies are empirical methods divided into?

Chapter 2
Empirical Strategies

There are two types of research paradigms that have different approaches to empirical studies. *Exploratory research* is concerned with studying objects in their natural setting and letting the findings emerge from the observations. This implies that a *flexible research design* [1] is needed to adapt to changes in the observed phenomenon. Flexible design research is also referred to as *qualitative research*, as it primarily is informed by qualitative data. Inductive research attempts to interpret a phenomenon based on explanations that people bring forward. It is concerned with discovering causes noticed by the subjects in the study, and understanding their view of the problem at hand. The subject is the person, which is taking part in an empirical study in order to evaluate an object.

Explanatory research is mainly concerned with quantifying a relationship or to compare two or more groups with the aim to identify a cause-effect relationship. The research is often conducted through setting up controlled experiment. This type of study is a *fixed design* [1] study, implying that factors are fixed before the study is launched. Fixed design research is also referred to as *quantitative research*, as it primarily is informed by quantitative data. Quantitative investigations are appropriate when testing the effect of some manipulation or activity. An advantage is that quantitative data promotes comparisons and statistical analyses. It is possible for qualitative and quantitative research to investigate the same topics but each of them will address a different type of question. For example, a quantitative investigation could be launched to investigate how much a new inspection method decreases the number of faults found in test. To answer questions about the sources of variations between different inspection groups, a qualitative investigation could be launched.

As mentioned earlier, fixed design strategies, such as controlled experiments, are appropriate when testing the effects of a treatment while a flexible design study of beliefs, understandings, and multiple perspectives are appropriate to find out why the results from a quantitative investigation are as they are. The two approaches should be regarded as complementary rather than competitive.

C. Wohlin et al., *Experimentation in Software Engineering*,
DOI 10.1007/978-3-642-29044-2_2, © Springer-Verlag Berlin Heidelberg 2012

The objectives of this chapter are: (1) to introduce empirical research strategies, (2) to highlight some important aspects in relation to the empirical strategies, and (3) to illustrate how the strategies can be used in the context of technology transfer and improvement. To fulfil the first objective, an overview of empirical strategies is provided, see Sect. 2.1, and then surveys, case studies and experiments are discussed in some more detail. The different empirical strategies are presented briefly in Sects. 2.2–2.4, and a comparison of them is provided in Sect. 2.5. The second objective is addressed by addressing replications of experiments in Sect. 2.6, theories in relation to empirical studies are briefly discussed in Sect. 2.7, and aggregation of empirical studies are elaborated in Sect. 2.8. Finally, the use of the research strategies within a technology transfer process and as being part of an improvement program is discussed in Sect. 2.9.

2.1 Overview of Empirical Strategies

Depending on the purpose of the evaluation, whether it is techniques, methods or tools, and depending on the conditions for the empirical investigation, there are three major different types of investigations (strategies) that may be carried out, *survey, case study* and *experiment* [144].

Definition 2.1. A **survey** is a system for collecting information from or about people to describe, compare or explain their knowledge, attitudes and behavior [58].

A survey is often an investigation performed in retrospect, when, for example, a tool or technique, has been in use for a while [133]. The primary means of gathering qualitative or quantitative data are interviews or questionnaires. These are done through taking a sample which is representative from the population to be studied. The results from the survey are then analyzed to derive descriptive and explanatory conclusions. They are then generalized to the population from which the sample was taken. Surveys are discussed further by Fink [58] and Robson [144].

Definition 2.2. **Case study** in software engineering is: an empirical enquiry that draws on multiple sources of evidence to investigate one instance (or a small number of instances) of a contemporary software engineering phenomenon within its real-life context, especially when the boundary between phenomenon and context cannot be clearly specified [146].

Case studies are used to research projects, activities or assignments. Data is collected for a specific purpose throughout the study. Based on the data collection, statistical analyses can be carried out. The case study is normally aimed at tracking a specific attribute or establishing relationships between different attributes. The level of control is lower in a case study than in an experiment. A case study is an observational study while the experiment is a controlled study [181]. A case study may, for example, be aimed at building a model to predict the number of faults in testing [2]. Multivariate statistical analysis is often applied in this type of studies. The analysis methods include linear regression and principal component analysis [118]. Case study research is further discussed in general by, for example, Robson [144], Stake [165], and Yin [180], and specifically for software engineering by Pfleeger [133], Kitchenham et al. [97], Verner et al. [173], Runeson and Höst [145], and Runeson et al. [146].

For the empirical investigation strategy in main focus of this book, experiment, we define:

Definition 2.3. Experiment (or controlled experiment) in software engineering is an empirical enquiry that manipulates one factor or variable of the studied setting. Based in randomization, different treatments are applied to or by different subjects, while keeping other variables constant, and measuring the effects on outcome variables. In human-oriented experiments, humans apply different treatments to objects, while in technology-oriented experiments, different technical treatments are applied to different objects.

Experiments are mostly done in a laboratory environment, which provides a high level of control. When experimenting, subjects are assigned to different treatments at random. The objective is to manipulate one or more variables and control all other variables at fixed levels. The effect of the manipulation is measured, and based on this a statistical analysis can be performed. In cases where it is impossible to randomly assign treatments to subjects, we may use quasi-experiments.

Definition 2.4. Quasi-experiment is an empirical enquiry similar to an experiment, where the assignment of treatments to subjects cannot be based on randomization, but emerges from the characteristics of the subjects or objects themselves.

In experimental studies, methods for statistical inference are applied with the purpose of showing with statistical significance that one method is better than the other [125, 144, 157]. The statistical methods are further discussed in Chap. 10.

Surveys are very common within social sciences where, for example, attitudes are polled to determine how a population will vote in the next election. A survey provides no control of the execution or the measurement, though it is possible to compare it with similar ones, but it is not possible to manipulate variables as in the other investigation methods [6].

Case study research is a technique where key factors that may have any effect on the outcome are identified and then the activity is documented [165, 180]. Case study research is an observational method, i.e. it is done by observation of an ongoing project or activity.

An experiment is a formal, rigorous and controlled investigation. In an experiment the key factors are identified and manipulated, while other factors in the context are kept unchanged, see Sect. 6.1. The separation between case studies and experiment can be represented by the level of control of the context [132]. In an experiment, different situations are deliberately enforced and the objective is normally to distinguish between two situations, for example, a control situation and the situation under investigation. Examples of the manipulated factors could be, for example, the inspection method or experience of the software developers. In a case study, the context is governed by the actual project under study.

Table 2.1 Design type and qualitative vs. quantitative data in empirical strategies

Strategy	Design type	Qualitative/quantitative
Survey	Fixed	Both
Case study	Flexible	Both
Experiment	Fixed	Quantitative

Some of the research strategies could be informed by qualitative or quantitative data, depending on the design of the investigation, see Table 2.1. The classification of a survey depends on the design of the questionnaires, i.e. which data is collected and if it is possible to apply any statistical methods. This is also true for case studies but the difference is that a survey is done in retrospect while a case study is done while a project is executed. A survey could also be launched before the execution of a project. In the latter case, the survey is based on previous experiences and hence conducted in retrospect to these experiences although the objective is to get some ideas of the outcome of the forthcoming project.

Experiments is almost purely quantitative since they have a focus on measuring different variables, change them and measure them again. During these investigations quantitative data is collected and then statistical methods are applied. However, qualitative data may be collected to help interpretation of the data [93]. The following sections give an introduction to each empirical strategy.

2.2 Surveys

Surveys are conducted when the use of a technique or tool already has taken place [133] or before it is introduced. It could be seen as a snapshot of the situation to capture the current status. Surveys could, for example, be used for opinion polls and market research.

When performing survey research the interest may be, for example, in studying how a new development process has improved the developers attitudes towards quality assurance or prioritizing quality attributes [94]. Then a sample of developers is selected from all the developers at the company. A questionnaire is constructed to obtain information needed for the research. The questionnaires are answered by the sample of developers. The information collected are then arranged into a form that can be handled in a quantitative or qualitative manner.

2.2.1 Survey Characteristics

Sample surveys are almost never conducted to create an understanding of the particular sample. Instead, the purpose is to understand the population, from which the sample was drawn [6]. For example, by interviewing 25 developers on what they think about a new process, the opinion of the larger population of 100 developers in the company can be assessed. Surveys aim at the development of generalized conclusions.

Surveys have the ability to provide a large number of variables to evaluate, but it is necessary to aim at obtaining the largest amount of understanding from the fewest number of variables since this reduction also eases the data collection and analysis work. Surveys with many questions are tedious for respondents to fill out, and the data quality may consequently decline. On the other hand, surveys aim at providing broad overviews, which may require questions in several fields.

2.2.2 Survey Purposes

The general objectives for conducting a survey is either of the following [6]:

- Descriptive
- Explanatory
- Explorative

Descriptive surveys can be conducted to enable assertions about some population. This could be determining the distribution of certain characteristics or attributes. The concern is not about why the observed distribution exists, but instead what that distribution is.

Explanatory surveys aim at making explanatory claims about the population. For example, when studying how developers use a certain inspection technique, we might want to explain why some developers prefer one technique while others prefer another. By examining the relationships between different candidate techniques and several explanatory variables, we may try to explain why developers choose one of the techniques.

Finally, explorative surveys are used as a pre-study to a more thorough investigation to assure that important issues are not foreseen. Creating a loosely structured questionnaire and letting a sample from the population answer it could do this. The information is gathered and analyzed, and the results are used to improve the full investigation. In other words, the explorative survey does not answer the basic research question, but it may provide new possibilities that could be analyzed and should therefore be followed up in the more focused or thorough survey.

2.2.3 Data Collection

The two most common means for data collection are questionnaires and interviews [58]. Questionnaires could both be provided in paper form or in some electronic form, for example, e-mail or web pages. The basic method for data collection through questionnaires is to send out the questionnaire together with instructions on how to fill it out. The responding person answers the questionnaire and then returns it to the researcher.

Letting interviewers handle the questionnaires (by telephone or face-to-face) instead of the respondents themselves, offers a number of advantages:

- Interview surveys typically achieve higher response rates than, for example, mail surveys.
- An interviewer generally decreases the number of "do not know" and "no answer", because the interviewer can answer questions about the questionnaire.
- It is possible for the interviewer to observe and ask questions. The disadvantage is the cost and time, which depend on the size of the sample, and they are also related to the intentions of the investigation.

2.3   Case Studies

A case study is conducted to investigate a single entity or phenomenon in its real-life context, with in a specific time space. Typically, the phenomenon may be hard to clearly distinguish from its environment. The researcher collects detailed information on, for example, one single project during a sustained period of time. During the performance of a case study, a variety of different data collection procedures, and analysis perspectives should be applied [146]. A brief introduction is provided in this chapter to set the context for the different types of empirical strategies, and a more in-depth introduction is provided in Chap. 5.

If we, for example, would like to compare two methods, the study may be defined as a case study or an experiment, depending on the scale of the evaluation, the ability to isolate factors, and feasibility for randomization. An example case study approach may be to use a pilot project to evaluate the effects of a change compared to some baseline [97].

Case studies are very suitable for industrial evaluation of software engineering methods and tools because they can avoid scale-up problems. The difference between case studies and experiments is that experiments sample over the variables that are being manipulated, while case studies select from the variables representing the typical situation. An advantage of case studies is that they are easier to plan and are more realistic, but the disadvantages are that the results are difficult to generalize and harder to interpret, i.e. it is possible to show the effects in a typical situation, but it requires more analysis to generalize to other situations [180].

If the effect of a process change is very widespread, a case study is more suitable. The effect of the change can only be assessed at a high level of abstraction because the process change includes smaller and more detailed changes throughout the development process [97]. Also, the effects of the change cannot be identified immediately. For example, if we would like to know if a new design tool increases the reliability, it may be necessary to wait until after delivery of the developed product to assess the effects on operational failures.

Case study research is a standard method used for empirical studies in various sciences such as sociology, medicine and psychology. Within software engineering, case studies should not only be used to evaluate how or why certain phenomena occur, but also to evaluate the differences between, for example, two design methods. This means in other words, to assess which of the two methods are most suitable in a certain situation [180]. An example of a case study in software engineering is an investigation if the use of perspective-based reading increases the quality of requirements specifications. A study like this cannot verify that perspective-based reading reduces the number of faults that reaches test, since this requires a reference group that does not use perspective-based techniques, but it may bring light to the mechanisms in play in an inspection setting.

2.3.1   Case Study Arrangements

A case study can be applied as a comparative research strategy, comparing the results of using one method or some form of manipulation, to the results of using another approach. To avoid bias and to ensure internal validity, it is necessary to create a solid base for assessing the results of the case study. Kitchenham et al. propose three ways to arrange the study to facilitate this [97]:

- A comparison of the results of using the new method against a company baseline is one solution. The company should gather data from standard projects and calculate characteristics like average productivity and defect rate. Then it is possible to compare the results from the case study with the figures from the baseline.
- A sister project can be chosen as a baseline. The project under study uses the new method and the sister project the current one. Both projects should have the same characteristics, i.e. the projects must be comparable.
- If the method applies to individual product components, it could be applied at random to some components and not to others. This is very similar to an experiment, but since the projects are not drawn at random from the population of all projects, it is not an experiment.

2.3.2   Confounding Factors and Other Aspects

When performing case studies it is necessary to minimize the effects of confounding factors. A confounding factor is a factor that makes it impossible to distinguish the effects of two factors from each other. This is important since we do not have the same control over a case study as in an experiment. For example, it may be difficult to tell if a better result depends on the tool or the experience of the user of the tool. Confounding effects could involve problems with learning how to use a tool or method when trying to assess its benefits, or using very enthusiastic or skeptical staff.

There are both pros and cons with case studies. Case studies are valuable because they incorporate qualities that an experiment cannot visualize, for example, scale, complexity, unpredictability, and dynamism. Some potential problems with case studies are:

- A small or simplified case study is seldom a good instrument for discovering software engineering principles and techniques. Increases in scale lead to changes in the type of problems that become most indicative. In other words, that the problem may be different in a small case study and in a large case study, although the objective is to study the same issues. For example, in a small case study the main problem may be the actual technique being studied, and in a large case study the major problem may be the amount of people involved and hence also the communication between people.
- Researchers are not in full control of a case study situation. This is good, from one perspective, because unpredictable changes frequently tell them much about the problems being studied. The problem is that we cannot be sure about the effects due to confounding factors.

Case studies are further elaborated in Chap. 5.

2.4   Experiments

Experiments are launched when we want control over the situation and want to manipulate behavior directly, precisely and systematically. Also, experiments involve more than one treatment to compare the outcomes. For example, if it is possible to control who is using one method and who is using another method, and when and where they are used, it is possible to perform an experiment. This type of manipulation can be made in an off-line situation, for example in a laboratory under controlled conditions, where the events are organized to simulate their appearance in the real world. Experiments may alternatively be made on-line, which means that the investigation is executed in the field in a real life context [6]. The level of control is more difficult in an on-line situation, but some factors may be possible to control while others may be impossible.

Experiments may be *human-oriented* or *technology-oriented*. In human-oriented experiments, humans apply different treatments to objects, for example, two inspection methods are applied to two pieces of code. In technology-oriented experiments, typically different tools are applied to different objects, for example, two test case generation tools are applied to the same programs. The human-oriented experiment has less control than the technology-oriented one, since humans behave differently at different occasions, while tools (mostly) are deterministic. Further, due to learning effects, a human subject cannot apply two methods to the same piece of code, which two tools can do without bias.

As mentioned earlier, considering the notion of context makes it possible to state the difference between case studies and experiments more rigorously. Examples of different contexts could be the application area and the system type [132]. In an experiment, we identify the contexts of interest, its variables and sample over them. This means that we select objects representing a variety of characteristics that are typical for the organization in which the experiment is conducted and design the research so that more than one value will be measured for each characteristic. An example could be to investigate the effect of an inspection method with respect to the faults found in test in two different systems, using two different programming languages, for example, in a situation where an organization has moved from one programming language to another. Then the different systems are the context for evaluating the inspection method, and hence similar objects are needed in the experiment. The inspection method becomes the independent variable and an experiment will involve objects where the different programming languages are used.

The design of the experiment should be made so that the objects involved represent all the methods we are interested in. Also, it is possible to consider the current situation to be the baseline (control), which means that the baseline represents one level (or value) of the independent variable, and the new situation to be the one we want to evaluate. Then the level of the independent variable for the new situation describes how the evaluated situation differs from the control. Though, the values of all the other variables should stay the same, for example, application domain and programming environment.

2.4.1 Characteristics

Experiments are appropriate to investigate different aspects [72, 162], including:

- Confirm theories, i.e. to test existing theories.
- Confirm conventional wisdom, i.e. to test people's conceptions.
- Explore relationships, i.e. to test that a certain relationship holds.
- Evaluate the accuracy of models, i.e. to test that the accuracy of certain models is as expected.
- Validate measures, i.e. to ensure that a measure actually measures what it is supposed to.

The strength of an experiment is that it can investigate in which situations the claims are true and they can provide a context in which certain standards, methods and tools are recommended for use.

2.4.2   Experiment Process

Carrying out an experiment involves several different steps. The different steps are:

1. Scoping
2. Planning
3. Operation
4. Analysis and interpretation
5. Presentation and package

The experiment process is presented in Chap. 6, and the different steps are discussed in more detail in Chaps. 7–11.

2.5   Empirical Strategies Comparison

The prerequisites for an investigation limit the choice of research strategy. A comparison of strategies can be based on a number of different factors. Table 2.2 is an extension of the different factors discussed by Pfleeger [133]. The factors are further described below.

Execution control describes how much control the researcher has over the study. For example, in a case study, data is collected during the execution of a project. If management decides to stop the studied project due to, for example, economical reasons, the researcher cannot continue carrying out the case study. The opposite is the experiment where the researcher is in control of the execution.

Measurement control is the degree to which the researcher can decide upon which measures to be collected, and to include or exclude during execution of the study. An example is how to collect data about requirement volatility. During the execution of a survey we cannot include this kind of measures, but in a case study or in an experiment it is possible to include them. In a survey, we can only collect data regarding people's opinion about requirement volatility.

Closely related, to the factors above, is the *investigation cost*. Depending on which strategy is chosen, the cost differs. This is related to, for example, the size of the investigation and the need for resources. The strategy with the lowest cost is the survey, since it does not require a large amount of resources. The difference between case studies and experiments is that if we choose to investigate a project in a case study, the outcome from the project is some form of product that may be retailed, i.e. it is an on-line investigation. In an off-line experiment the outcome is some form of experience or knowledge which is not directly profitable in the same way as a product.

Another important aspect to consider is the possibility to *replicate* the investigation. The purpose of a replication is to show that the result from the original experiment is valid for a larger population. A replication becomes a 'true' replication if it is possible to replicate both the design and the results. It is not

Table 2.2 Research strategy factors

Factor	Survey	Case study	Experiment
Execution control	No	No	Yes
Measurement control	No	Yes	Yes
Investigation cost	Low	Medium	High
Ease of replication	High	Low	High

uncommon that the objective is to perform a replication, but the results, to some extent, turn out differently than the results of the original study.

Another aspect related to replication, in the sense that it is concerned with studies over time, is longitudinal studies [141]. The main difference between a longitudinal study and a replication is that a longitudinal study is primarily conducted with the same subjects and a replication is mostly a study conducted with new subjects. In other words, replication means several studies and a longitudinal study is a single study. The longitudinal study is conducted over a period of time, for example, a survey can be done at several occasions, experiments can be repeated and the case study may also be longitudinal if it is conducted over a period of time. A longitudinal study is normally conducted to understand, describe or evaluate something that changes over time [144].

The choice of empirical strategy depends on the prerequisites for the investigation, the purpose of it, available resources and how we would like to analyze the collected data. Easterbrook et al. [50] provide more advice on selection of research strategies. Further, the borderline between different types of study is not always clear cut. For example, a comparative case study may also be referred to as a quasi-experiment in an industrial context, and a post-hoc observational study of software engineering course outcomes, may also be referred to as a student experiment.

2.6 Replications

The replication of an experiment involves repeating the investigation under similar conditions, while for example, varying the subject population. This helps finding out how much confidence it is possible to place in the results of the experiment. If the assumption of randomization is correct, i.e. the subjects are representative of a larger population, replications within this population show the same results as the previous performed experiment. If we do not get the same results, we have been unable to capture all aspects in the experiment design that affect the result. Even if it is possible to measure a certain variable or to replicate an experiment, it might be difficult and too costly.

Replications may be of different types [89, 155]:

- *Close* replications follow the original procedures as closely as possible. This type is sometimes referred to as *exact* replications [155].
- *Differentiated* replications study the same research questions, using different experimental procedures. They may also deliberately vary one or more major conditions in the experiment.

Basili et al. [20], proposed a more fine grained classification:

- Strict replications (synonym to close and exact)
- Replications that vary variables intrinsic to the study
- Replications that vary variables intrinsic to the focus of the study
- Replications that vary the context variables in the environment in which the solution is evaluated
- Replications that vary the manner in which the experiment is run
- Replications that extend the theory

In other fields of research, many different classifications schemes are used [64], and no standardized terminology exist across fields of research. Neither is the terminology in software engineering field established. The above presented distinction between *close* and *differentiated* replications is a starting point for specifying replications in software engineering.

The advantage of close replications is that the known factors are kept under control, building confidence in the outcome. However, close replications sometimes require the same researchers to conduct the study, as they have tacit knowledge about the experiment procedures which hardly can be documented [153, 154]. On the other hand, there is a substantial risk for experimenter bias in close replication studies [95]. Further, it is questioned that any replication in software engineering may be classified as close, since so many factors may vary in the complex setting of a software engineering experiment [89].

Differentiated replications on the other hand may be used for more exploratory studies. If the differences in factors and settings are well documented and analyzed, more knowledge may be gained from replicated studies. Factors to consider and report for differentiated replication studies include [89]:

- *Site* where the experiment is conducted
- *Experimenters* conducting the experiment
- *Design* chosen for the experiment
- *Instrumentation* i.e. forms and other material
- *Variables* measured
- *Subjects* conducting the experiment

These factors are discussed in detail Chap. 8. Arguments are raised for replicating original hypotheses, rather than specific experimental designs [123], i.e. in favor of differentiated replications rather than close replications.

2.7 Theory in Software Engineering

"A theory provides explanations and understanding in terms of basic concepts and underlying mechanisms, which constitute an important counterpart to knowledge of passing trends and their manifestation" [72]. Experiments may be conducted to generate, confirm and extend theories, as mentioned above. However, the use of theory is scarce in software engineering, as concluded by Hannay et al. in their systematic literature review of software engineering experiments, 1993–2002 [72]. They found 40 theories in 23 articles, out of the 113 articles in the review. Only two of the theories were used in more than one article!

Endres and Rombach [53] identifies a list of 50 findings which they refer to as 'laws', which is a notion for a description of a repeatable phenomenon in a natural sciences context. Endres and Rombach apply this notion to software engineering. Many of the listed 'laws' are more general than software engineering, for example, "it takes 5,000 h to turn a novice into an expert". In their notion, *theories* explain the 'laws', *hypotheses* propose a tentative explanation for why the phenomenon behaves as observed, while a *conjecture* is a guess about the phenomenon. Endres and Rombach list 25 hypotheses and 12 conjectures appearing in the software engineering literature.

Zendler [182] takes another approach, and defines a "preliminary software engineering theory", composed of three fundamental hypotheses, six central hypotheses, and four elementary hypotheses. There is a hierarchical relation between the hypotheses, the fundamental being the most abstract, and elementary the most concrete ones, originating from outcomes of experimental studies.

Gregor [70] describes five general types of theory, which may be adapted to the software engineering context [72]:

1. *Analysis:* Theories of this type describe the object of study, and include, for example, taxonomies, classifications and ontologies.
2. *Explanation:* This type of theories explains something, for example, why something happens.
3. *Prediction:* These theories aim at predicting what will happen, for example, in terms of mathematical or probabilistic models.
4. *Explanation and prediction:* These theories combine types 2 and 3, and is typically what is denoted an "empirically-based theory".
5. *Design and action:* Theories that describe how to do things, typically prescriptive in the form of design science [76]. It is debated whether this category should be denoted theory at all.

Sjøberg et al. [162] propose a framework for software engineering theories, comprising of four main parts:

- Constructs
- Propositions
- Explanations
- Scope

Table 2.3 Framework for software engineering theories, as proposed by Sjøberg et al. [162]

Archetype class	Subclasses
Actor	Individual, team, project, organisation or industry
Technology	Process model, method, technique, tool or language
Activity	Plan, create, modify or analyze (a software system)
Software system	Software systems may be classified along many dimensions, such as size, complexity, application domain, business/scientific/student project or administrative/embedded/real time, etc.

The *constructs* are the entities in which the theory are expressed, and to which the theory offers a description, explanation or prediction, depending on the type of theory as defined above. *Propositions* are made up from proposed relationships between the constructs. The *explanations* originate from logical reasoning or empirical observations of the propositions, that is, the relationship between the constructs.

The *scope* of the theory defines the circumstances, under which the theory is assumed to be applicable. Sjøberg et al. [162] suggest the scope being expressed in terms of four archetype classes: actor, technology, activity and software system, see Table 2.3.

Despite being attractive from a theoretical point of view, neither of these proposed theory systems have had any major impact on the software engineering field so far. Theories are important for the conceptualization and communication of knowledge within a field of research, and are useful when aggregating existing research and setting up replication studies. Theories may also be used for communication with practitioners in decision-making, whether it be strategic choices of technology, or project decisions based on prediction models. Hence, theory building in software engineering should be developed, in order for the field to develop into a mature field of science.

2.8 Aggregating Evidence from Empirical Studies

As the number of empirical studies grow, the need for aggregating evidence from multiple empirical studies appear, for example, replication studies. Firstly, the research should build upon each other so new research should always take existing knowledge into consideration as its starting point. Secondly, several empirical studies may together give answers to questions, which are not sufficiently answered by individual studies in isolation. The collection and synthesis of empirical evidence must meet scientific standards in itself.

Systematic literature reviews are means to collect and synthesize empirical evidence from different sources. Kitchenham and Charters define systematic literature reviews as "[a] form of secondary study that uses a well-defined methodology to identify, analyze and interpret all available evidence related to a specific research question in a way that is unbiased and (to a degree) repeatable" [96]. The empirical studies, searched for, are referred to as *primary studies* while the systematic literature review as such is referred to as a *secondary study*. Kitchenham and charters provide guidelines for such reviews, which are summarized in Chap. 4.

A systematic literature review has a specific research question, similar to a research question for a single empirical study. The research question is related to the *outcomes* of the reviewed empirical studies, and is typically on the form: "Is technology/method A better or not than B?" [106].

The search for empirical studies are done using database queries, as well as searching journals, conference proceedings and grey literature, like technical reports, based on keyword topics [96]. "Snowballing" procedures, i.e. following the references from or to one paper to find other relevant papers, are also proposed [145]. It should be noted that snowballing can be both backward and forward. Backward snowballing means following the reference list and forward snowballing refers to looking at papers citing the paper that has been found relevant.

If the research question is more general, or if the field of research is less explored, a *mapping study* (also referred to as *scoping study*) may be launched instead. Mapping studies have broader research questions, aiming to identify the state of practice or research on a topic and typically identify research trends [106]. Due to their broader scope, the search and classification procedures are less stringent, and have more qualitative characteristics.

Both systematic literature reviews and mapping studies must have clear criteria for inclusion and exclusion of studies as well as taxonomies for their classification. For systematic literature reviews, a natural criterion is that the studies are empirical, while mapping studies also may include non-empirical work.

When a set of empirical studies is collected on a topic, the synthesis or aggregation takes place. Syntheses based on statistical methods are referred to as *meta-analysis*. Examples of meta-analyses in software engineering include defect detection methods [74, 121], agile methods [46], and pair programming [73].

If the meta-analysis procedures do not apply, descriptive synthesis has to be used. These include visualization and tabulation of data and descriptive statistics of the data [96]. The broader research question for a literature review, the more qualitative methods are needed for its synthesis. Cruzes and Dybå present an overview of qualitative synthesis methods [39].

The interest for and conduct of systematic literature reviews in software engineering have grown substantially during the first decade of the twenty-first century. Kitchenham et al. report 53 unique systematic literature reviews being published between 2004 and 2008 [103, 104]. In addition to the synthesis of empirical findings, the conduct of the reviews lead to identification of improvement proposals, both in the reporting of empirical studies as such, and to the databases in which they are stored.

Systematic literature reviews are elaborated in more depth in Chap. 4.

2.9   Empiricism in a Software Engineering Context

Why should we perform experiments and other empirical studies in software engineering? The major reasons for carrying out quantitative empirical studies is the opportunity of getting objective and statistically significant results regarding the understanding, controlling, prediction, and improvement of software development. Empirical studies are an important input to the decision-making in an improvement seeking organization.

Before introducing new techniques, methods, or other ways of working, an empirical assessment of the virtues of such changes is preferred. In this section, a framework for evaluation of software process changes is presented, where different empirical strategies are suggested in three different contexts: desktop, laboratory, and development projects.

To be successful in software development there are some basic requirements [7, 8, 42]:

1. Understanding of the software process and product.
2. Definition of process and product qualities.
3. Evaluation of successes and failures.
4. Information feedback for project control.
5. Learning from experience.
6. Packaging and reuse of relevant experience.

Empirical studies are important to support the achievement of these requirements, and fit into the context of industrial and academic software engineering research, as well as in a learning organization, seeking continuous improvement. An example of a learning organization, called Experience Factory, is proposed by Basili in conjunction with the Quality Improvement Paradigm [7], as further described in the sequel of this section. This approach also includes a mechanism for defining and evaluating a set of operational goals using measurement. This mechanism is called Goal/Question/Metric (GQM) method [17], which is further described below. The GQM method is described in more detail by van Solingen and Berghout [172].

2.9.1   Empirical Evaluation of Process Changes

An improvement seeking organization wants to assess the impact of process changes (e.g., a new method or tool) before introducing them to improve the way of working. Empirical studies are important in order to get objective and quantifiable information on the impact of changes. In Sects. 2.2–2.4, three empirical strategies are described: surveys, case studies and experiments, and they are compared in Sect. 2.5. This section describes how the strategies may be used when software process changes are evaluated [177]. The objective is to discuss the strategies in terms of a suitable way of handling technology transfer from research to industrial

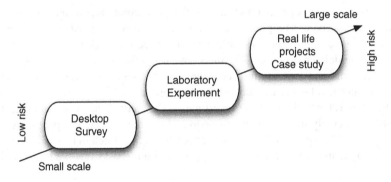

Fig. 2.1 Surveys, experiments and case studies

use. Technology transfer and some different steps in that process in relation to using empirical strategies are discussed in Sect. 2.10.

In Fig. 2.1, the strategies are placed in appropriate research environments. The order of the strategies is based on the 'normal' size of the study. The objective is to order the studies based on how they typically may be conducted to enable a controlled way of transferring research results into practice. As a survey does not intervene with the software development to any large extent, there is a small risk. An experiment is mostly rather limited in comparison to a real project and the case study is typically aimed at one specific project. Furthermore, an experiment may be carried out in a university environment prior to doing a study in industry, hence lowering the cost and risk, see also Linkman and Rombach [113].

The research environments are:

Desktop   The change proposal is evaluated off-line without executing the changed process. Hence, this type of evaluation does not involve people that apply the method, tool, etc. In the desktop environment, it is suitable to conduct surveys, for example, through interview-based evaluations and literature studies.

Laboratory The change proposal is evaluated in an off-line laboratory setting (in vitro[1]), where an experiment is conducted and a limited part of the process is executed in a controlled manner.

Real life   The change proposal is evaluated in a real life development situation, i.e. it is observed on-line (in vivo[2]). This involves, for example, pilot projects. In this environment it is often too expensive to conduct controlled experiments. Instead, case studies are often more appropriate.

In Fig. 2.1, the placement of the different research environments indicates an increase in scale and risk. In order to try out, for example a new design method

---

[1]Latin for "in the glass" and refers to chemical experiments in the test tube.

[2]Latin for "in life" and refers to experiments in a real environment.

in a large-scale design project and in a realistic environment, we may apply it in a development project as a pilot study. This is, of course, more risky compared to a laboratory or desktop study, as failure of the process change may, endanger the quality of the delivered product. Furthermore, it is often more expensive to carry out experiments and case studies, compared to desktop evaluation, as a desktop study does not involve the execution of a development process. It should be noted that the costs refer to the cost for investigating the same thing. For example, it is probably less costly to first interview people about the expected impact of a new review method than performing a controlled experiment, which in turn is less costly than actually using the new method in a project with the risks involved in adopting new technology.

Before a case study is carried out in a development project, limited studies in either or both desktop and laboratory environments should be carried out to reduce risks. However, there is no general conclusion on order and cost; for every change proposal, a careful assessment should be made of which empirical strategies are most effective for the specific situation. The key issue is to choose the best strategy based on cost and risk, and in many cases it is recommended to start in a small scale and then as the knowledge increases and the risk decreases the study is scaled up.

Independently of which research strategy we use, there is a need for methodology support in terms of how to work with improvement, how to collect data and to store the information. These issues are further discussed subsequently.

2.9.2   Quality Improvement Paradigm

The Quality Improvement Paradigm (QIP) [7] is a general improvement scheme tailored for the software business. QIP is similar to the Plan/Do/Study/Act cycle [23, 42], and includes six steps as illustrated in Fig. 2.2.

These steps are explained below [16].

1. *Characterize.* Understand the environment based upon available models, data, intuition, etc. Establish baselines with the existing business processes in the organization and characterize their criticality.
2. *Set goals.* On the basis of the initial characterization and of the capabilities that have a strategic relevance to the organization, set quantifiable goals for successful project and organization performance and improvement. The reasonable expectations are defined based upon the baseline provided by the characterization step.
3. *Choose process.* On the basis of the characterization of the environment and the goals that have been set, choose the appropriate processes for improvement, and supporting methods and tools, making sure that they are consistent with the goals that have been set.
4. *Execute.* Perform the product development and provide project feedback based upon the data on goal achievements that are being collected.

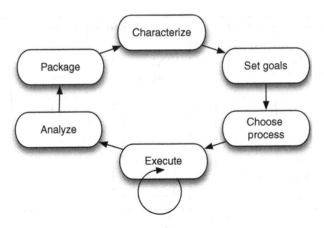

Fig. 2.2 The six steps of the Quality Improvement Paradigm [7]

5. *Analyze*. At the end of each specific project, analyze the data and the information gathered to evaluate the current practices, determine problems, record findings, and make recommendations for future project improvements.
6. *Package*. Consolidate the experience gained in the form of new, or updated and refined, models and other forms of structured knowledge gained from this and prior projects.

   The QIP implements two feedback cycles [16], see also Fig. 2.2:

- The *project feedback cycle* (*control cycle*) is the feedback provided to the project during the execution phase. Whatever the goals of the organization, the project used as a pilot should use its resources in the best possible way; therefore quantitative indicators at project and task level are useful in order to prevent and solve problems.
- The *corporate feedback cycle* (*capitalization cycle*) is the feedback loop that is provided to the organization. It has the double purpose of providing analytical information about project performance at project completion time by comparing the project data with the nominal range in the organization and analyzing concordance and discrepancy. Reusable experience is accumulated in a form that is useful and applicable to other projects.

2.9.3   Experience Factory

The QIP is based on that the improvement of software development requires continuous learning. Experience should be packaged into experience models that can be effectively understood and modified. Such experience models are stored in a repository, called *experience base*. The models are accessible and can be modified for reuse in current projects.

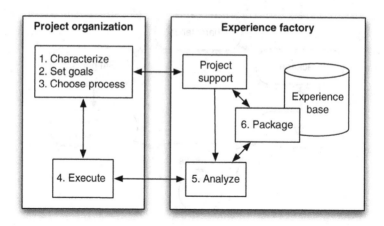

Fig. 2.3 Experience Factory

QIP focuses on a logical separation of project development (performed by the Project Organization) from the systematic learning and packaging of reusable experience (performed by the Experience Factory) [8]. The Experience Factory is thus a separate organization that supports product development by analyzing and synthesizing all kinds of experience, acting as a repository for such experience, and supplying that experience to various projects on demand, see Fig. 2.3.

The Experience Factory packages experience by "building informal, formal, or schematised models and measures of various processes, products, and other forms of knowledge via people, documents, and automated support" [16].

The goal of the Project Organization is to produce and maintain software. The project organization provides the Experience Factory with project and environment characteristics, development data, resource usage information, quality records, and process information. It also provides feedback on the actual performance of the models processed by the experience factory and utilized by the project.

The Experience Factory processes the information received from the development organization, and returns direct feedback to each project, together with goals and models tailored from similar projects. It also provides baselines, tools, lessons learned, and data, tailored to the specific project.

To be able to improve, a software developing organization needs to introduce new technology. It needs to experiment and record its experiences from development projects and eventually change the current development process. When the technology is substantially different from the current practice, the evaluation may be off-line in order to reduce risks. The change evaluation, as discussed above, may take the form of a controlled experiment (for detailed evaluation in the small) or of a case study (to study the scale effects). In both cases, the Goal/Question/Metric method, as described subsequently, provides a useful framework.

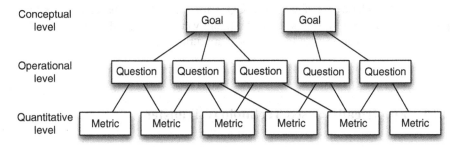

Fig. 2.4 GQM model hierarchical structure

2.9.4 Goal/Question/Metric Method

The Goal/Question/Metric (GQM) [17, 26, 172] method is based upon the assumption that for an organization to measure in a purposeful way it must:

1. Specify the goals for itself and its projects,
2. Trace those goals to the data that is intended to define those goals operationally, and
3. Provide a framework for interpreting the data with respect to the stated goals.

The result of the application of the GQM method is a specification of a measurement model targeting a particular set of issues and a set of rules for the interpretation of the measurement data.

The resulting measurement model has three levels, as illustrated by the hierarchical structure in Fig. 2.4:

1. *Conceptual level* (Goal). A goal is defined for an object, for a variety of reasons, with respect to various models of quality, from various points of view, relative to a particular environment. Objects of measurement are products, processes, and resources (see also Chap. 3).
2. *Operational level* (Question). A set of questions is used to characterize the way the assessment/achievement of a specific goal is going to be performed based on some characterization model. Questions try to characterize the objects of measurement (product, process and resource) with respect to a selected quality aspect and to determine its quality from the selected viewpoint.
3. *Quantitative level* (Metric). A set of data is associated with every question in order to answer it in a quantitative way (either objectively or subjectively).

The process of setting goals is critical to the successful application of the GQM method. Goals are formulated based on (1) policies and strategies of the organization, (2) descriptions of processes and products, and (3) organization models. When goals have been formulated, questions are developed based on these goals. Once the questions have been developed, we proceed to associating the questions with appropriate metrics.

Practical guidelines of how to use GQM for measurement-based process improvement are given by Briand et al. [26], and van Solingen and Berghout [172]. In Chap. 3, general aspects of measurement are further described.

2.10 Empirically-Based Technology Transfer

Empirical studies have a value stand-alone, but they can also be part of a knowledge exchange and improvement endeavor jointly between academia and industry, for example in technology transfer as also discussed above. Software engineering is an applied research area, and hence to perform research on industrially relevant problems is expected. It is in many cases insufficient to just do academic research on, for example, requirements engineering or software testing with the motivation that these areas are challenging in industry. Software engineering is preferably conducted jointly by academia and industry to enable transfer of knowledge in both directions and at the end transfer of new methods, technologies and tools from academia to industry. Joint research provides an excellent opportunity to improve industrial software development based on concrete evidence, and hence being a good example of evidence-based software engineering [48, 100].

Based on a long-term collaborative venture, a model for technology transfer was documented and presented by Gorschek et al. [66]. The seven steps in the model are summarized below to illustrate how different empirical studies and in particular experiments can be used in empirically driven improvement. The model is illustrated in Fig. 2.5. The model is closely related to the discussion about software process improvement in Sect. 2.9. The main focus of the model is on the usage of different empirical methods to create a solution to a real industrial problem and bring it to industrial application.

Identification of industrial problem/issue. The first step is to identify actual industrial challenges in a specific industrial context, which implies that the researcher is present at the industrial partner(s). The identification of challenges may be done using, for example, a survey or interviews, which are briefly presented in Sect. 2.2. The objective is to capture the challenges and in particular issues that are suitable for research. Any challenge identified must be possible to formulate as a research problem to avoid that the researcher ends up in the role of a consultant addressing short-term problems.

A major benefit with doing this step thoroughly is that it creates an opportunity to build a joint trust and ensures that the industrial partner(s) and its employees get used to have researchers present in their environment. At this stage, commitment from both management and other practitioners involved in the joint effort is crucial to ensure future success according to Wohlin et al. [179].

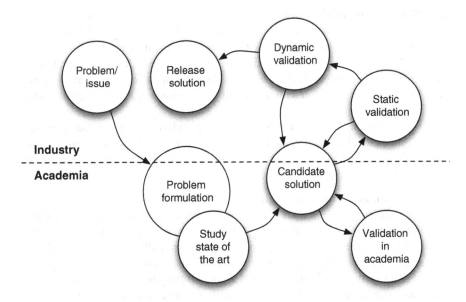

Fig. 2.5 Technology transfer model (Adapted from the description by Gorschek et al. [66])

Problem formulation. Based on the challenge(s) identified, the challenge should be formulated as a research problem and research questions should be specified. If several different challenges are identified there is a need to prioritize which to address. Furthermore, a main contact person for the chosen challenge should be identified. The person should preferably not only be appointed; it should be a person who would like to be the driver within the company and act as a champion for the research collaboration. This includes helping to get in contact with the right people in the company, and to help ensuring that the researchers get access to systems, documentation and data when needed.

As a natural part of the formulation of the research problem, the researchers conduct a literature search. This may be done as a systematic literature review as presented in Chap. 4. A literature survey is needed to know about existing approaches to the identified industrial challenge. It provides a basis for understanding the relationship between approaches available and the actual industrial needs.

Candidate solution. Based on available approaches and the actual needs, a candidate solution is developed, which may include tailoring to the current processes, methods, technologies and tools used at the company. The solution is preferably developed in close collaboration with the industrial partner(s) so that the applicability can be continuously ensured. Although a specific solution for a company may be derived, the intention of the researcher is to develop a generic solution, which then is instantiated in a specific context.

Validation in academia. A first validation of the proposed solution is preferably conducted in an academic environment to minimize the risk, i.e. an off-line validation. In many cases this may be conducted as an experiment as described in several chapters of this book or as a case study of a student project. An overview of case study research is provided in Chap. 5. The validation in an academic environment may be conducted with either students as subjects or with representatives from the industrial partner(s).

The main objective in this step is to capture any obvious flaws in the proposed solution and to identify improvements proposals of the candidate solution. This is done in an academic setting to ensure that the best possible solution is available when bringing it to industry.

Static validation. In the static validation, industry representatives evaluate the candidate solution off-line. This may be done through a presentation of the candidate solution followed by either interviews of different industry representatives, preferably in different affected roles, or joint workshops. In addition, it is preferable to make a general presentation to the organization to make them aware of the proposed solution at an early stage. This also gives an opportunity for the personnel to raise their voice at an early stage. Hopefully, this will help overcome any resistance once the new solution is going to be integrated to the way software is developed within the organization.

Based on the static validation, the new solution may need to be changed based on the feedback. The seven steps are all iterative, and hence it is more a matter of which order they start and they should definitively not be viewed as a waterfall approach without feedback cycles.

Dynamic validation. Once the new solution passes the static validation and there is agreement and commitment to implement the new solution, it is time to move to a dynamic validation. This is preferably done as a pilot evaluation. Exactly how to conduct the validation depends on the type of solution. The new solution may be used in a project, a subproject or for parts of a system, or for a specific activity. Independently, it is recommended that the dynamic validation be followed closely to evaluate the solution. The dynamic solution may be studied using a case study approach as described in Chap. 5.

Release solution. A generic solution must be tailored to each unique situation. There is a need to ensure that any research solution is properly handed over to an industrial champion and that the company has sufficient support in terms of descriptions, training and potential tool support. The latter is not primarily the responsibility of the researchers, but they must support their collaborative partner(s) to ensure that the transfer of the new solution is properly in place and integrated into the organization before moving to the next industrial challenge.

Preferably, the broader usage is also studied empirically through a case study. This will help obtaining empirical evidence for the new solution developed in the research collaboration.

Concluding remark. The transfer model outlined illustrates how different empirical strategies may be applied to support transfer of new research results from identification of needs to actual industrial usage.

Finally, it is interesting to note that the industrial representatives are primarily interested in the specific tailoring to their environment, while from a researchers perspective it becomes a case for the generic solution. Thus, the collaborative partners may have different main focuses, but at the end they both benefit from the joint effort. The industrial partner gets a solution to an identified challenge and the researchers are able to evaluate a research result in a real industrial environment. Gorschek and Wohlin [65] present an example of a generic solution for requirements abstraction and a particular industrial instantiation of the approach is presented by Gorschek et al. [67] separately.

2.11 Ethics in Experimentation

Any empirical research activity involving human subjects must take ethical aspects into consideration. Some aspects are regulated by national laws, others are not regulated at all. Andrews and Pradhan identified ethical issues in software engineering, and found existing policies to be insufficient [3]. Hall and Flynn surveyed ethical practice and awareness in the UK, and found alarming unawareness [71], and nothing indicates this country being an exception.

Singer and Vinson initiated a discussion on ethical issues [158], continued to discuss cases of ethical issues [159], and provided practical guidelines for the conduct of empirical studies [174]. They identified four key principles:

- Subjects must give *informed consent* to their participation, implying that they should have access to all relevant information about the study, before making their decision to participate or not. Their decision must be explicit and free, also with respect to implicit dependencies on managers, professors etc.
- The study should have *scientific value* in order to motivate subjects to expose themselves to the risks of the empirical study, even if these are minimal.
- Researchers must take all possible measures to maintain *confidentiality* of data and sensitive information, even when this is in conflict with the publication interests.
- Weighing risks, harms and benefits, the *beneficence* must overweigh, not only for the individual subjects, but also for groups of subjects and organizations.

These principles are turned into more practical guidelines below, related to planning, conduct and reporting of an experimental study. We also refer to Sieber [156] for a checklist of risks for subjects to be addressed in experimentation.

Ethical review. In countries where legislation require an ethical review for studies involving human subjects, like Canada, USA and Australia, the procedures and documentation for such studies have to be followed to enable the study. The review implies a proposal being put before an Ethical Review Board (ERB) at the university or government agency, for approval. These procedures are mostly derived from the needs in biomedical research, and thus generally not tailored to software engineering needs. Vinson and Singer mention, for example, that in Canada, it is not clear whether studies using source code (being written by humans and revealing information about them) and its data are subject to the review procedures [174].

The documentation needed in the review typically includes a description of the project, comprising details on subjects and treatments, documentation of how informed consent is obtained, and a review of ethical aspects of the project.

Informed consent. The basis for a human-oriented empirical study (e.g. an experiment) is that subjects are participating voluntarily, and that they have enough information to make the decision to participate or not. Further, this includes the option to withdraw from the study any time, without any penalty for the subject. In order to make this decision process clear and explicit, consent should be given in writing.

A consent form typically comprises the following elements [174]:

- *Research project title:* for identification purposes.
- *Contact information:* both research and ethics contact.
- *Consent and comprehension:* the subjects state that they understand the conditions for the project and accept them.
- *Withdrawal:* states the right to withdraw without penalties.
- *Confidentiality:* defined the promises about confidential handling of data and participation.
- *Risks and benefits:* explicitly listing what the subjects risk and gain.
- *Clarification:* the right for the subject to ask questions for clarification of their role in the study.
- *Signature:* mostly by both subject and researcher, one copy for each, to indicate it is a mutual agreement.

In some experimental designs, *full disclosure* of the research goal and procedures may compromise the conduct of the experiment as such. For example, knowing the hypothesis beforehand, the subjects may change their behavior accordingly. Then, *partial disclosure* may be used, meaning that the experimental goals and procedures are presented at a higher level of abstraction.

For empirical studies in companies (in vivo), the consent must include both the organization and the individual subjects. In particular, the subjects cannot be ordered to participate, and are free to withdraw without penalties. Further, issues of confidentiality and sensitive results *within* the company also must be taken into consideration.

The consent may be differentiated on whether it is given for the goals of the current study, or if data may be used for further studies with different goals.

Confidentiality. The subjects must be sure that any information they share with researchers will remain confidential. Three aspects on confidentiality are [174]:

- *Data privacy*, referring to restricted access to data, imposed by for example password protection and encryption.
- *Data anonymity*, addressed by keeping the identities of subjects apart from the data.
- *Anonymity of participation*, meaning that the consent decision should be kept secret.

Since the empirical studies (including experiments) aim at drawing general conclusions, there is no principal conflict with keeping the specifics confidential. Data privacy issues can also be solved by good working practices. However, as the number of subjects often are small, there is a risk that information may be traced to individuals, even if anonymized, thereby threatening anonymity. Further, for the external validity of the study (see Sect. 8.7), information about the study context should be reported, which may conflict the anonymity.

The anonymity of participation is the hardest to achieve. Students in a class, which are enrolled in experiments, may have the formal right to decline participation, but it is hard to hide from the researcher which students participate or not. Similarly in companies, managers would easily know who is participating in the study. Vinson and Singer advice that "for studies involving students, researchers should avoid recruiting students in the classroom setting and should avoid trying to recruit their own students" [174] – an advice followed by few.

Sensitive results. Outcomes from any empirical study may be sensitive in different respects for different stakeholders. The individual performance of a subject is one example, which managers or professors would like to see. The conclusions from the empirical study may also be sensitive, especially if a sponsor of the project has a stake in it. The results may also be sensitive to the researchers, for example, if an experiment does not support their hypotheses.

These situations stress the moral standards of the stakeholders. Possible measures to take to prepare for these situations include different kinds of independency. For results sensitive to:

- *Subjects*, make sure that confidentiality procedures apply, independently of facts revealed (crime exempted [159]),
- *Sponsors*, include clear statements on rights for independent publications of the anonymized results in the informed consent form for companies, and in research project contracts,
- *Researchers*, consider having peers to perform statistical analyses on anonymized data (both subjects and scales) independently from the experimenters, especially when the treatment is designed by the experimenters themselves. This also reduces the threat of experimenter expectancies.

These actions reduce the risk of being stuck in ethical dilemmas, and increases the validity of all empirical studies.

Inducement. In recruiting subjects for an experiment, there must be inducements to motivate their participation. The experience and knowledge gained by applying a new method may be inducement enough. In order to treat all participants fair, all subjects should be given the opportunity to learn about all treatments, even if the experimental design does not require it.

Some monetary inducement may also be involved, for example, in the form of cash payment, participation in a lottery, or, for professional subjects, their ordinary salary. Independently of form, the inducement must be balanced to ensure that the consent to participate really is voluntary, and not forced by too large economic or other inducements.

Feedback. To maintain long term relationships and trust with the subjects of a study, feedback of results and analysis are important. Subjects must not agree on the analysis, but should be given the opportunity to get information about the study and its results. If feasible, from a confidentiality point of view, data from individual's performance may be reported back together with the overall analysis.

Conclusion on ethics. Singer and Vinson ask in their early work for a code of ethics for empirical software engineering [159]. Still, 10 years later, the community has not yet developed one; the closest is Vinson and Singer's guidelines [174], which are summarized above. Research funding agencies start to require general codes of ethics be applied, which may not fit the purpose. Concrete and tailored ethical guidelines for empirical software engineering research would benefit both the subjects, which they aim to protect, and the development of the research field as such.

2.12 Exercises

2.1. What is the difference between qualitative and quantitative research?

2.2. What is a survey? Give examples of different types of surveys in software engineering.

2.3. Which role plays replications and systematic literature reviews in building empirical knowledge?

2.4. How can the Experience Factory be combined with the Goal/Question/Metrics method and empirical studies on a technology transfer context?

2.5. Which are the key ethical principles to observe then conducting experiments?

Chapter 3
Measurement

Software measurement is crucial to enable control of projects, products and processes, or as stated by DeMarco: *"You cannot control what you cannot measure"* [41]. Moreover, measurement is a central part in empirical studies. Empirical studies are used to investigate the effects of some input to the object under study. To control the study and to see the effects, we must be able to both measure the inputs in order to describe what causes the effect on the output, and to measure the output. Without measurements, it is not possible to have the desired control and therefore an empirical study cannot be conducted.

Measurement and measure are defined as [56]: "Measurement *is the process by which numbers or symbols are assigned to attributes of entities in the real world in such a way as to describe them according to clearly defined rules.*" A measure is the number or symbol assigned to an entity by this relationship to characterize an attribute.

Instead of making judgement directly on the real entity, we study the measures and make the judgement on them. The word metric or metrics is also often used in software engineering. Two different meanings can be identified. First of all, software metrics is used as a term for denoting the field of measurement in software engineering. The book by Fenton and Pfleeger [56] is an example of this. Secondly, the word metric is used to denote an entity which is measured, for example, lines of code (LOC) is a product metric. More precisely, it is a measure of the size of the program. Software measurement is also further discussed by Shepperd [150].

In this chapter, basic measurement theory is presented. Section 3.1 describes the basic concept of measurement theory, and the different scale types of measures. Examples of measures in software engineering and the relation to the statistical analysis are presented in Sect. 3.2, while practical aspects of measurements are discussed in Sect. 3.3.

C. Wohlin et al., *Experimentation in Software Engineering*,
DOI 10.1007/978-3-642-29044-2_3, © Springer-Verlag Berlin Heidelberg 2012

3.1 Basic Concepts

A measure is a mapping from the attribute of an entity to a measurement value, usually a numerical value. Entities are objects we can observe in the real world. The purpose of mapping the attributes into a measurement value is to characterize and manipulate the attributes in a formal way. One of the basic characteristics of a measure is therefore that it must preserve the empirical observations of the attribute [57]. That is, if object A is longer than object B, the measure of A must be greater than the measure of B.

When we use a measure in empirical studies, we must be certain that the measure is valid. To be *valid*, the measure must not violate any necessary properties of the attribute it measures and it must be a proper mathematical characterization of the attribute.

A valid measure allows different objects to be distinguished from one another, but within the limits of measurement error, objects can have the same measurement value. The measure must also preserve our intuitive notions about the attribute and the way in which it distinguishes different objects [97]. A measure must be valid both analytically and empirically. Analytical validity of a measure relates to its ability to capture accurately and reliably the item of interest. Empirical validity (sometimes referred to as statistical or predictive ability) describes how well, for example, a score correlates to something measured in another context.

Effect size is a simple way of quantifying the difference between two groups. This is particularly important in experimentation, since it may be possible to show a statistical significant difference between two groups, but it may not be meaningful from a practical point of view. In most cases, it is possible to show statistically significant differences with a sufficiently large number of subjects in an experiment, but it does not necessarily mean that it is meaningful from a practical point of view. It may be the case that the difference is too small or the cost to exploit the difference is simply too high.

The mapping from an attribute to a measurement value can be made in many different ways, and each different mapping of an attribute is a *scale*. If the attribute is the length of an object, we can measure it in meters, centimeters or inches, each of which is a different scale of the measure of the length.

As a measure of an attribute can be measured in different scales, we sometimes want to transform the measure into another scale. If this transformation from one measure to another preserves the relationship among the objects, it is called an admissible transformation [56]. An *admissible transformation* is also called *rescaling*.

With the measures of the attribute, we make statements about the object or the relation between different objects. If the statements are true even if the measures are rescaled, they are called *meaningful*, otherwise they are *meaningless* [27]. For example, if we measure the lengths of objects A and B to 1 m and 2 m respectively, we can make the statement that B is twice as long as A. This statement is true even if we rescale the measures to centimeters or inches, and is therefore meaningful. Another example, we measure the temperature in room A and room B to 10°C and 20°C, and make the statement that room B is twice as warm as room A. If we rescale the temperatures to the Fahrenheit scale, we get the temperatures 50°F and 68°F. The statement is no longer true and is therefore meaningless.

Depending on which admissible transformation that can be made on a scale, different scale types can be defined. Scales belonging to a scale type, share the same properties and the scale types are more or less powerful in the sense that more meaningful statements can be made the more powerful the scale is. The most commonly used scale types are described below.

Measures can also be classified in two other ways: (1) if the measure is direct or indirect, or (2) if the measure is objective or subjective. These classifications are further discussed later in this chapter.

3.1.1 Scale Types

The most common scale types are the following[1] [27, 56, 57]:

Nominal   The nominal scale is the least powerful of the scale types. It only maps the attribute of the entity into a name or symbol. This mapping can be seen as a classification of entities according to the attribute.
          Possible transformations for nominal scales are those that preserve the fact that the entities only can be mapped one-to-one.
          Examples of a nominal scale are classification, labeling and defect typing.
Ordinal   The ordinal scale ranks the entities after an ordering criterion, and is therefore more powerful than the nominal scale. Examples of ordering criteria are "greater than", "better than", and "more complex".
          The possible transformations for the ordinal scale are those that preserve the order of the entities, i.e. $M' = F(M)$ where M' and M are different measures on the same attribute, and F is a monotonic increasing function.
          Examples of an ordinal scale are grades and software complexity.
Interval The interval scale is used when the difference between two measures are meaningful, but not the value itself. This scale type orders the values in the same way as the ordinal scale but there is a notion of "relative distance" between two entities. The scale is therefore more powerful than the ordinal scale type.

---

[1]Fenton et al. [56,57] present a fifth scale type. The scale type is the absolute scale and is a special case of the ratio scale. The absolute scale is used when the value itself is the only meaningful transformation. An example of an absolute scale is counting.

Possible transformations with this scale type are those where the measures are a linear combination of each other, i.e. $M' = \alpha M + \beta$ where M' and M are different measures on the same attribute. Measures on this scale are uncommon in software engineering.

Examples of an interval scale are temperature measured in Celsius or Fahrenheit.

Ratio   If there exists a meaningful zero value and the ratio between two measures is meaningful, a ratio scale can be used.

Possible transformations are those that have the same zero and the scales only differs by a factor, i.e. $M' = \alpha M$ where M' and M are different measures on the same attribute.

Examples of a ratio scale are length, temperature measured in Kelvin and duration of a development phase.

The measurement scales are related to qualitative and quantitative research. Furthermore, it relates to which statistics can be used on the measures. This is further discussed in Chap. 10. According to Kachigan [90], qualitative research is concerned with measurement on the nominal and ordinal scales, and quantitative research treats measurement on the interval and ratio scales.

3.1.2   Objective and Subjective Measures

Sometimes, the measurement of an attribute cannot be measured without considering the viewpoint they are taken from. We can divide measures into two classes:

Objective   An objective measure is a measure where there is no judgement in the measurement value and is therefore only dependent on the object that is being measured. An objective measure can be measured several times and by different researchers, and the same value can be obtained within the measurement error. Examples of objective measures are lines of code (LOC), and delivery date.

Subjective   A subjective measure is the opposite of the objective measure. The person making the measurement contributes by making some sort of judgement. The measure depends on both the object and the viewpoint from which they are taken. A subjective measure can be different if the object is measured again. A subjective measure is mostly of nominal or ordinal scale type. Examples of subjective measures are personnel skill, and usability.

Subjective measures are always subject to potential bias. This is further discussed in Sect. 3.3.

3.1.3 Direct or Indirect Measures

The attributes that we are interested in are sometimes not directly measurable. These measures must be derived through other measures that are directly measurable. To distinguish the direct measurable measures from derived measures, we divide the measures into direct and indirect measures.

Direct   A direct measurement of an attribute is directly measurable and does not involve measurements on other attributes. Examples of direct measures are lines of code, and the number of defects found in test.

Indirect   An indirect measurement involves the measurement of other attributes. The indirect measure is derived from the other measures. Examples of indirect measures are defect density (number of defects divided by the number of lines of code), and programmers productivity (lines of code divided by the programmer's effort).

3.2 Measurements in Software Engineering

The objects that are of interest in software engineering can be divided into three different classes:

Process   The process describes which activities that are needed to produce the software.

Product   The products are the artifacts, deliverables or documents that results from a process activity.

Resources   Resources are the objects, such as personnel, hardware, or software, needed for a process activity.

In each of the classes we also make a distinction between internal and external attributes [55]. An internal attribute is an attribute that can be measured purely in terms of the object. The external attributes can only be measured with respect to how the object relates to other objects. Examples of different software measures are shown in Table 3.1.

Often in software engineering, software engineers want to make statements of an external attribute of an object. Unfortunately, the external attributes are mostly indirect measures and must be derived from internal attributes of the object. The internal attributes are mostly direct measures.

The measures are often part of a measurement program. Building software measurement programs is discussed by, for example, Grady and Caswell [68] and Hetzel [75].

Measurements in software engineering are different from measurements in other domains, for example, physics. In those domains, it is often clear, which the attributes are, and how they are measured. In software engineering, however, it is sometimes difficult to define an attribute in a measurable way with which everyone

Table 3.1 Examples of measures in software engineering

Class	Examples of objects	Type of attribute	Example of measures
Process	Testing	Internal	Effort
		External	Cost
Product	Code	Internal	Size
		External	Reliability
Resource	Personnel	Internal	Age
		External	Productivity

agrees [56]. Another difference is that it is difficult to prove that the measures are anything else but nominal or ordinal scale types in software engineering. Validation of the indirect measures is more difficult as both the direct measures and the models to derive the external measure have to be validated.

When conducting empirical studies, we are interested in the scale types of the measures as the statistical analysis depends on them. Formally, the statistical analysis methods depend upon the scale type, but the methods are mostly rather robust regarding scale type. The basic rule is that the more powerful scale types we use, the more powerful analysis methods we may use, see Chap. 10.

Many measures in software engineering are often measured with nominal or ordinal scales, or it is not proven that it is a more powerful scale type. This means that we cannot use the most powerful statistical analysis methods, which requires interval or ratio scales, for the empirical studies we conduct.

Briand et al. [27] argue that we can use the more powerful statistical analysis even if we cannot prove that we have interval or ratio scales. Many of the more powerful statistical methods are robust to non-linear distortions of the interval scale if the distortions are not too extreme. If we take care and carefully consider the risks, we can make use of the more powerful statistical methods and get results that otherwise would be infeasible without a very large sample of measures.

3.3   Measurements in Practice

In practice metrics are defined by the researcher and then collected during the operation phase of the empirical study. When it comes to how the metrics should be collected it is an advantage if it does not require too much effort by the subjects in the study. In many experiments subjects fill out forms in order to provide the data, but it is also possible to define instrumenting systems where data is automatically collected, for example, by the development environment. Lethbridge et al. [111] discuss several general techniques for collection.

Since the collected metrics are the basis for the further analysis, the quality of the collected metrics is important for the continued analysis of the study. This means that it is important to really understand what kind of metrics are collected and to be certain about what scale-type they belong to. It is also important to understand what distribution they represent, in particular if they are normally distributed or not.

When it comes to the distribution, this could be investigated by descriptive statistics. The data can, for example, be plotted in a graph, or another technique for analyzing to what extent the data is normally distributed can be used. This is further elaborated in Chap. 10. When it comes to the scale-type, this is based on how the metrics are defined and must be understood by the researcher when the metrics are defined.

How the metrics are defined can greatly affect how good they are in displaying what the researcher is interested in. For example, Kitchenham et al. [102] compare two ways of displaying productivity and show that a scatter plot displaying effort versus size gives better information than a chart showing productivity over time. A general advice is to not use metrics that are constructed from the ratio of two independent measures unless one is sure to understand the measure's implication.

During the operation of the study it is important to make sure that the collected data is correct. This means that the researcher should apply quality assurance procedures during the experiment, for example, by reviewing how subjects fill out forms, checking consistencies between different values, etc. Data validation is further discussed in Chap. 8.

A factor related to this concerns who is the inventor or owner of the aspects that are investigated in an experiment. Ideally someone else than the inventor of new methods should evaluate them in experiments and other research approaches, as recommended by Kitchenham et al. [98]. The inventor of a method naturally wants the method to perform well and there is always a risk that the researcher consciously or unconsciously selects metrics that are favorable for the investigated method. If it is known by the subjects that the researcher is the inventor of the investigated method this may also affect their performance. If experiments are carried out where own methods are studied, the design and selection of metrics could be reviewed by external researchers.

3.4 Exercises

3.1. What are measure, measurement and metric and how do they relate?

3.2. Which are the four main measurement scale types?

3.3. What are the difference between a direct and an indirect measure?

3.4. Which three classes are measurements in software engineering divided into?

3.5. What are internal and external attributes and how are they mostly related to direct and indirect measures?

Chapter 4
Systematic Literature Reviews

Systematic literature reviews are conducted to "*identify, analyse and interpret all available evidence related to a specific research question*" [96]. As it aims to give a complete, comprehensive and valid picture of the existing evidence, both the identification, analysis and interpretation must be conducted in a scientifically and rigorous way. In order to achieve this goal, Kitchenham and Charters have adapted guidelines for systematic literature reviews, primarily from medicine, evaluated them [24] and updated them accordingly [96]. These guidelines, structured according to a three-step process for *planning, conducting* and *reporting* the review, are summarized below.

4.1 Planning the Review

To plan a systematic literature review includes several actions:

Identification of the need for a review. The need for a systematic review originates from a researcher aiming to understand the state-of-the-art in an area, or from practitioners wanting to use empirical evidence in their strategic decision-making or improvement activities. If there are more or less systematic literature reviews available in the field, they should be appraised regarding scope and quality, to evaluate if they are sufficient to meet the current needs for a review. A systematic literature review may be viewed as a research method for making a literature review.

Specifying the research question(s). The area of the systematic review and the specific research questions set the focus for the identification of the primary studies, the extraction of data from the studies and the analysis. Hence, the research questions must be well thought through and phrased. Aspects to take into account in phrasing the research questions include [96]:

- The *population* in which the evidence is collected, i.e. which group of people, programs or businesses are of interest for the review?

C. Wohlin et al., *Experimentation in Software Engineering*,
DOI 10.1007/978-3-642-29044-2_4, © Springer-Verlag Berlin Heidelberg 2012

- The *intervention* applied in the empirical study, i.e. which technology, tool or procedure is under study?
- The *comparison* to which the intervention is compared, i.e. how is the control treatment defined? In particular the 'placebo' intervention is critical, as "not using the intervention" is mostly not a valid action in software engineering.
- The *outcomes* of the experiment should not only be statistically significant, but also be significant from a practical point of view. For example, it is probably not interesting that an outcome is 10% better in some respect if it is twice as time consuming.
- The *context* of the study must be defined, which is an extended view of the population, including whether it is conducted in academia or industry, in which industry segment, and also the incentives for the subjects [78, 132].
- The *experimental designs* to include in the research question must also be defined.

Staples and Niazi recommend the scope of a systematic literature review be limited by clear and narrow research questions to avoid inmanagable studies [166].

Developing a review protocol. The review protocol defines the procedures for the systematic literature review. It also acts as a log for conducting the review. Hence, it is a "living" document that is of importance both for the practical conduct of the review, and for its validity. Kitchenham and Charters propose the following items be covered in a review protocol [96]:

- Background and rationale
- Research questions
- Search strategy for primary studies
- Study selection criteria
- Study selection procedures
- Study quality assessment checklists and procedures
- Data extraction strategy
- Synthesis of the extracted data
- Dissemination strategy
- Project timetable

The protocol is preferably reviewed by peers to ensure its consistency and validity. Experience from systematic literature review stresses the importance of a pre-review study to help scoping the research questions, as well as being open to modifying research questions during the protocol development, as the problem under study becomes clearer [24].

4.2 Conducting the Review

Conducting the review means setting the review protocol into practice. This includes:

Identification of research. The main activity in this step involves specifying search strings and applying them to databases. However, it also includes manual searches in journals and conference proceedings, as well as searching researchers' web sites or sending questions to researchers. Systematically searching for primary studies based on references to and from other studies, is called "snowballing" [145].

The search strategy is a trade-off between finding all relevant primary studies, and not getting an overwhelming number of false positives, which must be excluded manually [43]. A false positive is an outcome that is wrongly positive when it should not be; in this case, it means that a paper is found and hence assumed to be of interest, and later it turns out that it is not and therefore it has to be removed. The search string is developed from the area to be covered and the research questions. Using multiple databases is a necessity to cover all relevant literature, but it also creates duplicates, which must be identified and removed. At the end, it must be accepted that the papers found are a sample of the population of all papers on a specific topic. The key issue is that the sample is indeed from the intended population.

The published primary studies tend to have a *publication bias*, which means that (in some sense) *positive* results are more likely to be published than *negative* results. Hence, also grey literature, like technical reports, theses, rejected publications, and work in progress, should be searched for [96].

The search results and a log of the actions taken should be stored, preferably using a reference management system.

Selection of primary studies. The basis for the selection of primary studies is the inclusion and exclusion criteria. The criteria should be developed beforehand, to avoid bias. However, they may have to be adjusted during the course of the selection, since all aspects of inclusion and exclusion are not apparent in the planning stage.

The identified set of candidate studies are processed related to the selection criteria. For some studies, it is sufficient to read the title or abstract to judge the paper, while other papers need a more thorough analysis of, for example, the methodology or conclusions to determine its status. Structured abstracts [30] may help the selection process.

As the selection process is a matter of judgments, also with well defined selection criteria, it is advised that two or more researchers assess each paper, or at least a random sample of the papers. Then the inter-rater agreement may be measured using the Cohen Kappa statistic [36] and be reported as a part of the quality assessment of the systematic literature review. However, it should be noted that a relatively high Cohen Kappa statistics may be obtained due to that many papers found in the automatic search are easily excluded by the researchers when assessing them manually. Thus, it may be important to conduct the assessment in several steps, i.e. start by removing those papers that are obviously not relevant although found in the search.

Study quality assessment. Assessing the quality of the primary studies is important, especially when the studies report contradictory results. The quality of the primary studies may be used to analyze the cause of contradicting results or to weight the importance of individual studies when synthesizing results.

There is no universally agreed and applicable definition of "study quality". Attempts to map quality criteria from medicine did not map to the quality range of software engineering studies [47].

The most practically useful means for quality assessment are checklists, even though their empirical underpinning may be weak. A study by Kitchenham et al. also showed that at least three reviewers are needed to make a valid assessment [105]. Checklists used in quality assessment of empirical studies are available in the empirical software engineering literature [96, 105, 145].

The quality assessment may lead to some primary studies being excluded, if the study quality is part of the selection criteria. It is also worth noting that the quality of the primary studies should be assessed, not the quality of the reporting. However, it is often hard to judge the quality of a study if it is poorly reported. Contacts with authors may be needed to find or clarify information, lacking in the reports.

Data extraction and monitoring. Once the list of primary studies is decided, the data from the primary studies is extracted. A data extraction form is designed to collect the information needed from the primary study reports. If the quality assessment data is used for study selection, the extraction form is separated into two parts, one for quality data, which is filled out during quality assessment, and one for the study data to be filled out during data extraction.

The data extraction form is designed based on the research questions. For pure meta-analytical synthesis, the data is a set of numerical values, representing number of subjects, objects characteristics, treatment effects, confidence intervals, etc. For less homogeneous sets of studies, more qualitative descriptions of the primary studies must be included. In addition to the raw data, the name of the reviewer, date of data extraction and publication details are logged for each primary study.

The data extraction form should be piloted before being applied to the full set of primary studies. If possible, the data extraction should be performed independently by two researchers, at least for a sample of the studies, in order to assess the quality of the extraction procedure.

If a primary study is published in more than one paper, for example, if a conference paper is extended to a journal version, only one instance should be counted as a primary study. Mostly, the journal version is preferred, as it is most complete, but both versions may be used in the data extraction. Supporting technical reports, or communication with authors may also serve as data sources for the extraction.

Data synthesis. The most advanced form of data synthesis is *meta-analysis*. This refers to statistical methods being applied to analyze the outcome of several independent studies. Meta-analysis assumes that the synthesized studies are homogenous, or the cause of the in-homogeneity being well known [135]. A meta-analysis compare *effect sizes* and p values to assess the synthesized outcome. It is primarily

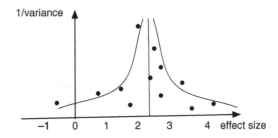

Fig. 4.1 An example funnel plot for 12 hypothetical studies

applicable to replicated experiments, if any, due to the requirement on homogeneity. In summary, the studies to be included in a meta-analysis must [135]:

- Be of the same type, for example, formal experiments
- Have the same test hypothesis
- Have the same measures of the treatment and effect constructs
- Report the same explanatory factors

Meta-analysis procedures involve three main steps [135]:

1. Decide which studies to include in the meta-analysis.
2. Extract the effect size from the primary study report, or estimate if there is no effect size published.
3. Combine the effect sizes from the primary studies to estimate and test the combined effect.

In addition to the primary study selection procedures presented above, the meta-analysis should include an analysis of *publication bias*. Such methods include the *funnel plot*, as illustrated in Fig. 4.1 where observed effect sizes are plotted against a measure of study size, for example, the inverse of the variance or another dispersion measure (see Sect. 10.1.2). The data points should scatter around a 'funnel' pattern if the set of primary studies is complete. Gaps in the funnel indicate some studies not being published or found [135].

The *effect size* is an indicator, independent of the unit or scale that is used in each of the primary studies. It depends on the type of study, but could typically be the difference between the mean values of each treatment. This measure must be normalized to allow for comparisons with other scales, that is, divided by the combined standard deviation [135].

The analysis assumes homogeneity between studies, and is then done with a *fixed effects* model. The meta-analysis estimates the true effect size by calculating an average value of the individual study effect sizes, which are averages themselves. There are tests to identify heterogeneity, such as the Q test and the Likelihood Ratio test, which should be applied to ensure model conditions are met [135].

For inhomogenous data, there are a *random effects* model, which allow for variability due to an unknown factor, which influences the effect sizes for the primary studies. This model provides estimates both for the sampling error, as the fixed effects model, and for the variability in the inhomogenous sub-populations.

Fig. 4.2 An example forest plot for three hypothetical studies

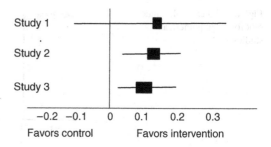

Less formal methods for data synthesis include *descriptive* or *narrative synthesis*. These methods tabulate data from the primary studies in a manner that brings light to the research question. As a minimum requirement on tabulated data, Kitchenham and Charters propose the following items be presented [96]:

- Sample size for each intervention
- Estimates of effect size for each intervention with standard errors for each effect
- Difference between the mean values for each intervention, and the confidence interval for the difference
- Units used for measuring the effect

Statistical results may be visualized using *forest plots*. A forest plot presents the means and variance of the difference between treatments for each study. An example forest plot is shown in Fig. 4.2.

Synthesizing inhomogenous studies and mixed-method studies require qualitative approaches. Cruzes and Dybå [39] surveyed secondary studies in software engineering, which included synthesis of empirical evidence. They identified several synthesis methods, many from medicine of which seven methods were used in software engineering. These methods are briefly introduced below. For more detail, refer to Cruzes and Dybå [39] and related references.

- *Thematic analysis* is a method that aims at identifying, analyzing and reporting patterns or themes in the primary studies. At minimum, it organizes and presents the data in rich detail, and interprets various aspects of the topic under study.
- *Narrative synthesis*, mentioned above, tells a 'story' which originates from the primary evidence. Raw evidence and interpretations are structured, using for example tabulation of data, groupings and clustering, or vote-counting as a descriptive tool. Narrative synthesis may be applied to studies with qualitative or quantitative data, or combinations thereof.
- The *comparative analysis* method is aimed at analyzing complex causal connections. It uses Boolean logic to explain relations between cause and effect in the primary studies. The analysis lists necessary and sufficient conditions in each of the primary studies and draws conclusions from presence/absence of independent variables in each of the studies. This is similar to Noblit and Hare's [127] *Line of argument synthesis*, referred to by Kitchenham and Charters [96].

- The *case survey* method is originally defined for case studies, but may apply to inhomogenous experiments too. It aggregates existing research by applying a survey instrument of specific questions to each primary study [114], similar to the data extraction mentioned above. The data from the survey is quantitative, and hence the aggregation is performed using statistical methods [108].
- *Meta-ethnography* translates studies into one another, and synthesize the translations into concepts that go beyond individual studies. Interpretations and explanations in the primary studies are treated as data in the meta-ethnography study. This is similar to Noblit and Hare's [127] *Reciprocal translation* and *Refutational synthesis*, referred to by Kitchenham and Charters [96].
- *Meta-analysis* is, as mentioned above, based on statistical methods to integrate quantitative data from several cases.
- *Scoping analysis* aims at giving an overview of the research in a field, rather than synthesizing the findings from the research. Scoping are also referred to as mapping studies, which are further discussed in Sect. 4.4.

Independently of synthesis method, a *sensitivity analysis* should take place to analyze whether the results are consistent across different subsets of studies. Subsets of studies may be, for example, high quality primary studies only, primary studies of particular type, or primary studies with good reports, presenting all detail needed.

4.3 Reporting the Review

Like any other empirical study, the systematic literature review may be reported to different audiences. In particular, if the purpose of the review is to influence practitioners, the format of the report has to be tailored well to its audience. Kitchenham and Charters [96] list the following forms for dissemination targeting practitioners:

1. Practitioner-oriented journals and magazines
2. Press Releases to the popular and specialist press
3. Short summary leaflets
4. Posters
5. Web pages
6. Direct communication to affected bodies

For academic audiences, the detailed reporting of procedures for the study is critical for the ability to assess and evaluate the quality of the systematic literature review. The reporting ideally includes changes to the study protocol, complete lists of included and excluded primary studies, data on their classification, as well as the raw data derived from each of the primary studies. If space constraints do not allow all details being published, a supporting technical report is recommended to be published online. A detailed structure for the academic report is proposed by Kitchenham and Charters [96].

4.4 Mapping Studies

If the research question for the literature review is broader, or the field of study is less explored, a *mapping study* may be launched instead of a systematic literature review. A mapping study [131], sometimes referred to as *scoping study* [96], searches a broader field for any kind of research, in order to get an overview of the state-of-art or state-of-practice on a topic.

A mapping study follows the same principled process as systematic literature reviews, but have different criteria for inclusions/exclusions and quality. Due to its broader scope and varying type of studies, the collected data and the synthesis tend to be more qualitative than for systematic literature reviews. However, it is important for the contribution and relevance of a mapping study that the analysis goes beyond the pure descriptive statistics and relates the trends and observations to real-world needs.

Kitchenham et al. [106] provided a summary of the key characteristics for mapping studies compared to systematic literature reviews, which is presented in Table 4.1.

4.5 Example Reviews

Kitchenham et al. report 53 unique systematic literature reviews in software engineering being published between 2004 and 2008 [103, 104]. They conclude that there is a growth of the number of systematic literature reviews being published, and that the quality of the reviews tend to be increasing too. However, still there is large variation between those who are aware of and use any systematic guidelines for its conduct, and those who are not referring to any guidelines.

In one of those systematic literature reviews, Sjøberg et al. [161] survey the experimental studies conducted in software engineering. They searched nine journals and three conference proceedings in the decade from 1993 to 2002, scanning through 5,453 articles to identify 103 experiments, i.e. 1.9% of the papers presented experiments. The two most frequently research categories are Software life-cycle/engineering (49%) and Methods/Techniques (32%) classified according to Glass et al's scheme [63]. This is due to the relatively large number of experiments on inspection techniques and object-oriented design techniques, respectively.

Using the same set of primary studies, Dybå et al. [49] reviewed the statistical power in software engineering experiments, and Hannay et al. [72] reviewed the use of theory in software engineering. Dieste et al. [43] investigated different search strategies on the same set of studies, whether titles, abstracts or full texts should be searched, and also aspects related to which databases to search.

Early attempts at synthesizing five experiment on inspection techniques by Hayes [74] and Miller [121] indicate that the software engineering experiments in this field are not sufficiently homogenous to allow for application of statistical

Table 4.1 Difference between mapping studies and systematic literature reviews, according to Kitchenham et al. [106]

SLR elements	Systemic mapping study	Systematic literature review
Goals	Classification and thematic analysis of literature on a software engineering topic	Identifying best practice with respect to specific procedures, technologies, methods or tools by aggregating information from comparative studies
Research question	Generic – related to research trends. Of the form: which researchers, how much activity, what type of studies, etc.	Specific – related to outcomes of empirical studies. Of the form: Is technology/method A better or not than B?
Search process	Defined by topic area	Defined by research question which identifies the specific technologies being investigated
Scope	Broad – all papers related to a topic area are included but only classification data about these are collected	Focused – only empirical papers related to a specific research question are included and detailed information about individual research outcomes is extracted from each paper
Search strategy requirements	Often less stringent if only research trends are of interest, for example authors may search only a targeted set of publications, restrict themselves to journal papers, or restrict themselves to one or two digital libraries	Extremely stringent – all relevant studies should be found. Usually systematic literature review teams need to use techniques other than simply searching data sources, such as looking at the references in identified primary studies and/or approaching researchers in the field to find out whether they are undertaking new research in the area
Quality evaluation	Not essential. Also complicated by the inclusive nature of the search which can include theoretical studies as well as empirical studies of all types making the quality evaluation of primary studies complicated	Important to ensure that results are based on best quality evidence
Results	A set of papers related to a topic area categorized in a variety of dimensions and counts of the number of papers in various categories	The outcomes of the primary studies are aggregated to answer the specific research question(s), possibly with qualifiers (e.g. results apply to novices only)

meta-analysis. They also conclude that raw data must be made available for meta-analysts, as well as additional non-published information from the primary study authors.

In a more recent literature review on the effectiveness of pair programming, Hannay et al. [73] conducted meta-analysis on data from 18 primary studies. They report separate analyses for three outcome constructs: quality, duration, and effort. They also visualize the outcomes using forest plots.

4.6 Exercises

4.1. What is the difference between a systematic literature review, and a more general literature review?

4.2. What search strategies exist for primary studies?

4.3. Why should two researchers conduct some of the same steps in a systematic literature review?

4.4. What requirements are set on the primary studies to be included in a meta-analysis?

4.5. Which are the key differences between as systematic literature study and a mapping study?

Chapter 5
Case Studies

The term "case study" appears every now and then in the title or in the abstracts of software engineering research papers. However, the presented studies range from very ambitious and well-organized studies in the field, to small toy examples that claim to be case studies. The latter should preferably be termed examples or illustrations. Additionally, there are different taxonomies used to classify research. The term case study is used in parallel with terms like field study and observational study, each focusing on a particular aspect of the research methodology. For example, Lethbridge et al. use *field studies* as the most general term [111], while Easterbrook et al. call *case studies* one of five "classes of research methods" [50]. Zelkowitz and Wallace propose a terminology that is somewhat different from what is used in other fields, and categorize project monitoring, case study and field study as *observational methods* [181]. This plethora of terms causes confusion and problems when trying to aggregate multiple empirical studies.

The case study methodology is well suited for many kinds of software engineering research, as the objects of study are contemporary phenomena, which are hard to study in isolation. Case studies do not generate the same results on, for example, causal relationships as controlled experiments do, but they provide deeper understanding of the phenomena under study in its real context. As they are different from analytical and controlled empirical studies, case studies have been criticized for being of less value, impossible to generalize from, being biased by researchers etc. The critique may be addressed by applying proper research methodology practices and accepting that knowledge is not only statistical significance [59, 109].

The objective of this chapter is to provide some guidance for the researcher conducting case studies. This chapter is based on Runeson and Höst [145] and more details on case studies in software engineering may be obtained from Runeson et al. [146]. Specifically, checklists for researchers are derived through a systematic analysis of existing checklists [79, 145], and later evaluated by Ph.D. students as well as by members of the International Software Engineering Research Network and updated accordingly.

The chapter does not provide absolute statements for what is considered a 'good' case study in software engineering. Rather it focuses on a set of issues that all

C. Wohlin et al., *Experimentation in Software Engineering*,
DOI 10.1007/978-3-642-29044-2_5, © Springer-Verlag Berlin Heidelberg 2012

contribute to the quality of the research. The minimum requirement for each issue must be judged in its context, and will most probably evolve over time.

The chapter is outlined as follows. We first introduce the context of case study research, discuss the motivations for software engineering case studies and define a case study research process in Sect. 5.1. Section 5.2 discusses the design of a case study and planning for data collection. Section 5.3 describes the process of data collection. In Sect. 5.4 issues on data analysis are treated, and reporting is discussed in Sect. 5.5.

5.1 Case Studies in Its Context

Three commonly used definitions of case study research are provided by Robson [144], Yin [180] and Benbasat et al. [22] respectively. The three definitions agree on that case study is an empirical method aimed at *investigating contemporary phenomena* in their context. Robson calls it a research strategy and stresses the use of *multiple sources of evidence*, Yin denotes it an inquiry and remarks that *the boundary between the phenomenon and its context may be unclear*, while Benbasat et al. make the definitions somewhat more specific, mentioning *information gathering from few entities* (people, groups, organizations), and the *lack of experimental control*.

Action research is closely related to case study research with its purpose to "influence or change some aspect of whatever is the focus of the research" [144]. More strictly, a case study is purely observational while action research is focused on and involved in the change process. In software process improvement [44, 85] and technology transfer studies [66], the research method could be characterized as action research if the researcher actively participates in the improvements. However, when studying the effects of a change, for example, in pre- and post-event studies, we classify the methodology as case study. In information system research, where action research is widely used, there is a discussion on finding the balance between action and research, see for example Baskerville and Wood-Harper [21] or Avison et al. [5]. For the research part of action research, these guidelines for case studies may be used too.

Easterbrook et al. [50] also count ethnographic studies among the major research methodologies. We prefer to consider ethnographic studies as a specialized type of case studies with focus on cultural practices [50] or long duration studies with large amounts of participant-observer data [98]. Zelkowitz and Wallace define four different "observational methods" in software engineering [181]; project monitoring, case study, assertion and field study. We prefer to see project monitoring as a part of a case study and field studies as multiple case studies, while assertion is not considered an accepted research method.

Robson summarizes his view, which seems functional in software engineering as well: "Many flexible design studies, although not explicitly labeled as such, can be usefully viewed as case studies" [144].

A case study may contain elements of other research methods, for example, a survey may be conducted within a case study, a literature search often precede a case study and archival analyses may be a part of its data collection. Ethnographic methods, like interviews and observations, are mostly used for data collection in case studies.

Yin adds specifically to the characteristics of a case study that it [180]:

- "Copes with the technically distinctive situation in which there will be many more variables than data points, and as one result
- Relies on multiple sources of evidence, with data needing to converge in a triangulating fashion, and as another result
- Benefits from the prior development of theoretical propositions to guide data collection and analysis."

Hence, a case study will never provide conclusions with statistical significance. On the contrary, many different kinds of evidence, figures, statements, documents, are linked together to support a strong and relevant conclusion.

In summary, the key characteristics of a case study are that [146]:

1. It is of flexible type, coping with the complex and dynamic characteristics of real world phenomena, like software engineering,
2. Its conclusions are based on a clear chain of evidence, whether qualitative or quantitative, collected from multiple sources in a planned and consistent manner, and
3. It adds to existing knowledge by being based on previously established theory, if such exist, or by building theory.

5.1.1   Why Case Studies in Software Engineering?

The area of software engineering involves development, operation, and maintenance of software and related artifacts. Research on software engineering is to a large extent aimed at investigating how development, operation, and maintenance are conducted by software engineers and other stakeholders under different conditions. Individuals, groups and organizations, carry out software development, and social and political questions are of importance for this development. That is, software engineering is a multidisciplinary discipline involving areas where case studies are conducted, like psychology, sociology, political science, social work, business, and community planning (e.g. [180]). This means that many research questions in software engineering are suitable for case study research.

The definition of case study in Sect. 2.1 focuses on studying phenomena in their context, especially when the boundary between the phenomenon and its context is unclear. This is particularly true in software engineering. Experimentation in software engineering has clearly shown that there are many factors impacting the outcome of a software engineering activity, for example, when trying to replicate studies, see Sect. 2.6. Case studies offer an approach that does not need a strict boundary between the studied object and its environment; perhaps the key to understanding is in the interaction between the two?

5.1.2 Case Study Research Process

When conducting a case study, there are five major process steps to go through:

1. Case study design: objectives are defined and the case study is planned.
2. Preparation for data collection: procedures and protocols for data collection are defined.
3. Collection of data: execution with data collection on the studied case.
4. Analysis of collected data
5. Reporting

This process is almost the same for any kind of empirical study; compare, for example, to the process outlined in Chap. 6 and further elaborated in Chaps. 7–11 for experiments and Kitchenham et al. [98]. However, as case study methodology is a flexible design strategy, there is a significant amount of iteration over the steps [2]. The data collection and analysis may be conducted incrementally. If insufficient data is collected for the analysis, more data collection may be planned etc. Eisenhardt adds two steps between 4 and 5 above in her process for building theories from case study research [52] (a) shaping hypotheses and (b) enfolding literature, while the rest except for terminological variations are the same as above.

The five process steps are presented in Sects. 5.2–5.5, where preparation and collection of data is presented in a joint section, i.e. Sect. 5.3.

5.2 Design and Planning

Case study research is of flexible type but this does not mean that planning is unnecessary. On the contrary, good planning for a case study is crucial for its success. There are several issues that need to be planned, such as what methods to use for data collection, what departments of an organization to visit, what documents to read, which persons to interview, how often interviews should be conducted, etc. These plans can be formulated in a case study protocol, see Sect. 5.2.2.

5.2.1 Case Study Planning

A plan for a case study should at least contain the following elements [144]:

- *Objective:* what to achieve?
- *The case:* what is studied?

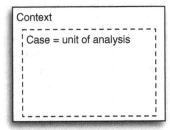 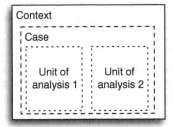

Fig. 5.1 Holistic case study (*left*) and embedded case study (*right*)

- *Theory:* frame of reference
- *Research questions:* what to know?
- *Methods:* how to collect data?
- *Selection strategy:* where to seek data?

The objective of the study may be, for example, exploratory, descriptive, explanatory, or improving. The objective is naturally more generally formulated and less precise than in fixed research designs. The objective is initially more like a focus point that evolves during the study. The research questions state what is needed to know in order to fulfill the objective of the study. Similar to the objective, the research questions evolve during the study and are narrowed to specific research questions during the study iterations [2].

In software engineering, the case may be a software development project, which is the most straightforward choice. It may alternatively be an individual, a group of people, a process, a product, a policy, a role in the organization, an event, a technology, etc. The project, individual, group etc. may also constitute a unit of analysis within a case. Studies on "toy programs" or similarly are of course excluded due to its lack of real-life context.

Yin [180] distinguishes between holistic case studies, where the case is studied as a whole, and embedded case studies where multiple units of analysis are studied within a case, see Fig. 5.1. Whether to define a study consisting of two cases as holistic or embedded depends on what we define as the context and research goals. For example if studying two projects in two different companies and in two different application domains, both using agile practices. On the one hand, the projects may be considered two units of analysis in an embedded case study if the context is software companies in general and the research goal is to study agile practices. On the other hand, if the context is considered being the specific company or application domain, they have to be seen as two separate holistic cases.

Using theories to develop the research direction is not well established in the software engineering field, as discussed in Sect. 2.7. However, defining the frame of reference of the study makes the context of the case study research clear, and helps both those conducting the research and those reviewing the results of it. In lack of theory, the frame of reference may alternatively be expressed in terms of the viewpoint taken in the research and the background of the researchers. Grounded theory case studies naturally have no specified theory [38].

The principal decisions on methods for data collection are defined at design time for the case study, although detailed decisions on data collection procedures are taken later. Lethbridge et al. [111] define three categories of methods: direct (e.g. interviews), indirect (e.g. tool instrumentation) and independent (e.g. documentation analysis). These are further elaborated in Sect. 5.3.

In case studies, the case and the units of analysis should be selected intentionally. This is in contrast to surveys and experiments, where subjects are sampled from a population to which the results are intended to be generalized. The purpose of the selection may be to study a case that is expected to be 'typical', 'critical', 'revelatory' or 'unique' in some respect [22], and the case is selected accordingly. In a comparative case study, the units of analysis must be selected to have the variation in properties that the study intends to compare. However, in practice, many cases are selected based on availability [22], which is similar for experiments [161].

Case selection is particularly important when replicating case studies. A case study may be literally replicated, i.e. the case is selected to predict similar results, or it is theoretically replicated, i.e. the case is selected to predict contrasting results for predictable reasons [180].

5.2.2 Case Study Protocol

The case study protocol is a container for the design decisions on the case study as well as field procedures for carrying through the study. The protocol is a continuously changed document that is updated when the plans for the case study are changed and serves several purposes:

1. It serves as a guide when conducting the data collection, and in that way prevents the researcher from missing to collect data that were planned to be collected.
2. The processes of formulating the protocol makes the research concrete in the planning phase, which may help the researcher to decide what data sources to use and what questions to ask.
3. Other researchers and relevant people may review it in order to give feedback on the plans. Feedback on the protocol from other researchers can, for example, lower the risk of missing relevant data sources, interview questions or roles to include in the research and to question the relation between research questions and interview questions.
4. It can serve as a log or diary where all data collection and analysis is recorded together with change decisions based on the flexible nature of the research. This can be an important source of information when the case study later on is reported. In order to keep track of changes during the research project, the protocol should be kept under some form of version control.

Table 5.1 Outline of case study protocol according to Brereton et al. [25]

Section	Content
Background	Previous research, main and additional research questions
Design	Single or multiple case, embedded or holistic design; object of study; propositions derived from research questions
Selection	Criteria for case selection
Procedures and roles	Field procedures; Roles for research team members
Data collection	Identify data, define collection plan and data storage
Analysis	Criteria for interpretation, linking between data and research questions, alternative explanations
Plan validity	Tactics to reduce threats to validity
Study limitations	Specify remaining validity issues
Reporting	Target audience
Schedule	Estimates for the major steps
Appendices	Any detailed information

Brereton et al. [25] propose an outline of a case study protocol, which is summarized in Table 5.1. As the proposal shows, the protocol is quite detailed to support a well-structured research approach.

5.3 Preparation and Collection of Data

There are several different sources of information that can be used in a case study. It is important to use several data sources in a case study in order to limit the effects of one interpretation of one single data source. If the same conclusion can be drawn from several sources of information, i.e. triangulation (briefly described in the context of experiments in Sect. 6.2), this conclusion is stronger than a conclusion based on a single source. In a case study, it is also important to take into account viewpoints of different roles, and to investigate differences for example between different projects and products. Commonly, conclusions are drawn by analyzing differences between data sources.

According to Lethbridge et al. [111], data collection techniques can be divided into three levels:

- *First degree:* Direct methods means that the researcher is in direct contact with the subjects and collect data in real time. This is the case with, for example interviews, focus groups, Delphi surveys [40], and observations with "think aloud protocols" [129].
- *Second degree:* Indirect methods where the researcher directly collects raw data without actually interacting with the subjects during the data collection. Examples are logging of the usage of software engineering tools, and observations through video recording.

• *Third degree:* Independent analysis of work artifacts where already available and sometimes compiled data is used. This is for example the case when documents such as requirements specifications and failure reports from an organization are analyzed or when data from organizational databases such as time accounting is analyzed.

First degree methods are mostly more expensive to apply than second or third degree methods, since they require significant effort both from the researcher and the subjects. An advantage of first and second degree methods is that the researcher can to a large extent exactly control what data is collected, how it is collected, in what form the data is collected, which the context is etc. Third degree methods are mostly less expensive, but they do not offer the same control to the researcher; hence the quality of the data is not under control either, neither regarding the original data quality nor its use for the case study purpose. In many cases the researcher must, to some extent, base the details of the data collection on what data is available. For third degree methods, it should also be noticed that the data has been collected and recorded for another purpose than that of the research study, contrary to general metrics guidelines [172]. It is not certain that requirements on data validity and completeness were the same when the data was collected as they are in the research study.

In Sects. 5.3.1–5.3.4, we discuss specific data collection methods, where we have found interviews, observations, archival data and metrics being applicable to software engineering case studies [22, 146, 180].

5.3.1 Interviews

In interview-based data collection, the researcher asks a series of questions to a set of subjects about the areas of interest in the case study. In most cases one interview is conducted with every single subject, but it is possible to conduct group-interviews. The dialogue between the researcher and the subject(s) is guided by a set of interview questions.

The interview questions are based on the research questions (although not phrased in the same way). Questions can be *open*, i.e. allowing and inviting a broad range of answers and issues from the interviewed subject, or *closed* offering a limited set of alternative answers.

Interviews can be divided into *unstructured, semi-structured* and *fully structured* interviews [144]. In an unstructured interview, the interview questions are formulated as general concerns and interests from the researcher. In this case the interview conversation will develop based on the interest of the subject and the researcher. In a fully structured interview all questions are planned in advance and all questions are asked in the same order as in the plan. In many ways, a fully structured interview is similar to a questionnaire-based survey. In a semi-structured interview, questions are planned, but they are not necessarily asked in the same order as they are listed.

Table 5.2 Overview of interview types

	Unstructured	Semi-structured	Fully structured
Typical foci	How individuals qualitatively experience the phenomenon	How individuals qualitatively and quantitatively experience the phenomenon	Researcher seeks to find relations between constructs
Interview questions	Interview guide with areas to focus on	Mix of open and closed questions	Closed questions
Objective	Exploratory	Descriptive and explanatory	Descriptive and explanatory

The development of the conversation in the interview can decide which order the different questions are handled, and the researcher can use the list of questions to be certain that all questions are handled, i.e. more or less as a checklist. Additionally, semi-structured interviews allow for improvisation and exploration of the studied objects. Semi-structured interviews are common in case studies. The three types of interviews are summarized in Table 5.2.

An interview session may be divided into a number of phases. First the researcher presents the objectives of the interview and the case study, and explains how the data from the interview will be used. Then a set of introductory questions is asked about the background etc. of the subject; these questions are relatively simple to answer. After the introduction, the main interview questions are posed, which take up the largest part of the interview. If the interview contains personal and maybe sensitive questions, for example, concerning economy, opinions about colleagues, why things went wrong, or questions related to the interviewees own competence [80], it is important that the interviewee is ensured confidentiality and that the interviewee trusts the interviewer. It is not recommended to start the interview with these questions or to introduce them before a climate of trust has been obtained. It is recommended that the researcher summarizes the major findings towards the end of the interview, in order to get feedback and avoid misunderstandings.

During the interview sessions, it is recommended to record the discussion in a suitable audio or video format. Even if notes are taken, it is in many cases hard to record all details, and it is impossible to know what is important to record during the interview. When the interview has been recorded it needs to be transcribed into text before it is analyzed. In some cases it may be advantageous to have the transcripts reviewed by the interview subject.

During the planning phase of an interview study it is decided whom to interview. Due to the qualitative nature of the case study it is recommended to select subjects based on differences instead of trying to replicate similarities, as discussed in Sect. 5.2. This means that it is good to try to involve different roles, personalities, etc. in the interview. The number of interviewees has to be decided during the study. One criterion for when sufficient interviews are conducted is 'saturation', i.e. when no new information or viewpoint is gained from new subjects [38].

Table 5.3 Different approaches to observations

	High awareness of being observed	Low awareness of being observed
High degree of interaction by the researcher	Category 1	Category 2
Low degree of interaction by the researcher	Category 3	Category 4

5.3.2 Observations

Observations can be conducted in order to investigate how software engineers conduct a certain task. This is a first or second degree method according to the classification above. There are many different approaches for observation. One approach is to monitor a group of software engineers with a video recorder and later on analyze the recording. Another alternative is to apply a "think aloud" protocol, where the researcher are repeatedly asking questions like "What is your strategy?" and "What are you thinking?" to remind the subjects to think aloud. This can be combined with recording of audio and keystrokes as proposed, for example, by Wallace et al. [176]. Observations in meetings are another type, where meeting attendants interact with each other, and thus generate information about the studied object. Karahasanoviĉ et al. [93] present an alternative approach where a tool for sampling is used to obtain data and feedback from the participants.

Approaches for observations can be divided into high or low interaction of the researcher and high or low awareness of the subjects of being observed, see Table 5.3.

Observations according to category 1 or category 2 are typically conducted in action research or classical ethnographic studies where the researcher is part of the team, and not only seen as a researcher by the other team members. The difference between category 1 and category 2 is that in category 1 the researcher is seen as an "observing participant" by the other subjects, while she is more seen as a "normal participant" in category 2. In category 3 the researcher is seen only as a researcher. The approaches for observation typically include observations with first degree data collection techniques, such as a "think aloud" protocol as described above. In category 4 the subjects are typically observed with a second degree technique such as video recording (sometimes called video ethnography).

An advantage of observations is that they may provide a deep understanding of the phenomenon that is studied. Further, it is particularly relevant to use observations, where it is suspected that there is a deviation between an 'official' view of matters and the 'real' case [142]. It should however be noted that it produces a substantial amount of data which makes the analysis time consuming.

5.3.3 Archival Data

Archival data refers to, for example, meeting minutes, documents from different development phases, failure data, organizational charts, financial records, and other previously collected measurements in an organization.

Archival data is a third degree type of data that can be collected in a case study. For this type of data a configuration management tool is an important source, since it enables the collection of a number of different documents and different versions of documents. As for other third degree data sources it is important to keep in mind that the documents were not originally developed with the intention to provide data for the research. It is of course hard for the researcher to assess the quality of the data, although some information can be obtained by investigating the purpose of the original data collection, and by interviewing relevant people in the organization.

5.3.4 Metrics

The above mentioned data collection techniques are mostly focused on qualitative data. However, quantitative data is also important in a case study. Collected data can either be defined or collected for the purpose of the case study, or already available data can be used in a case study. The first case gives, of course, most flexibility and the data that is most suitable for the research questions under investigation. The definition of what data to collect should be based on a goal-oriented measurement technique, such as the Goal Question Metric method (GQM) [11, 172], which is presented in Chap. 3.

Examples of already available data are effort data from older projects, sales figures of products, metrics of product quality in terms of failures etc. This kind of data may, for example, be available in a metrics database in an organization. However, note that the researcher can neither control nor assess the quality of the data, since it was collected for another purpose, and as for other forms of archival analysis there is a risk of missing important data.

5.4 Data Analysis

5.4.1 Quantitative Data Analysis

Data analysis is conducted differently for quantitative and qualitative data. For quantitative data, the analysis typically includes analysis of descriptive statistics, correlation analysis, development of predictive models, and hypothesis testing. All of these activities are relevant in case study research. Quantitative data analysis, although primarily in an experimental context, is further described in Chap. 10.

Descriptive statistics, such as mean values, standard deviations, histograms and scatter plots, are used to get an understanding of the data that has been collected. Correlation analysis and development of predictive models are conducted in order to describe how a measurement from a later process activity is related to an earlier process measurement. Hypothesis testing is conducted in order to determine if there is a significant effect of one or several variables (independent variables) on one or several other variables (dependent variables).

It should be noticed that methods for quantitative analysis assume a fixed research design. For example, if a question with a quantitative answer is changed halfway in a series of interviews, this makes it impossible to interpret the mean value of the answers. Further, quantitative data sets from single cases tend to be very small, due to the number of respondents or measurement points, which causes special concerns in the analysis.

5.4.2   Qualitative Data Analysis

The basic objective of the qualitative analysis is to derive conclusions from the data, keeping a clear chain of evidence. The chain of evidence means that a reader should be able to follow the derivation of results and conclusions from the collected data [180]. This means that sufficient information from each step of the study and every decision taken by the researcher must be presented.

In addition, analysis of qualitative research is characterized by having analysis carried out in parallel with the data collection and the need for systematic analysis techniques. Analysis must be carried out in parallel with the data collection since the approach is flexible and that new insights are found during the analysis. In order to investigate these insights, new data must often be collected, and instrumentation such as interview questionnaires must be updated. The need to be systematic is a direct result of that the data collection techniques can be constantly updated, while the same time being required to maintain a chain of evidence.

In order to reduce bias by individual researchers, the analysis benefits from being conducted by multiple researchers. The preliminary results from each individual researcher are merged into a common analysis result in a second step. Keeping track and reporting the cooperation scheme helps increasing the validity of the study.

General techniques for analysis. There are two different parts of data analysis of qualitative data, hypothesis generating techniques and hypothesis confirmation techniques [148].

Hypothesis *generation* is intended to find hypotheses from the data. When using these kinds of techniques, the researcher should try to be unbiased and open for whatever hypotheses are to be found in the data. The results of these techniques are the hypotheses as such. Examples of hypotheses generating techniques are "constant comparisons" and "cross-case analysis" [148]. Hypothesis *confirmation* techniques denote techniques that can be used to confirm that a hypothesis is really true, for example, through analysis of more data. Triangulation and replication are examples of approaches for hypothesis confirmation [148]. *Negative case analysis* tries to find alternative explanations that reject the hypotheses. These basic types of techniques are used iteratively and in combination. First hypotheses are generated and then they are confirmed. Hypothesis generation may take place within one cycle of a case study, or with data from one unit of analysis, and hypothesis confirmation may be done with data from another cycle or unit of analysis [2].

This means that analysis of qualitative data is conducted in a series of steps (based on Robson [144]). First the data is coded, which means that parts of the text can be given a code representing a certain theme, area, construct, etc. One code is usually assigned to many pieces of text, and one piece of text can be assigned more than one code. Codes can form a hierarchy of codes and sub-codes. The coded material can be combined with comments and reflections by the researcher (i.e. 'memos'). When this has been done, the researcher can go through the material to identify a first set of hypotheses. This can, for example, be phrases that are similar in different parts of the material, patterns in the data, differences between sub-groups of subjects, etc. The identified hypotheses can then be used when further data collection is conducted in the field, i.e. resulting in an iterative approach where data collection and analysis is conducted in parallel as described above. During the iterative process a small set of generalizations can be formulated, eventually resulting in a formalized body of knowledge, which is the final result of the research attempt. This is, of course, not a simple sequence of steps. Instead, they are executed iteratively and they affect each other.

One example of a useful technique for analysis is tabulation, where the coded data is arranged in tables, which makes it possible to get an overview of the data. The data can, for example be organized in a table where the rows represent codes of interest and the columns represent interview subjects. However, how to do this must be decided for every case study.

There are specialized software tools available to support qualitative data analysis, for example, NVivo[1] and Atlas.[2] However, in some cases standard tools such as word processors and spreadsheet tools are useful when managing the textual data.

Level of formalism. A structured approach is, as described above, important in qualitative analysis. However, the analysis can be conducted at different levels of formalism. Robson [144] mentions the following approaches:

- *Immersion approaches:* These are the least structured approaches, with very low level of structure, more reliant on intuition and interpretive skills of the researcher. These approaches may be hard to combine with requirements on keeping and communicating a chain of evidence.
- *Editing approaches:* These approaches include few a priori codes, i.e. codes are defined based on findings of the researcher during the analysis.

---

[1] http://www.qsrinternational.com

[2] http://www.atlasti.com

- *Template approaches:* These approaches are more formal and include more a priori based on research questions.
- *Quasi-statistical approaches:* These approaches are much formalized and include, for example, calculation of frequencies of words and phrases.

In our experience editing approaches and template approaches are most suitable in software engineering case studies. It is hard to present and obtain a clear chain of evidence in informal immersion approaches. It is also hard to interpret the result of, for example, frequencies of words in documents and interviews.

5.4.3 Validity

The validity of a study denotes the trustworthiness of the results, and to what extent the results are true and not biased by the researchers' subjective point of view. It is, of course, too late to consider the validity during the analysis. The validity must be addressed during all previous phases of the case study.

There are different ways to classify aspects of validity and threats to validity in the literature. Here we chose a classification scheme, which is also used by Yin [180] for case studies, and similar to what is usually used in controlled experiments in software engineering as further elaborated in Sect. 8.7. Some researchers have argued for having a different classification scheme for flexible design studies (credibility, transferability, dependability and confirmability), while we prefer to operationalize this scheme for flexible design studies, instead of changing the terms [144]. This scheme distinguishes between four aspects of the validity, which can be summarized as follows:

- *Construct validity:* This aspect of validity reflect to what extent the operational measures that are studied really represent what the researcher has in mind and what is investigated according to the research questions. If, for example, the constructs discussed in the interview questions are not interpreted in the same way by the researcher and the interviewed persons, there is a threat to construct validity.
- *Internal validity:* This aspect of validity is of concern when causal relations are examined. When the researcher is investigating whether one factor affects an investigated factor there is a risk that the investigated factor is also affected by a third factor. If the researcher is not aware of the third factor and/or does not know to what extent it affects the investigated factor, there is a threat to internal validity.
- *External validity:* This aspect of validity is concerned with to what extent it is possible to generalize the findings, and to what extent the findings are of interest to other people outside the investigated case. During analysis of external validity, the researcher tries to analyze to what extent the findings are of relevance for other cases. In case studies, there is no population from which a statistically representative sample has been drawn. However, for case studies, the intention is

to enable analytical generalization where the results are extended to cases which have common characteristics and hence for which the findings are relevant, i.e. defining a theory.

- *Reliability:* This aspect is concerned with to what extent the data and the analysis are dependent on the specific researchers. Hypothetically, if another researcher later on conducted the same study, the result should be the same. Threats to this aspect of validity are, for example, if it is not clear how to code collected data or if questionnaires or interview questions are unclear. For quantitative analysis, the counterpart to reliability is conclusion validity, see further Sect. 8.7.

It is, as described above, important to consider the validity of the case study from the beginning. Examples of ways to improve validity are triangulation; developing and maintaining a detailed case study protocol; having designs, protocols, etc. reviewed by peer researchers; have collected data and obtained results reviewed by case subjects; spending sufficient time with the case, and giving sufficient concern to analysis of "negative cases", i.e. looking for theories that contradict your findings.

5.5 Reporting

An empirical study cannot be distinguished from its reporting. The report communicates the findings of the study, but is also the main source of information for judging the quality of the study. Reports may have different audiences, such as peer researchers, policy makers, research sponsors, and industry practitioners [180]. This may lead to the need of writing different reports for difference audiences. Here, we focus on reports with peer researchers as main audience, i.e. journal or conference articles and possibly accompanying technical reports [22]. Guidelines for reporting software engineering case studies to other audiences and in other formats are provided by Runeson et al. [146]. Benbasat et al. propose that due to the extensive amount of data generated in case studies, "books or monographs might be better vehicles to publish case study research" [22].

For case studies, the same high-level structure may be used, see Chap. 11, but since they are more flexible and mostly based on qualitative data, the low-level detail is less standardized and more depending on the individual case. Below, we first discuss the characteristics of a case study report and then a proposed structure.

5.5.1 Characteristics

Robson defines a set of characteristics that a case study report should have [144], which in summary implies that it should:

- Tell what the study was about.
- Communicate a clear sense of the studied case.

- Provide a "history of the inquiry" so the reader can see what was done, by whom and how.
- Provide basic data in focused form, so the reader can make sure that the conclusions are reasonable.
- Articulate the researchers conclusions and set them into a context they affect.

In addition, this must take place under the balance between researchers duty and goal to publish their results, and the companies' and individuals' integrity [3].

Reporting the case study objectives and research questions is quite straightforward. If they are changed substantially over the course of the study, this should be reported to help understanding the case.

Describing the case might be more sensitive, since this might enable identification of the case or its subjects. For example, "a large telecommunications company in Sweden" is most probably a branch of the Ericsson Corporation. However, the case may be better characterized by other means than only application domain and country. Internal characteristics, like size of the studied unit, average age of the personnel etc. may be more interesting than external characteristics like domain and turnover. Either the case constitutes a small subunit of a large corporation, and then it can hardly be identified among the many subunits, or it is a small company and hence it is hard to identify it among many candidates. Still, care must be taken to find this balance.

Providing a "history of the inquiry" requires a level of substantially more detail than pure reporting of used methodologies, for example, "we launched a case study using semi-structured interviews". Since the validity of the study is highly related to what is done, by whom and how, it must be reported about the sequence of actions and roles acting in the study process. On the other hand, there is no room for every single detail of the case study conduct, and hence a balance must be found. Data is collected in abundance in a qualitative study, and the analysis has as its main focus to reduce and organize data to provide a chain of evidence for the conclusions. However, to establish trust in the study, the reader needs relevant snapshots from the data that support the conclusions. These snapshots may be in the form of, for example, citations (typical or special statements), pictures, or narratives with anonymized subjects. Further, categories used in the data classification, leading to certain conclusions may help the reader follow the chain of evidence.

Finally, the conclusions must be reported and set into a context of implications, for example, by forming theories. A case study cannot be generalized in the meaning of being representative of a population, but this is not the only way of achieving and transferring knowledge. Conclusions can be drawn without statistics, and they may be interpreted and related to other cases. Communicating research results in terms of theories is an underdeveloped practice in software engineering [72], as discussed in Sect. 2.7.

Table 5.4 Proposed reporting structure for case studies based on Jedlitschka and Pfahl [86] and adaptations to case study reporting according to Runeson et al. [146]

Section headings	Subsections
Title	
Authorship	
Structured abstract	
Introduction	Problem statement
	Research objectives
	Context
Related work	Earlier studies
	Theory
Case study design	Research questions
	Case and subject selection
	Data collection procedure(s)
	Analysis procedure(s)
	Validity procedure(s)
Results	Case and subject descriptions, covering execution, analysis and interpretation issues
	Subsections, which may be structured e.g. according to coding scheme, each linking observations to conclusions
	Evaluation of validity
Conclusions and future work	Summary of findings
	Relation to existing evidence
	Impact / implications
	Limitations
	Future work
Acknowledgements	
References	
Appendices	

5.5.2 Structure

For the academic reporting of case studies, the linear-analytic structure (problem, related work, methods, analysis and conclusions) is the most accepted structure. The high level structure for reporting experiments in software engineering proposed by Jedlitschka and Pfahl [86] therefore also fits the purpose of case study reporting. However, some changes are needed, based on specific characteristics of case studies and other issues based on an evaluation conducted by Kitchenham et al. [101]. The resulting structure is presented in Table 5.4.

In a case study, the theory may constitute a framework for the analysis; hence, there are two kinds of related work: (a) earlier studies on the topic and (b) theories on which the current study is based. The design section corresponds to the case study protocol, i.e. it reports the planning of the case study including the measures taken to ensure the validity of the study. Since the case study is of flexible design, and data collection and analysis are more intertwined, and hence these topics may be combined into one section (as was done in Sect. 5.3).

Consequently, the contents at the lower level must be adjusted, as proposed in Table 5.4. Specifically for the combined data section, the coding scheme often constitutes a natural subsection structure. Alternatively, for a comparative case study, the data section may be structured according to the compared cases, and for a longitudinal study, the time scale may constitute the structure of the data section. This combined results section also includes an evaluation of the validity of the final results.

In the next chapter, an overview of the process for conducting experiments is outlined and then each step in the process is presented in more detail in the subsequent chapters.

5.6   Exercises

5.1. When is case study a feasible research methodology?

5.2. What role has planning in case studies, being a flexible research methodology?

5.3. Which criteria govern the selection of cases for a study?

5.4. List three types of interviews, and explain which type is suitable for different situations.

5.5. Describe a typical process for qualitative analysis.

Chapter 6
Experiment Process

Experimentation is not simple; we have to prepare, conduct and analyze experiments properly. One of the main advantages of an experiment is the control of, for example, subjects, objects and instrumentation. This ensures that we are able to draw more general conclusions. Other advantages include ability to perform statistical analysis using hypothesis testing methods and opportunities for replication. To ensure that we make use of the advantages, we need a process supporting us in our objectives in doing experiments correctly (the notion of experiments include quasi-experiments, unless clearly stated otherwise). The basic principles behind an experiment are illustrated in Fig. 6.1.

The starting point is that we have an idea of a cause and effect relationship, i.e. we believe that there is a relationship between a cause construct and an effect construct. We have a theory or are able to formulate a hypothesis. A hypothesis means that we have an idea of, for example, a relationship, which we are able to state formally in a hypothesis.

In order to evaluate our beliefs, we may use an experiment. The experiment is created, for example, to test a theory or hypothesis. In the design of the experiment, we have a number of treatments (values that the studied variable can take, see below) over which we have control. The experiment is performed and we are able to observe the outcome. This means that we test the relationship between the treatment and the outcome. If the experiment is properly set up, we should be able to draw conclusions about the relationship between the cause and the effect for which we stated a hypothesis.

The main objective of an experiment is mostly to evaluate a hypothesis or relationship, see also Sect. 2.4.1. Hypothesis testing normally refers to the former, and the latter is foremost a matter of building a relational model based on the data collected. The model may be derived using multivariate statistical methods, for example, regression techniques and then we evaluate it in an experiment. The focus in this book is primarily on hypothesis testing. Multivariate statistical methods are treated by, for example, Kachigan [90, 91] and Manly [118].

The experiment process presented in this chapter is formulated to make sure that the proper actions are taken to ensure a successful experiment. It is unfortunately not

C. Wohlin et al., *Experimentation in Software Engineering*,
DOI 10.1007/978-3-642-29044-2_6, © Springer-Verlag Berlin Heidelberg 2012

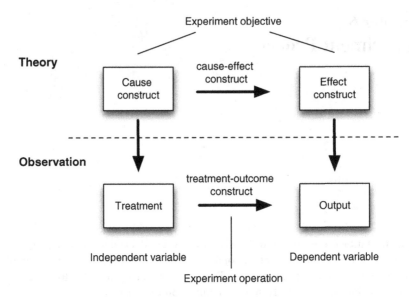

Fig. 6.1 Experiment principles (Adapted from Trochim [171])

uncommon that some factor is overlooked before the experiment, and the oversight prevents us from doing the planned analysis and hence we are unable to draw valid conclusions. The objective, of having a process, is to provide support in setting up and conducting an experiment. The activities in an experiment are briefly outlined in this chapter and treated in more detail in the following chapters, see Chaps. 7–11.

6.1 Variables, Treatments, Objects and Subjects

Before discussing the experiment process, it is necessary to introduce a few definitions in order to have a vocabulary for experimentation. When conducting a formal experiment, we want to study the outcome when we vary some of the input variables to a process. There are two kinds of variables in an experiment, independent and dependent variables, see Fig. 6.2.

Those variables that we want to study to see the effect of the changes in the independent variables are called *dependent variables* (or response variables). Often there is only one dependent variable in an experiment. All variables in a process that are manipulated and controlled are called *independent variables*.

Example. We want to study the effect of a new development method on the productivity of the personnel. We may have chosen to introduce an object-oriented design method instead of a function-oriented approach. The *dependent variable* in

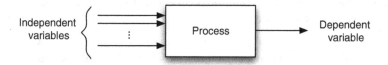

Fig. 6.2 Illustration of independent and dependent variables

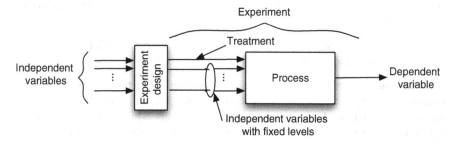

Fig. 6.3 Illustration of an experiment

the experiment is the productivity. *Independent variables* may be the development method, the experience of the personnel, tool support, and the environment.

An experiment studies the effect of changing one or more independent variables. Those variables are called *factors*. The other independent variables are controlled at a fixed level during the experiment, or else we cannot say if the factor or another variable causes the effect. A *treatment* is one particular value of a factor.

Example. The factor for the example experiment above, is the development method since we want to study the effect of changing the method. We use two treatments of the factor: the old and the new development method.

The choice of treatment, and at which levels the other independent variable shall have, is part of the experiment design, see Fig. 6.3. Experiment design is described in more detail in Chap. 8.

The treatments are being applied to the combination of *objects* and *subjects*. An object can, for example, be a document that shall be reviewed with different inspection techniques. The people that apply the treatment are called *subjects*.[1] The characteristics of both the objects and the subjects can be independent variables in the experiment.

---

[1] Sometimes the term *participant* is used instead of the term subject. The term subject is mainly used when people are considered with respect to different treatments and with respect to the analysis and the term participant mainly when it deals with how to engage and motivate people in a study.

Example. The *objects* in the example experiment are the programs to be developed and the *subjects* are the personnel.

An experiment consists of a set of *tests* (sometimes called trials) where each test is a combination of treatment, subject and object. It should be observed that this type of test should not be confused with the use of statistical tests, which is further discussed in Chap. 10. The number of tests affects the experimental error, and provides an opportunity to estimate the mean effect of any experimental factor. The experimental error helps us to know how much confidence we can place in the results of the experiment.

Example. A *test* can be that person N (*subject*) uses the new development method (*treatment*) for developing program A (*object*).

In human-oriented experiments, humans are the subjects, applying different treatments to objects. This implies several limitations to the control of the experiment. Firstly, humans have different skills and abilities, which in itself may be an independent variable. Secondly, humans learn over time, which means that if one subject applies two methods, the order of application of the methods may matter, and also the same object cannot be used for both occasions. Thirdly, human-oriented experiments are impacted by all sorts of influences and threats, due to the subject's ability to guess what the experimenter expects, their motivation for doing the tasks etc. Hence it is critical for the outcome of the experiment how subjects are selected and treated.

Technology-oriented experiments are easier to control, since the technology may be made deterministic. The independent variable out of control in this type of experiments may instead be the objects selected for the experiment. One tool or technique may be well suited for one type of programs, and not for another. Hence it is critical for the outcome how objects are selected.

6.2 Process

A process provides steps that support an activity, for example, software development. Processes are important as they can be used as checklists and guidelines of what to do and how to do it. To perform an experiment, several steps have to be taken and they have to be in a certain order. Thus, a process for how to perform experiments is needed.

The process presented is focused on experimentation, but the same basic steps must be performed in any empirical study, as illustrated for the case study process in Sect. 5.1.2. The main difference is the work within a specific activity, for example, the design of a survey, experiment and case study differ, but they all need to be designed. Further, as case studies are flexible design studies, there are several iterations over the process steps, while experiments and surveys, as fixed design studies, primarily execute the steps once. Thus, the basic process may be used for

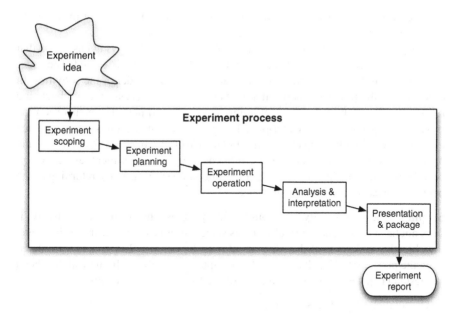

Fig. 6.4 Overview of the experiment process

other types of studies than experiments, but it has to be tailored to the specific type of study being conducted, for example, a survey using e-mail or a case study of a large software project. The process is as it is presented, however, suited for both randomized experiments and quasi-experiments. The latter are often used in software engineering when random samples of, for example, subjects (participants) are infeasible.

The starting point for an experiment is insight, and the idea that an experiment would be a possible way of evaluating whatever we are interested in. In other words, we have to realize that an experiment is appropriate for the question we are going to investigate. This is by no means always obvious, in particular since empirical studies are not frequently used within computer science and software engineering [170, 181]. Some argumentation regarding why computer scientist should experiment more is provided by Tichy [169]. If we assume that we have realized, that an experiment is appropriate then it is important to plan the experiment carefully to avoid unnecessary mistakes, see Sect. 2.9.

The experiment process can be divided into the following main activities. *Scoping* is the first step, where we scope the experiment in terms of problem, objective and goals. *Planning* comes next, where the design of the experiment is determined, the instrumentation is considered and the threats to the experiment are evaluated. *Operation* of the experiment follows from the design. In the operational activity, measurements are collected which then are analyzed and evaluated in *analysis and interpretation*. Finally, the results are presented and packaged in *presentation and package*. The activities are illustrated in Fig. 6.4 and further elaborated below, and then each of the activities is treated in-depth in Chaps. 7–11. An overview of the experiment process including the activities, is presented in Fig. 6.5.

The process is not supposed to be a 'true' waterfall model; it is not assumed that an activity is necessarily finished prior to that the next activity is started. The order of activities in the process primarily indicates the starting order of the activities. In other words, the process is partly iterative and it may be necessary to go back and refine a previous activity before continuing with the experiment. The main exception is when the operation of the experiment has started, then it is not possible to go back to the scoping and planning of the experiment. This is not possible since starting the operation means that the subjects are influenced by the experiment, and if we go back there is risk that it is impossible to use the same subjects when returning to the operation phase of the experiment process.

Scoping. The first activity is scoping. The hypothesis has to be stated clearly. It does not have to be stated formally at this stage, but it has to be clear. Furthermore, the objective and goals of the experiment must be defined. The goal is formulated from the problem to be solved. In order to capture the scope, a framework has been suggested [13]. The framework consists of the following constituents:

- Object of study (what is studied?),
- Purpose (what is the intention?),
- Quality focus (which effect is studied?),
- Perspective (whose view?), and
- Context (where is the study conducted?).

These are further discussed in Chap. 7.

Planning. The planning activity is where the foundation for the experiment is laid. The context of the experiment is determined in detail. This includes personnel and the environment, for example, whether the experiment is run in a university environment with students or in an industrial setting. Moreover, the hypothesis of the experiment is stated formally, including a null hypothesis and an alternative hypothesis.

The next step in the planning activity is to determine variables (both independent variables (inputs) and the dependent variables (outputs). An important issue regarding the variables is to determine the values the variables actually can take. This also includes determining the measurement scale, which puts constraints on the method that we later can apply for statistical analysis. The subjects of the study are identified.

Furthermore, the experiment is designed, which includes choosing a suitable experiment design including, for example, randomization of subjects. An issue closely related to the design is to prepare for the instrumentation of the experiment. We must identify and prepare suitable objects, develop guidelines if necessary and define measurement procedures. These issues are further discussed in Chap. 8.

As a part of the planning, it is important to consider the question of validity of the results we can expect. Validity can be divided into four major classes: internal,

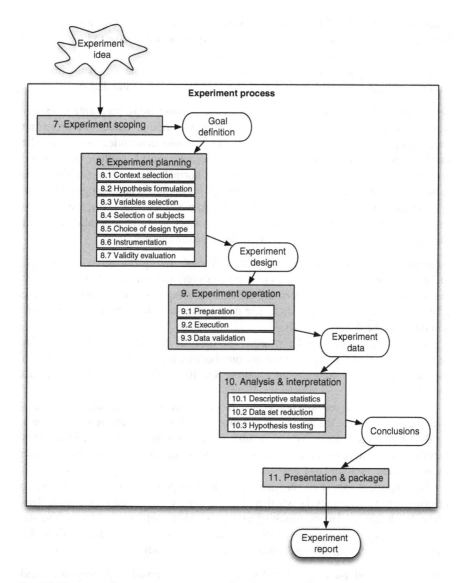

Fig. 6.5 Overview of the experiment process and artefacts with references to chapters and sections of this book

external, construct and conclusion validity. Internal validity is concerned with the validity within the given environment and the reliability of the results. The external validity is a question of how general the findings are. Many times, we would like to state that the results from an experiment are valid outside the actual context in which the experiment was run. The construct validity is a matter of judging if the treatment reflects the cause construct and the outcome provides a true picture of the effect construct, see Fig. 6.1. The conclusion validity is concerned with the relationship between the treatment and the outcome of the experiment. We have to judge if there is a relationship between the treatment and the outcome.

The planning is a crucial step in an experiment to ensure that the results from the experiment become useful. Poor planning may ruin any well-intended study.

Operation. The operation consists in principle of three steps: preparation, execution and data validation. In the preparation step, we are concerned with preparing the subjects as well as the material needed, for example, data collection forms. The participants must be informed about the intention; we must have their consent and they must be committed. The actual execution is normally not a major problem. The main concern is to ensure that the experiment is conducted according to the plan and design of the experiment, which includes data collection. Finally, we must try to make sure that the actually collected data is correct and provide a valid picture of the experiment. The operation activity is discussed in Chap. 9.

Analysis and interpretation. The data collected during operation provide the input to this activity. The data can now be analyzed and interpreted. The first step in the analysis is to try to understand the data by using descriptive statistics. These provide a visualization of the data. The descriptive statistics help us to understand and interpret the data informally.

The next step is to consider whether the data set should be reduced, either by removing data points or by reducing the number of variables by studying if some of the variables provide the same information. Specific methods are available for data reduction.

After having removed data points or reduced the data set, we are able to perform a hypothesis test, where the actual test is chosen based on measurement scales, values on the input data and the type of results we are looking for. The statistical tests together with a more detailed discussion of descriptive statistics and data reduction techniques can be found in Chap. 10.

One important aspect of this activity is the interpretation. That is, we have to determine from the analysis whether the hypothesis was possible to reject. This forms the basis for decision-making and conclusions concerning how to use the results from the experiment, which includes motivation for further studies, for example, to conduct an enlarged experiment or a case study.

Presentation and package. The last activity is concerned with presenting and packaging of the findings. This includes primarily documentation of the results, which can be made either through a research paper for publication, a lab package for replication purposes or as part of a company's experience base. This last activity is important to make sure that the lessons learned are taken care of in an appropriate way. Moreover, an experiment will never provide the final answer to a question, and hence it is important to facilitate replication of the experiment. A comprehensive and thorough documentation is a prerequisite to achieve this objective. Having said that, the use of lab packages should done with care since using the same experimental design and documents may carry over some systematic problems and biases from the original experiment, as discussed in Sect. 2.6. Independently, we must take some time after the experiment to document and present it in a proper way. The presentation of an experiment is further elaborated in Chap. 11.

6.3 Overview

The steps in this experiment process are described in more detail subsequently, and to support the understanding of the process, an example is presented in Chap. 12. The objective of the example is to closely follow the defined process in order to illustrate the use of it. A summarizing overview of the experiment process can be found in Fig. 6.5.

6.4 Exercises

6.1. What is a cause and effect relationship?

6.2. What is a treatment, and why is it sometime necessary to apply treatments in a random order?

6.3. What are dependent and independent variables respectively?

6.4. What are quasi-experiments? Explain why these are common in software engineering.

6.5. Which are the main steps in the experiment process, and why is it important to have distinct steps?

Part II
Steps in the Experiment Process

Chapter 7
Scoping

Conducting an experiment is a labor-intensive task. In order to utilize the effort spent, it is important to ensure that the intention with the experiment can be fulfilled through the experiment. In the scoping phase the foundation of the experiment is determined, which is illustrated in Fig. 7.1. If the foundation is not properly laid, rework may be required, or even worse, the experiment cannot be used to study what was intended. The purpose of the scoping phase is to define the goals of an experiment according to a defined framework. Here we follow the GQM template for goal definition, originally presented by Basili and Rombach [13].

The scoping of an experiment is discussed in Sect. 7.1. An experiment goal definition example is presented in Sect. 7.2.

7.1 Scope Experiment

The scope of the experiment is set by defining its goals. The purpose of a goal definition template is to ensure that important aspects of an experiment are defined before the planning and execution take place. By defining the goal of the experiment according to this template, the foundation is properly laid. The goal template is [13]:

Analyze <Object(s) of study>
for the purpose of <Purpose>
with respect to their <Quality focus>
from the point of view of the <Perspective>
in the context of <Context>.

The object of study is the entity that is studied in the experiment. The object of study can be products, processes, resources, models, metrics or theories. Examples are the final product, the development or inspection process, or a reliability growth model. The purpose defines what the intention of the experiment is. It may be to evaluate the impact of two different techniques, or to characterize the learning curve of an organization. The quality focus is the primary effect under study in the

C. Wohlin et al., *Experimentation in Software Engineering*,
DOI 10.1007/978-3-642-29044-2_7, © Springer-Verlag Berlin Heidelberg 2012

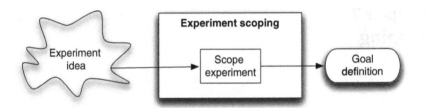

Fig. 7.1 Scoping phase overview

Table 7.1 Experiment context classification

		# Objects	
		One	More than one
# Subjects	One	Single object study	Multi-object variation study
per object	More than one	Multi-test within object study	Blocked subject-object study

experiment. Quality focus may be effectiveness, cost, reliability etc. The perspective tells the viewpoint from which the experiment results are interpreted. Examples of perspectives are developer, project manager, customer and researcher. The context is the 'environment' in which the experiment is run. The context briefly defines which personnel is involved in the experiment (subjects) and which software artifacts (objects[1]) are used in the experiment. Subjects can be characterized by experience, team size, workload etc. Objects can be characterized by size, complexity, priority, application domain etc.

The experiment context can be classified in terms of the number of subjects and objects involved in the study [10], see Table 7.1.

Single object studies are conducted on a single subject and a single object. Multi-object variation studies are conducted on a single subject across a set of objects. Multi-test within object studies examines a single object across a set of subjects. Blocked subject-object studies examine a set of subjects and a set of objects. All these experiment types can be run either as an experiment or a quasi-experiment. In a quasi-experiment there is a lack of randomization of either subjects or objects. The single-object study is a quasi-experiment if the single subject and object are not selected by random, but it is an experiment if the subject and object are chosen by random. The difference between experiments and quasi-experiments is discussed further by Robson [144].

Examples of the different experiment types are given by the series of experiments conducted at NASA-SEL [10], aimed at evaluation of Cleanroom principles and techniques. Cleanroom is a collection of engineering methods and techniques assembled with the objective to produce high-quality software. A brief introduction to Cleanroom is provided by Linger [112]. The experiment series consists of four distinct steps. First, a reading versus unit test experiment was conducted in a blocked

---

[1]Note that the "objects" here are generally different from the "objects of study" defined above.

Table 7.2 Example experiment context classification, from Basili [10]

		# Objects	
		One	More than one
# Subjects per object	One	3. Cleanroom project no. 1 at SEL [14]	4. Cleanroom projects no. 2-4 at SEL [14]
	More than one	2. Cleanroom experiment at University of Maryland [149]	1. Reading versus test [12] 5. Scenario based reading vs. checklist [18]

Table 7.3 Goal definition framework

Object of study	Purpose	Quality focus	Perspective	Context
Product	Characterize	Effectiveness	Developer	Subjects
Process	Monitor	Cost	Modifier	Objects
Model	Evaluate	Reliability	Maintainer	
Metric	Predict	Maintainability	Project manager	
Theory	Control	Portability	Corporate manager	
	Change		Customer	
			User	
			Researcher	

subject-object study [12], see 1 in Table 7.2. Secondly, a development project applying Cleanroom techniques was conducted in a student environment [149]. The experiment was a multi-test within object variation experiment, see 2 in Table 7.2. Thirdly, a project using Cleanroom was conducted at NASA-SEL [14] as a single object experiment, see 3 in Table 7.2. Fourthly, three Cleanroom projects were conducted in the same environment, constituting a multi-object variation study [14], see 4 in Table 7.2. The next round is a new reading experiment where different techniques are analyzed [18], see 5 in Table 7.2. This series of experiments is also discussed by Linkman and Rombach [113].

The example, in Table 7.2, illustrates how experiments (see 1 and 2) can be conducted as pre-studies prior to case studies (see 3 and 4). This is in line with the discussion regarding technology transfer and a suitable ordering based on cost and risk as discussed in Sects. 2.9 and 2.10.

7.2 Example Experiment

The goal definition framework can be filled out with different objects of study, purposes etc. In Table 7.3, examples of elements are given.

A study definition example is constructed by composing the elements of the framework and is presented below. The example defines an inspection experiment where different inspection techniques are evaluated, i.e. perspective-based reading vs. checklist-based reading. Perspective-based reading was introduced by Basili et al. [18], and it has been evaluated in several experiments including a comparison of perspective-based reading vs. an existing method at NASA by Maldonado et al. [117] and Laitenberger et al. [107] present a comparison between perspective-based reading and a checklist-based approach. Researchers have also compared other reading techniques such as a comparison between usage-based reading and checklist-based reading by Thelin et al. [168].

The objects studied are the Perspective-Based Reading (PBR) technique and a checklist-based technique. The purpose is to evaluate the reading techniques, in particular with respect to differences between perspectives in PBR. The quality focus is the effectiveness and efficiency of the reading techniques. The perspective is from the researcher's point of view. The experiment is run using M.Sc. and Ph.D. students as subjects based on a defined lab package with textual requirements documents. The study is conducted as a blocked subject-object study, see Table 7.1, since it involves many subjects and more than one requirements document.

The example is summarized as:

Analyze *the PBR and checklist techniques*
for the purpose of *evaluation*
with respect to *effectiveness and efficiency*
from the point of view of *the researcher*
in the context of *M.Sc. and Ph.D. students reading requirements documents.*

This example is used in Chaps. 8–10 to illustrate the progress of the experimental process. The summary of the experiment forms the goal definition of the experiment. It is the input to the planning step in the experiment process.

7.3   Exercises

7.1. Why is it important to have set up clear goals with an experiment from the beginning?

7.2. Write an example of a goal definition for an experiment you would like to conduct.

7.3. Why is the context in an experiment important?

7.4. How can the context be characterized?

7.5. Explain how a series of studies can be used for technology transfer.

Chapter 8
Planning

After the scoping of the experiment, the planning takes place. The scoping determines the foundation for the experiment – *why* the experiment is conducted – while the planning prepares for *how* the experiment is conducted.

As in all types of engineering activities, the experiment must be planned and the plans must be followed-up in order to control the experiment. The result of the experiment can be disturbed, or even destroyed if not planned properly.

The planning phase of an experiment can be divided into seven steps. The input to the phase is the goal definition for the experiment, see Chap. 7. Based on the goal definition, the *context selection* selects the environment in which the experiment will be executed. Next, the *hypothesis formulation* and the *variable selection* of independent and dependent variables take place. The *selection of subjects* is carried out. The *experiment design type* is chosen based on the hypothesis and variables selected. Next the *instrumentation* prepares for the practical implementation of the experiment. Finally the *validity evaluation* aims at checking the validity of the experiment. The planning process is iterated until a complete experiment design is ready. An overview of the planning phase is given in Fig. 8.1.

8.1 Context Selection

In order to achieve the most general results in an experiment, it should be executed in large, real software projects, with professional staff. However, conducting an experiment involves risks, for example that the new method to be examined is not as good as expected and causes delays. An alternative is to run off-line projects in parallel with the real projects. This reduces the risks but causes extra costs. A cheaper alternative is to run projects staffed by students. Such projects are cheaper, easier to control, but more directed to a certain context than projects staffed by professionals with more and various experience. Furthermore these projects do

C. Wohlin et al., *Experimentation in Software Engineering*,
DOI 10.1007/978-3-642-29044-2_8, © Springer-Verlag Berlin Heidelberg 2012

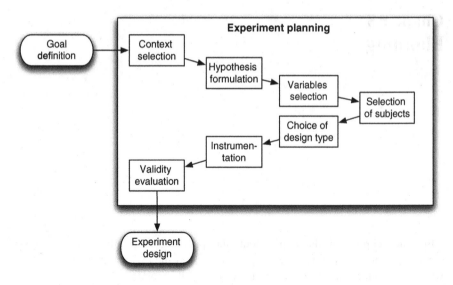

Fig. 8.1 Planning phase overview

seldom address real problems, but problems more of toy size due to constraints in cost and time. This trade-off involves a balance between making studies valid to a specific context or valid to the general software engineering domain, see further Sect. 8.7. Given this trade-off, experiments with students as subjects are discussed in literature, for example, by Höst et al. [77].

Hence, the context of the experiment can be characterized according to four dimensions:

- Off-line vs. on-line
- Student vs. professional
- Toy vs. real problems
- Specific vs. general

A common situation in an experiment is that something existing is compared to something new, for example an existing inspection method is compared to a new one [18, 136, 139]. There are two problems related to this type of studies. Firstly, what is the existing method? It has been applied for some period of time, but it is rarely well documented and there is no consistent application of the method. Secondly, learning a new method may influence how the old one is applied.

This and other issues related to that we are concerned with people have to be taken into account when planning for an experiment in order to make the results valid.

8.2 Hypothesis Formulation

The basis for the statistical analysis of an experiment is hypothesis testing. A hypothesis is stated formally and the data collected during the course of the experiment is used to, if possible, reject the hypothesis. If the hypothesis can be rejected then conclusions can be drawn, based on the hypothesis testing under given risks.

In the planning phase, the experiment definition is formalized into hypotheses. Two hypotheses have to be formulated:

Null   A null hypothesis, H_0, states that there are no real underlying trends or patterns in the experiment setting; the only reasons for differences in our observations are coincidental. This is the hypothesis that the experimenter wants to reject with as high significance as possible. An example hypothesis is that a new inspection method finds on average the same number of faults as the old one, i.e. $H_0 : \mu_{N_{old}} = \mu_{N_{new}}$, where μ denotes the average and N is the number of faults found.

Alternative   An alternative hypothesis, H_a, H_1, etc., is the hypothesis in favor of which the null hypothesis is rejected. An example hypothesis is that a new inspection method on average finds more faults than the old one, i.e. $H_1 : \mu_{N_{old}} < \mu_{N_{new}}$.

There are a number of different statistical tests described in the literature that can be used to evaluate the outcome of an experiment. They are all based on that the above hypotheses are formulated before the statistical tests are chosen and performed. The statistical tests are elaborated in Sect. 10.3.

Testing hypotheses involves different types of risks. Either the test rejects a true hypothesis or the test does not reject a false hypothesis. These risks are referred to as type-I-error and type-II-error:

Type-I-error   A type-I-error has occurred when a statistical test has indicated a pattern or relationship even if there actually is no real pattern. That is, the probability of committing a type-I-error can be expressed as: $P(\text{type-I-error}) = P(\text{reject } H_0 \mid H_0 \text{ true})$.
               In the example hypothesis above, the type-I-error is the probability of rejecting H_0 even though the two methods on average find the same number of faults.

Type-II-error A type-II-error has occurred when a statistical test has not indicated a pattern or relationship even if there actually is a real pattern. That is, the probability of committing a type-II-error can be expressed as: $P(\text{type-II-error}) = P(\text{not reject } H_0 \mid H_0 \text{ false})$.
               In the example hypothesis above, the type-II-error is the probability of not rejecting H_0 even though the two methods on average have different means.

The size of the errors depends on different factors. One example is the ability of the statistical test to reveal a true pattern in the collected data. This is referred to as the power of a test:

Power   The power of a statistical test is the probability that the test will reveal a true pattern if H_0 is false. An experimenter should choose a test with as high power as possible. The power can be expressed as:

Power $= P(\text{reject } H_0 \mid H_0 \text{ false}) = 1 - P(\text{type-II-error})$

All these factors have to be considered when planning an experiment.

8.3   Variables Selection

Before any design can start we have to choose the dependent and independent variables.

The *independent variables* are those variables that we can control and change in the experiment. Choosing the right variables is not easy and it usually requires domain knowledge. The variables should have some effect on the dependent variable and must be controllable. The choices of the independent and dependent variables are often done simultaneously or in reverse order. The choice of independent variables also includes choosing the measurement scales, the range for the variables and the specific levels at which tests will be made.

The effect of the treatments is measured in the *dependent variable(s)*. Often there is only one dependent variable and it should therefore be derived directly from the hypothesis. The variable is mostly not directly measurable and we have to measure it via an indirect measure instead. This indirect measure must be carefully validated, because it affects the result of the experiment. The hypothesis can be refined when we have chosen the dependent variable. The choice of dependent variable also means that the measurement scale and range of the variables are determined. A reason to have only one dependent variable is that if there are more there is a risk that the "fishing and the error rate" threat to conclusion validity may become too large as described in Sect. 8.8.1.

8.4   Selection of Subjects

The selection of subjects is important when conducting an experiment [144]. The selection is closely connected to the generalization of the results from the experiment. In order to generalize the results to the desired population, the selection must be representative for that population. The selection of subjects is also called a sample from a population.

The sampling of the population can be either a probability or a non-probability sample. The difference between the two is that in the probability sampling, the probability of selecting each subject is known and in the non-probability sampling it is unknown. Examples of *probability sampling techniques* are:

- *Simple random sampling:* Subjects are selected from a list of the population at random.
- *Systematic sampling:* The first subject is selected from the list of the population at random and then every n:th person is selected from the list.
- *Stratified random sampling:* The population is divided into a number of groups or strata with a known distribution between the groups. Random sampling is then applied within the strata.

Examples of *non-probability sampling techniques* are:

- *Convenience sampling:* The nearest and most convenient persons are selected as subjects.
- *Quota sampling:* This type of sampling is used to get subjects from various elements of a population. Convenience sampling is normally used for each element.

The size of the sample also impacts the results when generalizing. The larger the sample is, the lower the error becomes when generalizing the results. The sample size is also closely related to the power of the statistical test, see Sect. 10.3.1. There are some general principles for choosing the sample size:

- If there is large variability in the population, a larger sample size is needed.
- The analysis of the data may influence the choice of the sample size. It is therefore needed to consider how the data shall be analyzed already at the design stage of the experiment.

8.5 Experiment Design

To draw meaningful conclusions from an experiment, we apply statistical analysis methods on the collected data to interpret the results, as further described in Chap. 10. To get the most out of the experiment, it must be carefully planned and designed. Which statistical analyses we can apply depend on the chosen design, and the used measurement scales, see Chap. 3. Therefore design and interpretation are closely related.

8.5.1 Choice of Experiment Design

An experiment consists of a series of tests of the treatments. To get the most out of the experiment, the series of tests must be carefully planned and designed. A design of an experiment describes how the tests are organized and run. More formally, we can define an experiment as a set of tests.

As described above, the design and the statistical analysis are closely related. The choice of design affects the analysis and vice versa. To design the experiment, we have to look at the hypothesis to see which statistical analysis we have to perform to reject the null hypothesis. Based on the statistical assumptions, for example, the measurement scales, and on which objects and subjects we are able to use, we make the experiment design. During the design we determine how many tests the experiment shall have to make sure that the effect of the treatment is visible. A proper design also forms the basis to allow for replication. In the following two sections, general design principles and some standard design types are presented.

8.5.2 General Design Principles

When designing an experiment, many aspects must be considered. The general design principles are *randomization, blocking* and *balancing*, and most experiment designs use some combination of these. To illustrate the general design principles, we use an example.

Example. A company will conduct an experiment to investigate the effect on the reliability of a program when using object-oriented design instead of the standard company design principle. The experiment will use program A as the experiment object. The experiment design is of type "multi-test within object study", see Chap. 7.

Randomization. One of the most important design principles is randomization. All statistical methods used for analyzing the data require that the observations be from independent random variables. To meet this requirement, randomization is used. The randomization applies on the allocation of the objects, subjects and in which order the tests are performed. Randomization is used to average out the effect of a factor that may otherwise be present. Randomization is also used to select subjects that is representative of the population of interest.

Example. The selection of the persons (subjects) will be representative of the designers in the company, by random selection of the available designers. The assignment to each treatment (object-oriented design or the standard company design principle) is selected randomly.

Blocking. Sometimes we have a factor that probably has an effect on the response, but we are not interested in that effect. If the effect of the factor is known and controllable, we can use a design technique called blocking. Blocking is used to systematically eliminate the undesired effect in the comparison among the treatments. Within one block, the undesired effect is the same and we can study the effect of the treatments on that block. Blocking is used to eliminate the undesired effect in the study and therefore the effects between the blocks are not studied. This technique increases the precision of the experiment.

Example. The persons (subjects) used, for this experiment, have different experience. Some of them have used object-oriented design before and some have not. To minimize the effect of the experience, the persons are grouped into two groups (blocks), one with experience of object-oriented design and one without.

Balancing. If we assign the treatments so that each treatment has equal number of subjects, we have a balanced design. Balancing is desirable because it both simplifies and strengthens the statistical analysis of the data, but it is not necessary.

Example. The experiment uses a balanced design, which means that there is the same number of persons in each group (block).

8.5.3 Standard Design Types

In this section some of the most frequently used experiment designs are presented. The designs range from simple experiments with a single factor to more complex experiments with many factors. Experiment design is discussed in depth by, for example, Montgomery [125] and is elaborated in more depth for software engineering by Juristo and Moreno [88]. For most of the designs, an example hypothesis is formulated and statistical analysis methods are suggested for each design. The design types presented in this section are suitable for experiments with:

- One factor with two treatments.
- One factor with more than two treatments.
- Two factors with two treatments.
- More than two factors each with two treatments.

One factor with two treatments. With these experiments, we want to compare the two treatments against each other. The most common is to compare the means of the dependent variable for each treatment. The following notations are used:

μ_i The mean of the dependent variable for treatment i.

y_{ij} The j:th measure of the dependent variable for treatment i.

Example of an experiment: The aim is to investigate if a new design method produces software with higher quality than the previously used design method. The factor in this experiment is the design method and the treatments are the new and the old design method. The dependent variable can be the number of faults found in development.

Completely randomized design. This is a basic experiment design for comparing two treatment means. The design setup uses the same objects for both treatments and assigns the subjects randomly to each treatment, see Table 8.1. Each subject uses only one treatment on one object. If we have the same number of subjects per treatment the design is balanced.

Table 8.1 Example of assigning subjects to the treatments for a randomized design

Subjects	Treatment 1	Treatment 2
1	X	
2		X
3		X
4	X	
5		X
6	X	

Table 8.2 Example of assigning the treatments for a paired design

Subjects	Treatment 1	Treatment 2
1	2	1
2	1	2
3	2	1
4	2	1
5	1	2
6	1	2

Example of hypothesis:

$H_0 : \mu_1 = \mu_2$

$H_1 : \mu_1 \neq \mu_2, \mu_1 < \mu_2$ or $\mu_1 > \mu_2$

Examples of analysis: t-test, Mann-Whitney, see Sect. 10.3.

Paired comparison design. We can sometimes improve the precision of the experiment by making comparisons within matched pairs of experiment material. In this design, each subject uses both treatments on the same object. This is sometimes referred to as a crossover design. This type of design has some challenges, which is further discussed in relation to the example in Sect. 10.4. To minimize the effect of the order, in which the subjects apply the treatments, the order is assigned randomly to each subject, see Table 8.2. This design cannot be applied in every case of comparison as the subject can gain too much information from the first treatment to perform the experiment with the second treatment. The comparison for the experiment can be to see if the difference between the paired measures is zero. If we have the same number of subjects starting with the first treatment as with the second, we have a balanced design.

Example of hypothesis:

$d_j = y_{1j} - y_{2j}$ and μ_d is the mean of the difference.

$H_0 : \mu_d = 0$

$H_1 : \mu_d \neq 0, \mu_d < 0$ or $\mu_d > 0$

Examples of analysis: Paired t-test, Sign test, Wilcoxon, see Sect. 10.3.

One factor with more than two treatments. As with experiments with only two treatments, we want to compare the treatments with each other. The comparison is often performed on the treatment means.

Example of an experiment: The experiment investigates the quality of the software when using different programming languages. The factor in the experiment is the programming language and the treatments can be C, C++, and Java.

Table 8.3 Example of assigning the treatments to the subjects

Subjects	Treatment 1	Treatment 2	Treatment 3
1		X	
2			X
3	X		
4	X		
5		X	
6			X

Table 8.4 Example of assigning the treatments to the subjects

Subjects	Treatment 1	Treatment 2	Treatment 3
1	1	3	2
2	3	1	2
3	2	3	1
4	2	1	3
5	3	2	1
6	1	2	3

Completely randomized design. A completely randomized design requires that the experiment is performed in random order so that the treatments are used in an environment as uniform as possible. The design uses one object to all treatments and the subjects are assigned randomly to the treatments, see Table 8.3.

Example of hypothesis, where a is the number of subjects:

$H_0 : \mu_1 = \mu_2 = \mu_3 = \ldots = \mu_a$

$H_1 : \mu_i \neq \mu_j$ for at least one pair (i, j)

Examples of analysis: ANOVA (ANalysis Of VAriance) and Kruskal-Wallis, see Sect. 10.3.

Randomized complete block design. If the variability between the subjects is large, we can minimize this effect on the result by using a randomized complete block design. With this design, each subject uses all treatments and the subjects form a more homogeneous experiment unit, i.e. we block the experiment on the subjects, see Table 8.4. The blocks represent a restriction on randomization. The experiment design uses one object to all treatments and the order in which the subjects use the treatments are assigned randomly. The paired comparison design above is a special case of this design with only two treatments. The randomized complete block design is one of the most used experiment designs.

Example of hypothesis:

$H_0 : \mu_1 = \mu_2 = \mu_3 = \ldots = \mu_a$

$H_1 : \mu_i \neq \mu_j$ for at least one pair (i, j)

Examples of analysis: ANOVA (ANalysis Of VAriance) and Kruskal-Wallis, see Sect. 10.3.

Two factors. The experiment gets more complex when we increase from one factor to two. The single hypothesis for the experiments with one factor will split into three hypotheses: one hypothesis for the effect from one of the factors, one for the other and one for the interaction between the two factors. We use the following notations:

Table 8.5 Example of a 2*2 factorial design			Factor A	
			Treatment A1	Treatment A2
	Factor B	Treatment B1	Subject 4, 6	Subject 1, 7
		Treatment B2	Subject 2, 3	Subject 5, 8

τ_i The effect of treatment i on factor A.
β_j The effect of treatment j on factor B.
$(\tau\beta)_{ij}$ The effect of the interaction between τ_i and β_j.

2*2 factorial design. This design has two factors, each with two treatments. In this experiment design, we randomly assign subjects to each combination of the treatments, see Table 8.5.

Example of an experiment: The experiment investigates the understandability of the design document when using structured or object-oriented design based on one 'good' and one 'bad' requirements documents. The first factor, A, is the design method and the second factor, B, is the requirements document. The experiment design is a 2*2 factorial design as both factors have two treatments and every combination of the treatments are possible.

Example of hypothesis:
$H_0 : \tau_1 = \tau_2 = 0$
H_1 : at least one $\tau_i \neq 0$
$H_0 : \beta_1 = \beta_2 = 0$
H_1 : at least one $\beta_j \neq 0$
$H_0 : (\tau\beta)_{ij} = 0$ for all i, j
H_1 : at least one $(\tau\beta)_{ij} \neq 0$
Example of analysis: ANOVA (ANalysis Of VAriance), see Sect. 10.3.

Two-stage nested design. If one of the factors, for example B, in the experiment is similar but not identical for different treatments of the other factor, for example A, we have a design that is called nested or hierarchical design. Factor B is said to be nested under factor A. The two-stage nested design has two factors, each with two or more treatments. The experiment design and analysis are the same as for the 2*2 factorial design, see Table 8.6.

Example of an experiment: The experiment investigates the test efficiency of unit testing of a program when using function or object-oriented programming and if the programs are 'defect-prone' or 'non-defect-prone'. The first factor, A, is the programming language and the second factor, B, is the defect-proneness of the program. The experiment design has to be nested, as a 'defect-prone/nondefect-prone' functional program is not the same as a 'defect-prone/non-defectprone' object-oriented program.

More than two factors. In many cases, the experiment has to consider more than two factors. The effect in the dependent variable can therefore be dependent not only on each factor separately but also on the interactions between the factors.

Table 8.6 Example of a two-stage nested design where B is nested under A

Factor A			
Treatment A1		Treatment A2	
Factor B		Factor B	
Treatment B1′	Treatment B2′	Treatment B1″	Treatment B2″
Subject 1, 3	Subject 6, 2	Subject 7, 8	Subject 5, 4

Table 8.7 Example of a 2^3 factorial design

Factor A	Factor B	Factor C	Subjects
A1	B1	C1	2, 3
A2	B1	C1	1, 13
A1	B2	C1	5, 6
A2	B2	C1	10, 16
A1	B1	C2	7, 15
A2	B1	C2	8, 11
A1	B2	C2	4, 9
A2	B2	C2	12, 14

These interactions can be between two or more factors. This type of designs is called factorial designs. This section gives an introduction to designs where each factor has only two treatments each. Designs where the factors have more than two treatments are presented by Montgomery [125].

2^k *factorial design.* The 2*2 factorial design is a special case of the 2^k factorial design, i.e. when $k = 2$. The 2^k factorial design has k factors where each factor has two treatments. This means that there are 2^k different combinations of the treatments. To evaluate the effects of the k factors, all combinations have to be tested. The subjects are randomly assigned to the different combinations. An example of a 2^3 factorial design is shown in Table 8.7.

The hypotheses and the analyses for this type of design are of the same type as for the 2*2 factorial design. More details about the 2^k factorial design care presented by Montgomery [125].

2^k *fractional factorial design.* When the number of factor grows in a 2^k factorial design, the number of factor combinations grows rapidly, for example, there are 8 combinations for a 2^3 factorial design and 16 for a 2^4 factorial design. Often, it can be assumed that the effects of certain high-order interactions are negligible and that the main effects and the low-order interaction effects can be obtained by running a fraction of the complete factorial experiment. This type of design is therefore called fractional factorial design.

The fractional factorial design is based on three ideas:

- *The sparsity of effect principle:* It is likely that the system is primarily driven by some of the main and low-order interaction effects.

Table 8.8 Example of an one-half fraction of the 2^3 factorial design

Factor A	Factor B	Factor C	Subjects
A1	B1	C2	2, 3
A2	B1	C1	1, 8
A1	B2	C1	5, 6
A2	B2	C2	4, 7

Table 8.9 Example of an one-quarter fraction of the 2^5 factorial design

Factor A	Factor B	Factor C	Factor D	Factor E	Subjects
A1	B1	C1	D2	E2	3, 16
A2	B1	C1	D1	E1	7, 9
A1	B2	C1	D1	E2	1, 4
A2	B2	C1	D2	E1	8, 10
A1	B1	C2	D2	E1	5, 12
A2	B1	C2	D1	E2	2, 6
A1	B2	C2	D1	E1	11, 15
A2	B2	C2	D2	E2	13, 14

- *The projection property:* A stronger design can be obtained by taking a subset of significant factors from the fractional factorial design.
- *Sequential experimentation:* A stronger design can be obtained by combining sequential runs of two or more fractional factorial designs.

The major use of these fractional factorial designs is in screening experiments, where the purpose of the experiment is to identify the factors that have large effects on the system. Examples of fractional factorial designs are:

One-half fractional factorial design of the 2^k factorial design: Half of the combinations of a full 2^k factorial design is chosen. The combinations are selected so that if one factor is removed the remaining design is a full 2^{k-1} factorial design, see Table 8.8. The subjects are randomly assigned to the selected combinations. There are two alternative fractions in this design and if both fractions are used in sequence, the resulting design is a full 2^k factorial design.

One-quarter fractional factorial design of the 2^k factorial design: One quarter of the combinations of the full 2^k factorial design is chosen. The combinations are selected so that if two factors are removed the remaining design is a full 2^{k-2} factorial design, see Table 8.9. There are however dependencies between the factors in the one-quarter design due to that it is not a full factorial design.

For example, in Table 8.9, factor D is dependent on a combination of factor A and B. It can, for example, be seen that for all combinations of A1 and B1, we have D2, and so forth. In a similar way, factor E is dependent on a combination of factor A and C. Thus, if factor C and E (or B and D) are removed, the resulting design becomes two replications of a 2^{3-1} fractional factorial design and not a 2^3 factorial design. The latter design is obtained if D and E are removed. The two replications can be identified in Table 8.9 by noticing that the first four rows are equivalent to the four last rows in the table, when C and E are removed, and hence it becomes two replications of a 2^2 factorial design.

The subjects are randomly assigned to the selected combinations. There are four alternative fractions in this design and if all four fractions are used in sequence, the resulting design is a full 2^k factorial design. If two of the fractions are used in sequence a one-half fractional design is achieved.

More details on the fractional factorial designs are presented by Montgomery [125].

In summary, the choice of the correct experimental design is crucial, since a poor design will undoubtedly affect the possibility of being able to draw the correct conclusions after the study. Furthermore, the design puts constraints on the statistical methods that can be applied. Finally, it should be stressed that it is important to try to use a simple design if possible and try to make the best possible use of the available subjects.

8.6 Instrumentation

The instruments for an experiment are of three types, namely objects, guidelines and measurement instruments. In the planning of an experiment, the instruments are chosen. Before execution, the instruments are developed for the specific experiment.

Experiment objects may be, for example, specification or code documents. When planning for an experiment, it is important to choose objects that are appropriate. For example, in an inspection experiment, the number of faults must be known in the inspection objects. This can be achieved by seeding faults or by using a document with a known number of faults. Using a true early version of a document in which the faults are identified can do the latter.

Guidelines are needed to guide the participants in the experiment. Guidelines include, for example, process descriptions and checklists. If different methods are compared in the experiment, guidelines for the methods have to be prepared for the experiment. In addition to the guidelines, the participants also need training in the methods to be used.

Measurements in an experiment are conducted via data collection. In human-intensive experiments, data is generally collected via manual forms or in interviews. The planning task to be performed is to prepare forms and interview questions and to validate the forms and questions with some people having similar background and skills as the experiment participants. An example of a form used to collect information about the experience of subjects is shown among the exercises, see Table A.1 in Appendix A.

The overall goal of the instrumentation is to provide means for performing the experiment and to monitor it, without affecting the control of the experiment. The results of the experiment shall be the same independently of how the experiment is instrumented. If the instrumentation affects the outcome of the experiment, the results are invalid.

The validity of an experiment is elaborated in Sect. 8.7 and more about the preparation of instruments can be found in Sects. 9.1.2 and 9.2.2.

8.7 Validity Evaluation

A fundamental question concerning results from an experiment is how valid the results are. It is important to consider the question of validity already in the planning phase in order to plan for adequate validity of the experiment results. Adequate validity refers to that the results should be valid for the population of interest. First of all, the results should be valid for the population from which the sample is drawn. Secondly, it may be of interest to generalize the results to a broader population. The results are said to have adequate validity if they are valid for the population to which we would like to generalize.

Adequate validity does not necessarily imply most general validity. An experiment conducted within an organization may be designed to answer some questions for that organization exclusively, and it is sufficient if the results are valid within that specific organization. On the other hand, if more general conclusions shall be drawn, the validity must cover a more general scope as well.

There are different classification schemes for different types of threats to the validity of an experiment. Campbell and Stanley define two types, threats to internal and external validity [32]. Cook and Campbell extend the list to four types of threats to the validity of experimental results. The four threats are *conclusion, internal, construct* and *external validity* [37]. The former categorization is sometimes referred to in the literature, but the latter is preferable since it is easily mapped to the different steps involved when conducting an experiment, see Fig. 8.2.

Each of the four categories presented by Cook and Campbell [37] is related to a methodological question in experimentation. The basic principles of an experiment are presented in Fig. 8.2.

On the top, we have the theory area, and on the bottom, the observation area. We want to draw conclusions about the theory defined in the hypotheses, based on our observations. In drawing conclusions we have four steps, in each of which there is one type of threat to the validity of the results.

1. *Conclusion validity.* This validity is concerned with the relationship between the treatment and the outcome. We want to make sure that there is a statistical relationship, i.e. with a given significance.
2. *Internal validity.* If a relationship is observed between the treatment and the outcome, we must make sure that it is a causal relationship, and that it is not a result of a factor of which we have no control or have not measured. In other words that the treatment causes the outcome (the effect).

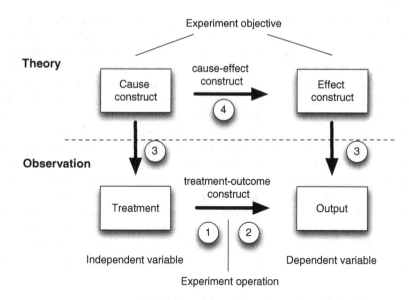

Fig. 8.2 Experiment principles (Adapted from Trochim [171])

3. *Construct validity.* This validity is concerned with the relation between theory and observation. If the relationship between cause and effect is causal, we must ensure two things: (1) that the treatment reflects the construct of the cause well (see left part of Fig. 8.2) and (2) that the outcome reflects the construct of the effect well (see right part of Fig. 8.2).
4. *External validity.* The external validity is concerned with generalization. If there is a causal relationship between the construct of the cause, and the effect, can the result of the study be generalized outside the scope of our study? Is there a relation between the treatment and the outcome?

Conclusion validity is sometimes referred to as statistical conclusion validity [37], and has its counterpart in reliability for qualitative analysis, see Sect. 5.4.3. Threats to conclusion validity are concerned with issues that affect the ability to draw the correct conclusion about relations between the treatment and the outcome of an experiment. These issues include, for example, choice of statistical tests, choice of sample sizes, care taken in the implementation and measurement of an experiment.

Threats to internal validity concern issues that may indicate a causal relationship, although there is none. Factors that impact on the internal validity are how the subjects are selected and divided into different classes, how the subjects are treated and compensated during the experiment, if special events occur during the experiment etc. All these factors can make the experiment show a behavior that is not due to the treatment but to the disturbing factor.

Threats to construct validity refer to the extent to which the experiment setting actually reflects the construct under study. For example, the number of courses taken at the university in computer science may be a poor measure of the subject's experience in a programming language, i.e. has poor construct validity. The number of years of practical use may be a better measure, i.e. has better construct validity.

Threats to external validity concern the ability to generalize experiment results outside the experiment setting. External validity is affected by the experiment design chosen, but also by the objects in the experiment and the subjects chosen. There are three main risks: having wrong participants as subjects, conducting the experiment in the wrong environment and performing it with a timing that affects the results.

A detailed list of threats to the validity is presented in Sect. 8.8. This list can be used as a checklist for an experiment design. In the validity evaluation, each of the items is checked to see if there are any threats. If there are any, they have to be addressed or accepted, since sometimes some threat to validity has to be accepted. It may even be impossible to carry out an experiment without certain threats and hence they have to be accepted and then addressed when interpreting the results. The priority between different types of threats is further discussed in Sect. 8.9.

8.8 Detailed Description of Validity Threats

Below, a list of threats to the validity of experiments is discussed based on Cook and Campbell [37]. All threats are not applicable to all experiments, but this list can be seen as a checklist. The threats are summarized in Table 8.10 and the alternative and limited classification scheme [32] is summarized in Table 8.11.

8.8.1 Conclusion Validity

Threats to the conclusion validity are concerned with issues that affect the ability to draw the correct conclusion about relations between the treatment and the outcome of an experiment.

Low statistical power. The power of a statistical test is the ability of the test to reveal a true pattern in the data. If the power is low, there is a high risk that an erroneous conclusion is drawn, see further Sect. 8.2 or more specifically we are unable to reject an erroneous hypothesis.

Violated assumptions of statistical tests. Certain tests have assumptions on, for example, normally distributed and independent samples. Violating the assumptions may lead to wrong conclusions. Some statistical tests are more robust to violated assumptions than others are, see Chap. 10.

Fishing and the error rate. This threat contains two separate parts. Searching or 'fishing' for a specific result is a threat, since the analyses are no longer independent and the researchers may influence the result by looking for a specific outcome.

Table 8.10 Threats to validity according to Cook and Campbell [37]

Conclusion validity	Internal validity
Low statistical power	History
Violated assumption of statistical tests	Maturation
Fishing and the error rate	Testing
Reliability of measures	Instrumentation
Reliability of treatment implementation	Statistical regression
Random irrelevancies in experimental setting	Selection
Random heterogeneity of subjects	Mortality
	Ambiguity about direction of causal influence
	Interactions with selection
	Diffusion of imitation of treatments
	Compensatory equalization of treatments
	Compensatory rivalry
	Resentful demoralization
Construct validity	**External validity**
Inadequate preoperational explication of constructs	Interaction of selection and treatment
Mono-operation bias	Interaction of setting and treatment
Mono-method bias	Interaction of history and treatment
Confounding constructs and levels of constructs	
Interaction of different treatments	
Interaction of testing and treatment	
Restricted generalizability across constructs	
Hypothesis guessing	
Evaluation apprehension	
Experimenter expectancies	

Table 8.11 Threats to validity according to Campbell and Stanley [32]

Internal validity	External validity
History	Interaction of selection and treatment
Maturation	Interaction of history and treatment
Testing	Interaction of setting and treatment
Instrumentation	Interaction of different treatments
Statistical regression	
Selection	

The error rate is concerned with the actual significance level. For example, conducting three investigations with a significance level of 0.05 means that the total significance level is $1 - (1 - 0.05)^3$, which equals 0.14. The error rate (i.e. significance level) should thus be adjusted when conducting multiple analyses.

Reliability of measures. The validity of an experiment is highly dependent on the reliability of the measures. This in turn may depend on many different factors, like poor question wording, bad instrumentation or bad instrument layout. The basic principle is that when you measure a phenomenon twice, the outcome shall be the same. For example, lines of code are more reliable than function points since it does not involve human judgement. In other words, objective measures, that can be repeated with the same outcome, are more reliable than subjective measures, see also Chap. 3.

Reliability of treatment implementation. The implementation of the treatment means the application of treatments to subjects. There is a risk that the implementation is not similar between different persons applying the treatment or between different occasions. The implementation should hence be as standard as possible over different subjects and occasions.

Random irrelevancies in experimental setting. Elements outside the experimental setting may disturb the results, such as noise outside the room or a sudden interrupt in the experiment.

Random heterogeneity of subjects. There is always heterogeneity in a study group. If the group is very heterogeneous, there is a risk that the variation due to individual differences is larger than due to the treatment. Choosing more homogeneous groups will on the other hand affect the external validity, see below. For example, an experiment with undergraduate students reduces the heterogeneity, since they have more similar knowledge and background, but also reduces the external validity of the experiment, since the subjects are not selected from a general enough population.

8.8.2 Internal Validity

Threats to internal validity are influences that can affect the independent variable with respect to causality, without the researcher's knowledge. Thus they threat the conclusion about a possible causal relationship between treatment and outcome. The internal validity threats are sometimes sorted into three categories, *single group threats, multiple group threats* and *social threats*.

Single group threats. These threats apply to experiments with single groups. We have no control group to which we do not apply the treatment. Hence, there are problems in determining if the treatment or another factor caused the observed effect.

History. In an experiment, different treatments may be applied to the same object at different times. Then there is a risk that the history affects the experimental results, since the circumstances are not the same on both occasions. For example if one of the experiment occasions is on the first day after a holiday or on a day when a very rare event takes place, and the other occasion is on a normal day.

Maturation. This is the effect of that the subjects react differently as time passes. Examples are when the subjects are affected negatively (tired or bored) during the experiment, or positively (learning) during the course of the experiment.

Testing. If the test is repeated, the subjects may respond differently at different times since they know how the test is conducted. If there is a need for familiarization to the tests, it is important that the results of the test are not fed back to the subject, in order not to support unintended learning.

Instrumentation. This is the effect caused by the artifacts used for experiment execution, such as data collection forms, document to be inspected in an inspection experiment etc. If these are badly designed, the experiment is affected negatively.

Statistical regression. This is a threat when the subjects are classified into experimental groups based on a previous experiment or case study, for example top-ten or bottom-ten. In this case there might be an increase or improvement, even if no treatment is applied at all. For example if the bottom-ten in an experiment are selected as subjects based on a previous experiment, all of them will probably not be among the bottom-ten in the new experiment due to pure random variation. The bottom-ten cannot be worse than remain among the bottom-ten, and hence the only possible change is to the better, relatively the larger population from which they are selected.

Selection. This is the effect of natural variation in human performance. Depending on how the subjects are selected from a larger group, the selection effects can vary. Furthermore, the effect of letting volunteers take part in an experiment may influence the results. Volunteers are generally more motivated and suited for a new task than the whole population. Hence the selected group is not representative for the whole population.

Mortality. This effect is due to the different kinds of persons who drop out from the experiment. It is important to characterize the dropouts in order to check if they are representative of the total sample. If subjects of a specific category drop out, for example, all the senior reviewers in an inspection experiment, the validity of the experiment is highly affected.

Ambiguity about direction of causal influence. This is the question of whether A causes B, B causes A or even X causes A and B. An example is if a correlation between program complexity and error rate is observed. The question is if high program complexity causes high error rate, or vice versa, or if high complexity of the problem to be solved causes both.

Most of the threats to internal validity can be addressed through the experiment design. For example, by introducing a control group many of the internal threats can be controlled. On the other hand, multiple group threats are introduced instead.

Multiple groups threats. In a multiple groups experiment, different groups are studied. The threat to such studies is that the control group and the selected experiment groups may be affected differently by the single group threats as defined above. Thus there are interactions with the selection.

Interactions with selection. The interactions with selection are due to different behavior in different groups. For example, the selection-maturation interaction means that different groups mature at different speed, for example if two groups apply one new method each. If one group learns its new method faster than the other, due to its learning ability, does, the selected groups mature differently. Selection-history means that different groups are affected by history differently, etc.

Social threats to internal validity. These threats are applicable to single group and multiple group experiments. Examples are given below from an inspection experiment where a new method (perspective-based reading) is compared to an old one (checklist-based reading).

Diffusion or imitation of treatments. This effect occurs when a control group learns about the treatment from the group in the experiment study or they try to imitate the behavior of the group in the study. For example, if a control group uses a checklist-based inspection method and the experiment group uses perspective-based methods, the former group may hear about the perspective-based method and perform their inspections influenced by their own perspective. The latter may be the case if the reviewer is an expert in a certain area.

Compensatory equalization of treatments. If a control group is given compensation for being a control group, as a substitute for that they do not get treatments; this may affect the outcome of the experiment. If the control group is taught another new method as a compensation for not being taught the perspective-based method, their performance may be affected by that method.

Compensatory rivalry. A subject receiving less desirable treatments may, as the natural underdog, be motivated to reduce or reverse the expected outcome of the experiment. The group using the traditional method may do their very best to show that the old method is competitive.

Resentful demoralization. This is the opposite of the previous threat. A subject receiving less desirable treatments may give up and not perform as good as it generally does. The group using the traditional method is not motivated to do a good job, while learning something new inspires the group using the new method.

8.8.3   Construct Validity

Construct validity concerns generalizing the result of the experiment to the concept or theory behind the experiment. Some threats relate to the design of the experiment, others to social factors.

Design threats. The design threats to construct validity cover issues that are related to the design of the experiment and its ability to reflect the construct to be studied.

Inadequate preoperational explication of constructs. This threat, despite its exten-sive title, is rather simple. It means that the constructs are not sufficiently defined, before they are translated into measures or treatments. The theory is not clear enough, and hence the experiment cannot be sufficiently clear. For example, if two inspection methods are compared and it is not clearly enough stated what being 'better' means. Does it mean to find most faults, most faults per hour, or most serious faults?

Mono-operation bias. If the experiment includes a single independent variable, case, subject or treatment, the experiment may under-represent the construct and thus not give the full picture of the theory. For example, if an inspection experiment is conducted with a single document as object, the cause construct is under-represented.

Mono-method bias. Using a single type of measures or observations involves a risk that if this measure or observation gives a measurement bias, then the experiment will be misleading. By involving different types of measures and observations they can be cross-checked against each other. For example, if the number of faults found is measured in an inspection experiment, where fault classification is based on subjective judgement, the relations cannot be sufficiently explained. The experimenter may bias the measures.

Confounding constructs and levels of constructs. In some relations it is not primarily the presence or absence of a construct, but the level of the construct which is of importance to the outcome. The effect of the presence of the construct is confounded with the effect of the level of the construct. For example, the presence or absence of prior knowledge in a programming language may not explain the causes in an experiment, but the difference may depend on if the subjects have 1, 3 or 5 years of experience with the current language.

Interaction of different treatments. If the subject is involved in more than one study, treatments from the different studies may interact. Then you cannot conclude whether the effect is due to either of the treatments or of a combination of treatments.

Interaction of testing and treatment. The testing itself, i.e. the application of treatments, may make the subjects more sensitive or receptive to the treatment. Then the testing is a part of the treatment. For example, if the testing involves measuring the number of errors made in coding, then the subjects will be more aware of their errors made, and thus try to reduce them.

Restricted generalizability across constructs. The treatment may affect the studied construct positively, but unintenionally affect other constructs negatively. This threat makes the result hard to generalize into other potential outcomes. For example, a comparative study concludes that improved productivity is achieved with a new method. On the other hand, it can be observed that it reduces the maintainability, which is an unintended side effect. If the maintainability is not measured or observed, there is a risk that conclusions are drawn based on the productivity attribute, ignoring the maintainability.

Social threats to construct validity. These threats are concerned with issues related to behavior of the subjects and the experimenters. They may, based on the fact that they are part of an experiment, act differently than they do otherwise, which gives false results from the experiment.

Hypothesis guessing. When people take part in an experiment they might try to figure out what the purpose and intended result of the experiment is. Then they are likely to base their behavior on their guesses about the hypotheses, either positively or negatively, depending on their attitude to the anticipated hypothesis.

Evaluation apprehension. Some people are afraid of being evaluated. A form of human tendency is to try to look better when being evaluated which is confounded to the outcome of the experiment. For example, if different estimation models are compared, people may not report their true deviations between estimate and outcome, but some false but 'better' values.

Experimenter expectancies. The experimenters can bias the results of a study both consciously and unconsciously based on what they expect from the experiment. The threat can be reduced by involving different people which have no or different expectations to the experiment. For example, questions can be raised in different ways in order to give the answers you want.

8.8.4   *External Validity*

Threats to external validity are conditions that limit our ability to generalize the results of our experiment to industrial practice. There are three types of interactions with the treatment: people, place and time:

Interaction of selection and treatment. This is an effect of having a subject population, not representative of the population we want to generalize to, i.e. the wrong people participate in the experiment. An example of this threat is to select only programmers in an inspection experiment when programmers as well as testers and system engineers generally take part in the inspections.

Interaction of setting and treatment. This is the effect of not having the experimental setting or material representative of, for example, industrial practice. An example is using old-fashioned tools in an experiment when up-to-date tools are common in industry. Another example is conducting experiment on toy problems. This means wrong 'place' or environment.

Interaction of history and treatment. This is the effect of that the experiment is conducted on a special time or day which affects the results. If, for example, a questionnaire is conducted on safety-critical systems a few days after a big software-related crash, people tend to answer differently than a few days before, or some weeks or months later.

The threats to external validity are reduced by making the experimental environment as realistic as possible. On the other hand, reality is not homogenous. Most important is to characterize and report the characteristics of the environment, such as staff experience, tools, methods in order to evaluate the applicability in a specific context.

8.9   Priority Among Types of Validity Threats

There is a conflict between some of the types of validity threats. The four types considered are internal validity, external validity, conclusion validity and construct validity. When increasing one type, another type may decrease. Prioritizing among the validity types is hence an optimization problem, given a certain purpose of the experiment.

For example, using undergraduate students in an inspection experiment will probably enable larger study groups, reduce heterogeneity within the group and give reliable treatment implementation. This results in high conclusion validity, while the external validity is reduced, since the selection is not representative if we want to generalize the results to the software industry.

Another example is to have the subjects measure several factors by filling out schemes in order to make sure that the treatments and outcomes really represent the constructs under study. This action will increase the construct validity, but there is a risk that the conclusion validity is reduced since more, tedious measurements have a tendency to reduce the reliability of the measures.

In different experiments, different types of validity can be prioritized differently, depending on the purpose of the experiment. Cook and Campbell [37] propose the following priorities for theory testing and applied research:

Theory testing. In theory testing, it is most important to show that there is a casual relationship (internal validity) and that the variables in the experiment represent the constructs of the theory (construct validity). Adding to the experiment size can generally solve the issues of statistical significance (conclusion validity). Theories are seldom related to specific settings, population or times to which the results should be generalized. Hence there is little need for external validity issues. The priorities for experiments in theory testing are in decreasing order: internal, construct, conclusion and external.

Applied research. In applied research, which is the target area for most of the software engineering experiments, the priorities are different. Again, the relationships under study are of highest priority (internal validity) since the key goal of the experiment is to study relationships between causes and effects. In applied research, the generalization – from the context in which the experiment is conducted to a wider context – is of high priority (external validity). For a researcher, it is not so interesting to show a particular result for company X, but rather that the result is valid for companies of a particular size or application domain. Third, the applied researcher is relatively less interested in which of the components in a complex treatment that really causes the effect (construct validity). For example, in a reading experiment, it is not so interesting to know if it is the increased understanding in general by the reviewer, or it is the specific reading procedure that helps the readers to find more faults. The main interest is in the effect itself. Finally, in practical settings it is hard to get sufficient size of data sets, hence the statistical conclusions may be drawn with less significance (conclusion validity).

The priorities for experiments in applied research are in decreasing order: internal, external, construct and conclusions.

It can be concluded that the threats to validity of experimental results are important to evaluate and balance during planning of an experiment. Depending on the purpose of the experiment, different validity types are given different priority. The threats to an experiment are also closely related to the practical importance of the results. We may, for example, be able to show a statistical significance, but the difference is of no practical importance. This issue is further elaborated in Sect. 10.3.14.

8.10 Example Experiment

This description is a continuation of the example introduced in Sect. 7.2. The input to the planning phase is the goal definition. Some of the issues related to planning have partially been addressed in the way the goal definition is formulated in the example. It is already stated that students will be the subjects and the text also indicates that the experiment will involve more than one requirements document. Planning is a key activity when conducting an experiment. A mistake in the planning step may affect the whole outcome of the experiment. The planning step includes seven activities as shown in Fig. 8.1.

Context selection. The type of context is in many cases at least partially decided by the way the goal definition is formulated. It is implicitly stated that the experiment will be run off-line, although it could potentially be part of a student project, which would have meant on-line although not as part of an industrial development project. The experiment will be run with a mixture of M.Sc. and Ph.D. students.

An off-line experiment with students implies that it may be difficult to have time to inspect a requirements document for a fully-fledged real system. In many cases, experiments of this type have to resort to a requirements document with limited features. In this specific case, two requirements documents from a lab package (material available on-line for replication purposes) will be used. The choice to use two requirements documents has some implications when it comes to the choice of design type, which we will come back to. The requirements documents have some limitations when it comes to features and hence they are to some extent to be considered as 'toy' requirements documents.

The experiment can be considered as general in the sense that the objective is to compare two reading techniques in general (from a research perspective), and it is not about comparing an existing reading technique in a company with a new alternative reading technique. The latter would have made the experiment specific for the situation at the company. In both these cases, there are some issues to take into account to ensure a fair comparison.

In the general research case, it is important that the comparison is fair in the sense that the support for the two techniques being investigated is comparable. It is of course easy to find a very poor checklist and then provide good support for PBR. This would favour PBR and hence the outcome of the experiment would definitively be challenged. This is also the reason why having "no support" is not a good control. An experimental comparison/evaluation must be based on having two comparable methods with similar support. Using "no support" as a control group should be avoided. It would only be interesting if the group having support performs worse than those not having any support, or it is the 'old' way of working at a company. However, this situation is quite rare and hence it is rarely worth performing an experiment under these circumstances.

In the specific case, there is no problem with fairness in the type of support provided, since as long as an existing technique is compared with a new alternative, then it is fine from a support perspective. The main challenge in the specific case is that the participants know the existing technique very well, while a new technique must be taught to them. Thus, the new technique may have a disadvantage since it is not as well known. On the other hand, it has the advantage of potentially being more interesting to the subjects, since it means learning a new technique. Thus, in this case the situation is not that clear-cut, but the potential biases in favour of one or the other technique must be taken into consideration by the researcher.

Hypothesis formulation. In the goal definition it is expressed that we would like to compare both effectiveness and efficiency when it comes to detecting faults when using two different reading techniques when conducting the inspection. The first method is Perspective-based Reading (PBR) and the second method is Checklist-based Reading (CBR). PBR is based on the reviewers having different perspectives when performing the inspection. CBR is based on having a checklist for different items that are likely to relate to faults in requirements documents.

The fact that the requirements documents to be used in the experiment have been used in prior experiments, means that the number of faults is assumed to be known, although it cannot be ruled out that new faults are found. It should also be noted that effectiveness refers to the number of faults found out of the total number of faults, while efficiency also includes time, i.e. whether more faults are found per time unit. To be able to formulate the formal hypotheses, we let N be the number of faults and Nt the number of faults found per time unit.

If we let:

- μ_{NPBR} and μ_{NCBR} be the number of faults found using PBR and CBR respectively, and
- μ_{NtPBR} and μ_{NtCBR} be the number of faults found per time unit using PBR and CBR respectively.

Then, the hypotheses are formulated as follows:

Effectiveness:
$H_0 : \mu_{NPBR} = \mu_{NCBR}$
$H_1 : \mu_{NPBR} <> \mu_{NCBR}$

It should be noted that we have chosen the alternative hypothesis as being any difference between the two reading techniques. In other words, the alternative hypothesis is formulated as a two-sided hypothesis with no assumption regarding one technique being better than the other.

Efficiency:
$H_0 : \mu_{NtPBR} = \mu_{NtCBR}$
$H_1 : \mu_{NtPBR} <> \mu_{NtCBR}$

The hypotheses mean that we would like to show with a statistical significance that the two reading techniques find a different number of faults and a different number of faults are found per time unit. We would like to refute the null hypothesis. It must be noted that not being able to refute the null hypothesis does *not* imply accepting the null hypothesis. This type of outcome may be due to having too few subjects and not due to the reading techniques being equally good at detecting faults.

Variables selection. The independent variable is the reading technique and it has two levels: PBR and CBR, respectively. The dependent variables are the number of faults found and the number of faults found per time unit. This means that we must ensure that the subjects can clearly mark faults found so that the researcher can compare the faults marked with the known set of faults. Furthermore, we must ensure that the subjects can keep track of time and fill in the time when a specific fault was found. It must be noted that it is important to keep track of the time for a specific fault, since a fault may be a false positive and hence we must know which time should be removed from the data set too.

Selection of subjects. Preferably it would be possible to find subjects for the experiment by random. However, in most experiments the researcher tends to be forced to use subjects that are available. This means often students participating in courses at the university become the subjects in experiments run at the university, which is the case in this example experiment. In this case, it is important that the subjects still have the freedom to deny participation, without any penalty for the individual. If the participation in the experiment gives course credit points, alternative options should be provided.

If the purpose of the experiment would be to compare how the two student groups perform using the different methods, then the treatment in the experiment is ruled by the selection of subjects, i.e. the characteristics of the student groups. In fact, this would make it a quasi-experiment. Independently, it is important to characterize the selected subjects to help assessing the external validity of the study.

Choice of design type. Once we know which subjects that are going to participate, it is time to take the next step when it comes to randomization and decide how the subjects should be divided into groups. A good approach is often to use a pre-test to try to capture the experience of the subjects and based on the outcome of the pre-test divide the subjects into experience groups from which we randomly select subjects to the groups in the experiment. This is done to try to ensure that the groups are as equal as possible when it comes to previous experiences, still maintaining the randomization over the subjects. This is referred to as blocking, i.e. we block on previous experience to try to ensure that it does not affect the outcome of the experiment. Finally, the objective is in most cases to have equally large groups, i.e. we want a balanced design. The choice of design type may be affected by the number of subjects available. If having many subjects, it is possible to consider more experimental combinations or consider using each subjects for only one treatment. With relatively few subjects, it becomes more challenging to design the experiment and to use the subjects wisely without compromising the objectives of the experiment.

The next step is to decide on the design type. The experiment includes one factor of primary interest (reading technique) with two treatments (PBR and CBR, respectively), and a second factor that is not really of interest in the experiment (requirements document). Based on the previous decisions taken, the natural design is a completely randomized design where each groups first uses either PBR or CBR on one of the requirements document and then uses the other reading technique on the other requirements document. However, decisions have to be taken on order too. We have two options: (1) either have both groups using different reading techniques on one of the requirements documents first and then switch reading techniques when inspecting the other requirements document, or (2) have both groups using the same reading technique on different requirements documents. In either case, there is an ordering issue. In the first case, one of the requirements document will be used before the other and in the second case one reading technique will be used before the other. Thus, we have to consider which poses the least threats to the experiment. Validity threats are further elaborated below.

Another design option would have been to allow one group to use PBR on a requirements document and the other group use CBR on the same document. The advantage would be that a larger requirements document could be used in the same time frame. The downside is that only half as many data points are generated. In an experiment it is often the case that a certain amount of time is available for running the experiment. Thus, it becomes a question of how to use the time in the most effective way, i.e. to get as good output from the experiment as possible to address the hypotheses stated. The choice of design is very important and it is always a trade-off. Different types of designs have different advantages and disadvantages. Furthermore, the choice also forms the basis for which statistical method that can be applied on the data. This is further discussed in Sect. 10.4.

In this specific case, a completely randomized design is chosen. One group is first assigned to using PBR on the first requirements document and the other group is assigned to use CBR on the same requirements document. This alternative is chosen since it is believed that an order between the reading techniques is worse than an order between the requirements documents. This is particular the case since the primary interest is in the difference between reading techniques and not any differences between the two requirements documents.

Instrumentation. Given that the experiment is based on a lab package, the requirements documents are already available and hence also a list of detected faults (at least known so far). Otherwise, suitable requirements documents should be identified, preferably with a known number of faults to be able to determine the effectiveness of the reading technique.

The guidelines for the two reading techniques must be developed or reused from elsewhere. Here it is important to ensure a fair comparison, as mentioned above, by providing comparable support for the two methods.

Forms for filling out faults found must be developed or reused from another experiment. It is crucial to ensure traceability between the requirements document and the form, for example by numbering the faults in the requirements document while capturing the information about the fault in the form.

Validity evaluation. Finally, the validity threats must be evaluated. This is important to do upfront to ensure that the threats are minimized. It is close to impossible to avoid all threats. Having said that, it still means that if possible all threats should be identified and whenever possible mitigated.

The evaluation of the threats in this specific example is left as an exercise; see Exercise 8.5 in Sect. 8.11.

Next step in the experiment process. Based on the steps described above for the example, we are hopefully ready to run the experiment. However, before doing so it is recommended that some colleagues review the experiment design. Furthermore, it is good if it is possible to run a trial run of the experiment, although it means using one or more persons that otherwise could have been subjects in the experiment. Thus, it is important to use potential subjects wisely.

8.11   Exercises

8.1. What are a null hypothesis and an alternative hypothesis?

8.2. What is type-I-error and type-II-error respectively, which is worst and why?

8.3. In which different ways may subjects be sampled?

8.4. What different types of experiment designs are available, and how do the design relate to the statistical methods to apply in the analysis?

8.5. Which are the threats (consider all four types of validity threats) that exist in the example in Sect. 8.10 and explain why they are threats, what is the trade-off between the different validity types?

Chapter 9
Operation

When an experiment has been designed and planned it must be carried out in order to collect the data that should be analyzed. This is what we mean with the operation of an experiment. In the operational phase of an experiment, the treatments are applied to the subjects. This means that this part of the experiment is the part where the experimenter actually meets the subjects. In most experiments in software engineering there are only a few other times when the subjects actually are involved. These occasions can, for example, be in a briefing before subjects commit to participate in the experiment and after the experiment when the results of the experiment are presented to the subjects. Since experiments in software engineering in most cases deal with humans, although it is possible to run technology-oriented experiments to as discussed in Sect. 2.4. This chapter deals to some extent with how to motivate people to participate and take part in experiments.

Even if an experiment has been perfectly designed and the collected data is analyzed with the appropriate analysis methods, the result will be invalid if the subjects have not participated seriously in the experiment. Since the field of experimental psychology also deals with experiments involving humans, guidelines for conducting experiments from that field [4, 29] are to some extent applicable also in software engineering.

The operational phase of an experiment consists of three steps: *preparation* where subjects are chosen and forms etc. are prepared, *execution* where the subjects perform their tasks according to different treatments and data is collected, and *data validation* where the collected data is validated. The three steps are displayed in Fig. 9.1 and they are further described in the sequel of this chapter.

9.1 Preparation

Before the experiment is actually executed there are some preparations that have to be made. The better these preparations are performed the easier it will be to execute the experiment. There are two important aspects in the preparation. The first is to

C. Wohlin et al., *Experimentation in Software Engineering*,
DOI 10.1007/978-3-642-29044-2_9, © Springer-Verlag Berlin Heidelberg 2012

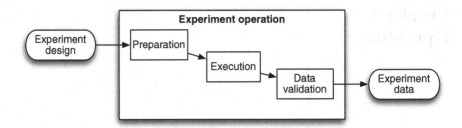

Fig. 9.1 Three steps in experiment operation

select and inform participants, and the second is to prepare material such as forms and tools.

9.1.1   Commit Participants

Before an experiment can be started, people who are willing to act as subjects have to be found. It is essential that the people are motivated and willing to participate throughout the whole experiment.

In many cases it is important to find people who work with tasks in the experiment that are similar to their ordinary work tasks. For example, if an experiment involves writing C-code with different kinds of tools, it would probably make sense to involve persons who are used to write C-code, and not to involve Java-programmers. If people are chosen that are not a representative set of the people that we want to be able to make statements about, this will be a threat to the external validity of the experiment, see Chap. 8. The selection of subjects, in terms of sampling technique, is discussed in Sect. 8.4.

When the right people are found and it is necessary to convince these people to participate in the experiment. Several ethical aspects have to be considered when people are participating as subjects.

Obtain consent. The participants have to agree to the research objectives. If the participants do not know the intention of the work or the work does not comply with what they thought they should do when they agreed to participate, there is a risk that they will not perform the experiment according to the objectives and their personal ability. This could result in that the data becomes invalid. It is important to describe how the result of the experiment will be used and published. It should be made clear to the participants that they are free to withdraw from the experiment. Sometimes a trade-off must be made between this aspect and the design with respect to validity. If the participants are affected by the experiment as such, this will affect the validity of the experiment.

Sensitive results. If the results obtained in the experiment are sensitive for the participants, it is important to assure the participants that the results of their personal performance in the experiment will be kept confidential. It is sometimes hard to judge if the result is sensitive or not, but generally it can be said that if the result would have a meaning for the participants outside the experiment it is in some way sensitive. For example, if the experiment measures the productivity of a programmer, the result would indicate how skilled the programmer is as a programmer and the result would be sensitive. On the other hand if participants are asked to use a method for acceptance testing and they normally never deal with this type of testing, the result of the experiment would probably not be that sensitive.

Inducements. One way to attract people to an experiment is to offer some kind of inducement. The value of it should however not be too large, since this could cause people to participate merely to receive the inducement. This would not motivate people to seriously participate in the experiment.

Disclosure. Disclosure means to reveal all details of the experiment as openly as possible to the experiment subjects. The opposite, to deceive or betray the participants, is generally not to acceptable. If alternative ways of conducting the experiment are available these methods should be used instead. If non-disclosure is the only alternative it should only be applied if it concerns aspects that are insignificant to the participants and do not affect their willingness to participate in the experiment. In case of partial disclosure, the situation should be explained and revealed to the participants as early as possible.

For more discussion on ethical aspects in experimentation, see Sect. 2.11.

9.1.2 Instrumentation Concerns

Before the experiment can be executed, all experiment instruments must be ready, see Sect. 8.6. This may include the experiment objects, guidelines for the experiment and measurement forms and tools. The required instruments are determined by the design of the experiment and the method that will be used for data collection.

If the subjects themselves should collect data, this means in most cases that some kind of forms must be handed out to the participants. One thing to determine when forms are constructed is whether they should be personal or the participants should fill them out anonymously. If there should be no additional studies and there hence is no real need for the experimenter to distinguish between different participants, it may be appropriate to use anonymous forms. This will however mean that there is no possibility to contact the participant if something is filled out in an unclear way.

In many cases it is appropriate to prepare one personal set of instruments for every participant. This is because many designs deal with randomization and repeated tests, such that different participants should be subject to different treatments. This can be done also when the participants are anonymous.

If data should be collected in interviews, questions should be prepared before the execution of the experiment. Here it may also be appropriate to prepare different questions for different participants.

9.2   Execution

The experiment can be executed in a number of different ways. Some experiments, such as simple inspection experiments can be carried out at one occasion when all participants are gathered at, for example, a meeting. The advantage of this is that the result of the data collection can be obtained directly at the meeting and there is no need to contact the participants and later on ask for their respective results. Another advantage is that the experimenter is present during the meeting and if questions arise they can be resolved directly.

Some experiments are, however, executed during a much longer time span, and it is impossible for the experimenter to participate in every detail of the experiment and the data collection. This is, for example, the case when the experiment is performed in relation to one or several large projects, where different methods for development are evaluated. An example of such an experiment is presented by Ohlsson and Wohlin [128], where a course in large-scale software development was studied during 2 years. Each year, seven projects were run in parallel with a total of approximately 120 students. The objective of the experiment by Ohlsson and Wohlin [128] was to evaluate different levels of formality when collecting effort data.

9.2.1   Data Collection

Data can be collected either manually by the participants that fill out forms, manually supported by tools, in interviews, or automatically by tools.

An advantage of using forms, is that it does not require so much effort for the experimenter, since the experimenter does not have to actively take part in the collection. A drawback is that there is no possibility for the experimenter to directly reveal inconsistencies, uncertainties and flaws in the forms etc. This type of faults cannot be revealed until after the data collection or if the participants raise attention to faults or have questions. An advantage with interviews is that the experimenter has the possibility to communicate better with the participants during the data collection. A drawback is of course that it requires more effort from the experimenter.

9.2.2   Experimental Environment

If an experiment is performed within a regular development project, the experiment should not affect the project more than necessary. This is because the reason for performing the experiment within the project is to see the effects of different treatments in an environment such as the one in the project. If the project environment is changed too much because of the experiment that effect will be lost.

There are however some cases where it is appropriate with some interaction between the experiment and the project. If the experimenter, for example, reveals that some parts of the project could be performed better or that estimations are not correct, it would be appropriate for the experimenter to tell the project leader. This type of direct feedback from the experiment to the project can help to motivate project personnel to participate in the experiment.

9.3 Data Validation

When data has been collected, the experimenter must check that the data is reasonable and that it has been collected correctly. This deals with aspects such as if the participants have understood the forms and therefore filled them out correctly. Another source of error is that some participants may not have participated in the experiment seriously and some data therefore should be removed before the analysis. Outlier analysis is further discussed in Sect. 10.2.

It is important to review that the experiment has actually been conducted in the way that was intended. It is, for example, important that the subjects have applied the correct treatments in the correct order. If this type of misunderstandings have occurred, the data is of course invalid.

One way to check that the participants have not misunderstood the intentions of the experimenter, is to give a seminar, or in some other way present the results of the data collection. This will give the participants the possibility to reflect on results that they do not agree with. It also helps building long term trust, as discussed in Sect. 2.11.

9.4 Example Operation

The experiment design from Sect. 8.10 is the input to the operation, which consists of three steps that must be addressed.

Preparation. First of all the subjects must be identified. In this example, Ph.D. and M.Sc. students are invited as subjects. Once having a potential set of participants, it is important to convince them to participate and get their commitment to participate in the experiment. After having an initial commitment, consent must be ensured from the participants. It is recommended that consent forms be used even if the formal rules may not require it. Other issues to take into account in relation to ethics are described in Sect. 9.1.1. Assigning subjects to treatment must be done using a randomization procedure. If the design includes a blocking factor (type of student), subjects should be split according to that factor, and then randomly assigned to treatments within each blocking group. If a balanced design is chosen, the selection must end up in the same number of subjects for each group.

The next step is to ensure that the infrastructure needed is in place. This includes having a suitable room booked, for example, providing sufficient distance between the subjects. Copies of all documents and forms must be available for all subjects. Given that time is going to be collected, a clock is needed in the room. It cannot be assumed that everybody has access to his or her own clock.

Execution. During the execution it is important to ensure the people are suitably spread out in the room. As it is an inspection experiment, it should be possible to run the experiment once with all subjects doing the inspection at the same time. This also means that it is easy to provide support for any questions that may arise during the experiment. Depending on whether the data should be collected by filling in forms by hand or by use of a computer, preparation has to be done accordingly.

Data validation. Finally, the data has to be validated. It may be the case that one or several subjects leave the experiment very early and their data forms have to be checked carefully to ensure that they have filled in the forms in a reasonable way. Furthermore, it must be checked that everybody has understood how to fill in the data in a correct way. If this is not the case, it may be the case that data from one or several subjects must be removed.

9.5   Exercises

9.1. Which factors should be considered when selecting subjects?

9.2. Why are ethical issues important in experimentation?

9.3. Why is it necessary to prepare the instrumentation carefully before an experiment?

9.4. What is data validation and why should it be done before the statistical analysis?

9.5. How should we handle subjects that have a personal interest in the outcome of the experiment?

Chapter 10
Analysis and Interpretation

The experiment data from the operation is input to the analysis and interpretation. After collecting experimental data in the operation phase, we want to be able to draw conclusions based on this data. To be able to draw valid conclusions, we must interpret the experiment data. Quantitative interpretation may be carried out in three steps, as depicted in Fig. 10.1.

In the first step, the data is characterized using *descriptive statistics*, which visualize central tendency, dispersion, etc. In step 2, abnormal or false data points are excluded, thus *reducing the data set* to a set of valid data points. In the third step, the data is analyzed by *hypothesis testing*, where the hypotheses of the experiment are evaluated statistically, at a given level of significance. These steps are described in more detail in the sequel of this chapter.

10.1 Descriptive Statistics

Descriptive statistics deal with the presentation and numerical processing of a data set. After collecting experimental data, descriptive statistics may be used to describe and graphically present interesting aspects of the data set. Such aspects include measures indicating, for example, where on some scale the data is positioned and how concentrated or spread out the data set is. The goal of descriptive statistics is to get a feeling for how the data set is distributed. Descriptive statistics may be used before carrying out hypothesis testing, in order to better understand the nature of the data and to identify abnormal or false data points (so called *outliers*).

In this section, we present a number of descriptive statistics and plotting techniques that may help to get a general view of a data set. The scale of measurement (see Chap. 3) restricts the type of statistics that are meaningful to compute. Table 10.1 shows a summary of some of these statistics in relation to the scales under which they are admissible. It should, however, be noted that measures of one scale type can be applied to the more powerful scales, for example, mode can be used for all four scales in Table 10.1.

C. Wohlin et al., *Experimentation in Software Engineering*,
DOI 10.1007/978-3-642-29044-2_10, © Springer-Verlag Berlin Heidelberg 2012

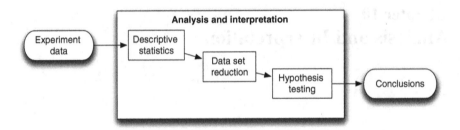

Fig. 10.1 Three steps in quantitative interpretation

Table 10.1 Some relevant statistics for each scale

Scale type	Measure of central tendency	Dispersion	Dependency
Nominal	Mode	Frequency	
Ordinal	Median, percentile	Interval of variation	Spearman corr. coeff. Kendall corr. coeff.
Interval	Mean, variance, and range	Standard deviation	Pearson corr. coeff.
Ratio	Geometric mean	Coefficient of variation	

10.1.1 Measures of Central Tendency

Measures of central tendency, such as mean, median, and mode, indicate a 'middle' of a data set. This 'midpoint' is often called average and may be interpreted as an estimation of the *expectation* of the stochastic variable from which the data points in the data set are sampled.

When describing the measures of central tendency, we assume that we have n data points $x_1 \ldots x_n$, sampled from some stochastic variable. The (arithmetic) *mean*, denoted $\bar{x}$, is calculated as:

$$\bar{x} = \frac{1}{n} \sum_{i=1}^{n} x_i$$

The mean value is meaningful for the interval and ratio scales. For example, we may compute the mean for the data set (1, 1, 2, 4) resulting in $\bar{x} = 2.0$.

The *median*, denoted $\tilde{x}$, represents the middle value of a data set, following that the number of samples that are higher than the median is the same as the number of samples that are lower than the median. The median is calculated by sorting the samples in ascending (or descending) order and picking the middle sample. This is well defined if n is odd. If n is even, the median may be defined as the arithmetic mean of the two middle values. The latter operation requires that the scale is at least interval. If the scale is ordinal, one of the two middle values may be selected by random choice, or the median may be represented as a pair of values.

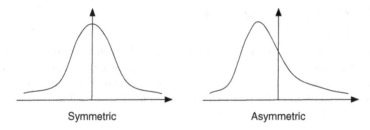

Fig. 10.2 A symmetric distribution has the same values of mean, median, and mode, while they may differ if the distribution is asymmetric

The median value is meaningful for the ordinal, interval, and ratio scales. As an example, we may compute the median for the data set $(1, 1, 2, 4)$ resulting in $\tilde{x} = 1.5$.

The median is a special case of the *percentile*, namely the 50%-percentile, denoted $x_{50\%}$, indicating that 50% of the samples lies below $x_{50\%}$. In general x_p denotes the percentile where $p\%$ of the samples lies below this value. The percentile value is meaningful for the ordinal, interval, and ratio scales.

The *mode* represents the most commonly occurring sample. The mode is calculated by counting the number of samples for each unique value and selecting the value with the highest count. The mode is well defined if there is only one value that is more common than all others are. If an odd number of samples have the same occurrence count, the mode may be selected as the middle value of the most common samples. The latter operation requires that the scale is at least ordinal. If the scale is nominal, the mode may be selected among the most common samples by random choice or represented as a pair of the most common values.

The mode value is meaningful for the nominal, ordinal, interval and ratio scales. As an example, we may compute the mode for the data set $(1, 1, 2, 4)$ giving a mode of 1.

A less common measure of central tendency is the *geometric mean*, which is calculated as the n:th root of the product of all samples, as shown below.

$$\sqrt[n]{\prod_{i=1}^{n} x_i}$$

The geometric mean is well defined if all samples are non-negative and meaningful for the ratio scale. The (arithmetic) mean and median are equal if the distribution of samples is symmetric. If the distribution is both symmetric and has one unique maximum, all these three measures of central tendency are equal. However, if the distribution of samples is skewed, the values of the mean, median and mode may differ, see Fig. 10.2.

If, for example, the higher tail of the distribution is long, the mean is increased, while the median and mode is unaffected. This indicates that the mean is a more sensitive measure. However, it requires at least an interval scale, and hence may not always be meaningful.

10.1.2   Measures of Dispersion

The measures of central tendency do not convey information of the dispersion of the data set. Thus, it is necessary to measure the level of variation from the central tendency, i.e. to see how spread or concentrated the data is. The (sample) *variance*, denoted s^2, is a common measure of dispersion, and is calculated as:

$$s^2 = \frac{1}{n-1} \sum_{i=1}^{n} (x_i - \bar{x})^2$$

Hence, the variance is the mean of the square distance from the sample mean. It may seem odd that the dividend is $n-1$ and not just n, but by dividing with $n-1$, the variance gets some desirable properties. In particular, the sample variance is an unbiased and consistent estimation of the variance of the stochastic variable. The variance is meaningful for the interval and ratio scales.

The *standard deviation*, denoted s, is defined as the square root of the variance:

$$s = \sqrt{\frac{1}{n-1} \sum_{i=1}^{n} (x_i - \bar{x})^2}$$

The standard deviation is often preferred over the variance as it has the same dimension (unit of measure) as the data values themselves. The standard deviation is meaningful for the interval and ratio scales.

The *range* of a data set is the distance between the maximum and minimum data value:

$$\text{range} = x_{max} - x_{min}$$

The range value is meaningful for the interval and ratio scales.

The *variation interval* is represented by the pair (x_{min}, x_{max}) including the minimum and maximum of the data values. This measure is meaningful for ordinal, interval and ratio scales.

Sometimes the dispersion is expressed in percentages of the mean. This value is called the *coefficient of variation* and is calculated as:

$$100 \frac{s}{x}$$

The coefficient of variation measure has no dimension and is meaningful for the ratio scale.

A general view of dispersion is given by the *frequency* of each data value. A frequency table is constructed by tabulating each unique value and the count of occurrence for each value. The *relative frequency* is calculated by dividing each frequency by the total number of samples. For the data set $(1, 1, 1, 2, 2, 3, 4, 4, 4, 5, 6, 6)$ with 13 samples we can construct the frequency table shown in Table 10.2. The frequency is meaningful for all scales.

Table 10.2 A frequency table example

Value	Frequency	Relative frequency
1	3	23%
2	2	15%
3	1	8%
4	3	23%
5	1	8%
6	2	15%
7	1	8%

10.1.3 Measures of Dependency

When the data set consists of related samples in pairs (x_i, y_i) from two stochastic variables, X and Y, it is often interesting to examine the dependency between these variables.

If X and Y are related through some function, $y = f(x)$, we want to estimate this function. If we suspect that the function $y = f(x)$ is linear and could be written on the form $y = \alpha + \beta x$, we could apply *linear regression*. Regression means fitting the data points to a curve, and in our case we will show how fitting a line that minimizes the sum of the quadratic distances to each data point makes linear regression. Before we present the formulas we define the following shorthands for some commonly occurring sums:

$$S_{xx} = \sum_{i=1}^{n}(x_i - \bar{x})^2$$

$$S_{yy} = \sum_{i=1}^{n}(y_i - \bar{y})^2$$

$$S_{xy} = \sum_{i=1}^{n}(x_i - \bar{x})(y_i - \bar{y}) = \left(\sum_{i=1}^{n} x_i y_i\right) - \frac{1}{n}\left(\sum_{i=1}^{n} x_i\right)\left(\sum_{i=1}^{n} y_i\right)$$

The sums can be used to compute the regression line $y = \bar{y} + \beta(x - \bar{x})$ where the slope of the line is:

$$\beta = \frac{S_{xy}}{S_{xx}}$$

and the line crosses the y-axis at $\alpha = \bar{y} - \beta\bar{x}$.

If the dependency is non-linear, it may be possible to find a *transformation* of data, so that the relation becomes linear, and linear regression can be used. If, for example, the relation is exponential, $y = \alpha x^\beta$, this implicates that a logarithmic transformation of the data results in the linear relation $log(y) = log(\alpha) + \beta log(x)$.

After the logarithmic transformation we can use linear regression to calculate the parameters of the line.

For a single number that quantifies how much two data sets, x_i and y_i, vary together, we can use the *covariance*. This measure of dependency, denoted c_{xy}, is defined as:

$$c_{xy} = \frac{S_{xy}}{n-1}$$

The covariance is meaningful for interval and ratio scales. The covariance is dependent on the variance of each variable, and to be able to compare dependencies between different related variables, the covariance may be normalized with the standard deviations of x_i and y_i. If we do this we get the *correlation coefficient* r (also called *Pearson correlation coefficient*), which is calculated as:

$$r = \frac{c_{xy}}{s_x s_y} = \frac{S_{xy}}{\sqrt{S_{xx}S_{yy}}} = \frac{(n \sum_{i=1}^{n} x_i y_i) - (\sum_{i=1}^{n} x_i)(\sum_{i=1}^{n} y_i)}{\sqrt{(n \sum_{i=1}^{n} x_i^2 - (\sum_{i=1}^{n} x_i)^2)(n \sum_{i=1}^{n} y_i^2 - (\sum_{i=1}^{n} y_i)^2)}}$$

The r-value is between -1 and $+1$, and if there is no correlation r equals zero. The opposite is however not true. The x_i and y_i values may be strongly correlated in a non-linear manner even if $r = 0$. The (Pearson) correlation coefficient measures only linear dependency and is meaningful if the scales of x_i and y_i are interval or ratio, and works good for data that is normally distributed.

If the scale is ordinal or if the data is far from normally distributed, the *Spearman rank-order correlation coefficient*, denoted r_s, can be used. The Spearman correlation is calculated in the same manner as the Pearson correlation except that the ranks (i.e., the order numbers when the samples are sorted) are used instead of the sample values, see for example Siegel and Castellan [157].

Another measure of dependency is the *Kendall rank-order correlation coefficient*, denoted T. The Kendall correlation is suitable as a measure for the same sort of data as the Spearman correlation, i.e. at least ordinal samples in pair. The Kendall correlation differs, however, in the underlying theory as it focuses on counting agreements and disagreements in ranks between samples, see for example Siegel and Castellan [157].

If we have more than two variables, we can apply *multivariate analysis*, including techniques such as *multiple regression, principal component analysis (PCA), cluster analysis*, and *discriminant analysis*. These techniques are described by, for example, Manly [118] and Kachigan [90, 91].

10.1.4   Graphical Visualization

When describing a data set, quantitative measures of central tendency, dispersion, and dependency, should be combined with graphical visualization techniques. Graphs are very illustrative and give a good overview of the data set.

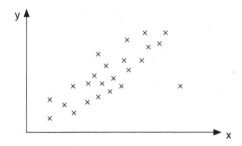

Fig. 10.3 A scatter plot

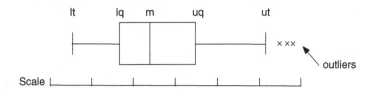

Fig. 10.4 A box plot

One simple but effective graph is the *scatter plot*, where pairwise samples (x_i, y_i) are plotted in two dimensions, as shown in Fig. 10.3.

The scatter plot is good for assessing dependencies between variables. By examining the scatter plot, it can be seen how spread or concentrated the data points are, and if there is a tendency of linear relation. Atypical values (outliers) may be identified, and the correlation may be observed. In Fig. 10.3, there is a linear tendency with a positive correlation, and we may observe potential outliers. In this particular case there is one candidate outlier.

The *box plot* is good for visualizing the dispersion and skewedness of samples. The box plot is constructed by indicating different percentiles graphically, as shown in Fig. 10.4. Box plots can be made in different ways. We have chosen an approach advocated by, for example Fenton and Pfleeger, and Frigge et al. [56, 60]. The main difference between the approaches is how to handle the whiskers. Some literature proposes that the whiskers should go to the lowest and highest values respectively, see for example Montgomery [125]. Fenton and Pfleeger [56] propose using a value, which is the length of the box, multiplied with 1.5 and added or subtracted from the upper and lower quartiles, respectively.

The middle bar in the box m, is the median. The lower quartile lq, is the 25% percentile (the median of the values that are less than m), and the upper quartile uq is the 75% percentile (the median of the values that are greater than m). The length of the box is $d = uq - lq$.

The tails of the box represent the theoretical bound within which it is likely to find all data points if the distribution is normal. The upper tail ut is $uq + 1.5d$ and the lower tail lt is $lq - 1.5d$ [60]. The tail values are truncated to the nearest actual data point, in order to avoid meaningless values (such as negative lines of code).

Fig. 10.5 A histogram

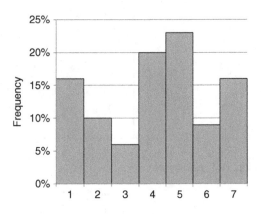

Fig. 10.6 A cumulative
histogram

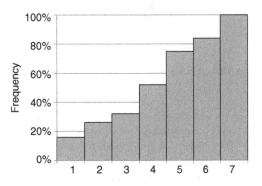

Values outside the lower and upper tails are called *outliers*, and are shown explicitly in the box plot. In Fig. 10.4, there are three outliers.

The *histogram* can be used to give an overview of the distribution density of the samples from one variable. A histogram consists of bars with heights that represent the frequency (or the relative frequency) of a value or an interval of values, as shown in Fig. 10.5. The histogram is thus a graphical representation of a frequency table. One distribution of particular interest is the normal distribution, since it is one aspect that should be taken into account when analyzing the data. Thus, a plot could provide a first indication whether the data resembles a normal distribution or not. It is also possible to test the data for normality. This is further discussed in Sect. 10.3 when introducing the Chi-2 test.

The *cumulative histogram*, illustrated in Fig. 10.6, may be used to give a picture of the probability distribution function of the samples from one variable. Each bar is the cumulative sum of frequencies up to the current class of values.

A *pie chart*, as illustrated in Fig. 10.7, shows the relative frequency of the data values divided into a specific number of distinct classes, by constructing segments in a circle with angles proportional to the relative frequency.

Fig. 10.7 A pie chart

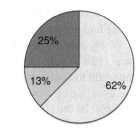

Fig. 10.8 An outlier detected
in a scatter plot

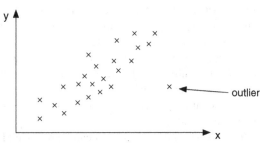

10.2   Data Set Reduction

In Sect. 10.3, a number of statistical methods are described. All methods have in
common that the result of using them, depend much on the quality of the input data.
If the data, that the statistical methods are applied on, does not represent what we
think it represents, then the conclusions that we draw from the results of the methods
are of course not correct.

Errors in the data set can occur either as systematic errors, or they can occur as
outliers, which means that the data point is much larger or much smaller than one
could expect looking at the other data points, see Fig. 10.8.

One effective way to identify outliers is to draw scatter plots, as shown in
Fig. 10.8. Another way is to draw box plots, as illustrated in Fig. 10.4. There
are some statistical methods available for detecting outliers. These methods can,
for example, be based on that the data comes from a normal distribution and
determining the probability of finding a value such as the largest or smallest value
from this distribution. This can, for example, be done by looking at the difference
between possible outliers and the mean of all values or at the difference between
the outlier and its closest value, and then determining the probability of finding as
large difference as was found. This study is conducted to evaluate if it is possible
that the outlier found can come from the normal distribution, although it seems like
an extreme value.

Notice that data reduction as discussed here is related to data validation as
discussed in Chap. 9. Data validation deals with identifying false data points based
on the execution of the experiment, such as determining if people have participated
seriously in the experiment. The type of data reduction discussed in this section is
concerned with identifying outliers not only based on the experiment execution, but

instead looking at the results from the execution in the form of collected data and taking into account, for example, descriptive statistics.

When outliers have been identified, it is important to decide what to do with them. This should not only be based on the coordinates in the diagram, here it is important to analyze the reasons for the outliers. If the outlier is due to a strange or rare event that never will happen again, the point could be excluded. This can, for example, be the case if the point is completely wrong or misunderstood.

If the outlier is due to a rare event that may occur again, for example, if a module was implemented by inexperienced staff, it is not advisable to exclude the value from the analysis, because there is much relevant information in the outlier. If the outlier is due to a variable that was not considered before, such as the staff experience, it may be considered to base the calculations and models also on this variable. It is also possible to derive two separate models. In the case with staff experience it means one model based on normal staff (with the outlier removed) and one separate model for inexperienced staff. How to do this must be decided for every special case.

It is not only invalid data that can be removed from the data set. It is sometimes ineffective to analyze redundant data if the redundancy is too large. One way to identify redundant data is through factor analysis and principal component analysis (PCA). These techniques identify orthogonal factors that can be used instead of the original factors. It would lead too far to describe this type of techniques in this book. Refer instead to, for example, Kachigan [90, 91] and Manly [118].

10.3   Hypothesis Testing

10.3.1   Basic Concept

The objective of hypothesis testing is to see if it is possible to reject a certain null hypothesis, H_0, based on a sample from some statistical distribution. That is, the null hypothesis describes some properties of the distribution from which the sample is drawn and the experimenter wants to reject that these properties are true with a given significance. The null hypothesis is also discussed in Chap. 8. A common case is that the distribution depends on a single parameter. Setting up H_0 then means formulating the distribution and assigning a value to the parameter, which will be tested.

For example, if an experimenter observes a vehicle and wants to show that the vehicle is not a car. The experimenter knows that all cars have four wheels, but also that there are other vehicles than cars that have four wheels. A very simple example of a null hypothesis can be formulated as "H_0: the observed vehicle is a car".

To test H_0, a test unit, t, is defined and a critical area, C, is given as well which is a part of the area over which t varies. This means that the significance test can be formulated as:

- If $t \in C$, reject H_0
- If $t \notin C$, do not reject H_0

In our example, the test unit t is the number of wheels and the critical area is $C = 1, 2, 3, 5, 6, \ldots$. The test is: if $t \leq 3$ or $t \geq 5$, reject H_0, otherwise do not reject H_0.

If it is observed that $t = 4$, it means that the hypothesis cannot be rejected and no conclusion can be drawn. This is because there may be other vehicles than cars with four wheels.

The null hypothesis should hence be formulated negatively, i.e. the intention of the test is to reject the hypothesis. If the null hypothesis is not rejected, nothing can be said about the outcome, while if the hypothesis is rejected, it can be stated that the hypothesis is false with a given significance (α), see below. When a test is carried out it is in many cases possible to calculate the lowest possible significance (often denoted the p-value) with which it is possible to reject the null hypothesis. This value is often reported from statistical analysis packages.

The critical area, C, may have different shapes, but it is very common that it has some form of intervals, for example $t \leq a$ or $t \geq b$. If C consists of one such interval it is one-sided. If it consists of two intervals ($t \leq a, t \geq b$, where $a < b$), it is two-sided.

Three important probabilities concerning hypothesis testing are:

$$\alpha = P(\text{type-I-error}) = P(\text{reject } H_0 \mid H_0 \text{ is true})$$

$$\beta = P(\text{type-II-error}) = P(\text{not reject } H_0 \mid H_0 \text{ is false})$$

$$\text{Power} = 1 - \beta = P(\text{reject } H_0 \mid H_0 \text{ is false})$$

These probabilities are also discussed in Chap. 8.

We try here to illustrate the concepts in a small example describing a simple but illustrative test called the *binomial test*. An experimenter has measured a number of failures during operation for a product and classified them as corruptive (faults that do corrupt the program's data) and non-corruptive (faults that do not corrupt the program's data). The experimenter's theory is that the non-corruptive faults are more common than the corruptive faults. The experimenter therefore wants to perform a test in order to see if the difference in the number of faults of the different types is due to coincident or if it reveals a systematic difference.

The null hypothesis is that there is no difference in the probability of receiving a corruptive fault and receiving a non-corruptive fault. That is, the null hypothesis can be formulated as:

$$H_0 : P(\text{corruptive fault}) = P(\text{non-corruptive fault}) = 1/2$$

It is decided that α should be less than 0.10. The experimenter has received the following data:

- There are 11 faults that are non-corruptive.
- There are four faults that are corruptive.

If the null hypothesis is true, the probability of obtaining as few as four (i.e., four or less) corruptive faults out of 15 is

$$P(\text{0-4 corruptive faults}) = \sum_{i=0}^{4} \binom{15}{i} \left(\frac{1}{2}\right)^i \left(\frac{1}{2}\right)^{15-i} = \frac{1}{2^{15}} \sum_{i=0}^{4} \binom{15}{i} = 0.059$$

That is, if the experimenter concludes that the data that has been received shows that the non-corruptive faults are more common than the corruptive faults, the probability of committing a type-I-fault is 0.059. In this case the experimenter can reject H_0 because $0.059 < 0.10$.

The probability of receiving five or less corruptive faults, if the null hypothesis is true, can be computed to be 0.1509. This is larger than 0.10, which means that 5 corruptive faults out of 15 would not be sufficient to reject H_0. The experimenter can therefore decide more formally to interpret the data in an experiment with 15 received faults as:

- If four or less faults are corruptive, reject H_0.
- If more than four faults are corruptive, do not reject H_0.

To summarize, the number of received corruptive faults (out of 15 faults) is the test unit and the critical area is 0, 1, 2, 3 and 4 (corruptive faults).

Based on this, it is interesting to determine the power of the formulated test. Since the power is the probability of rejecting H_0 if H_0 is not true, we have to formulate what we mean with that H_0 is not true. In our example this can be formulated as:

$$P(\text{corruptive fault}) < P(\text{non-corruptive fault})$$

Since the sum of the two probabilities equals 1, this can also be formulated as:

$$P(\text{corruptive fault}) = a < 1/2$$

The probability of receiving four or less corruptive faults out of 15 faults (i.e., the probability of rejecting H_0 if H_0 is false) is:

$$p = \sum_{i=0}^{4} \binom{15}{i} a^i (1-a)^{15-i}$$

This probability is plotted for different values of a in Fig. 10.9.

It can be seen that the power of the test is high if the difference between the probabilities of receiving a corruptive fault and a non-corruptive fault is large. If, for example, $a = 0.05$ there is a very great chance that there will be four or fewer corruptive faults. On the other hand, if the difference is very small, the power will be smaller. If, for example, $a = 0.45$ there is a great chance that there will be more than four corruptive faults.

Fig. 10.9 Power of a one sided binomial test

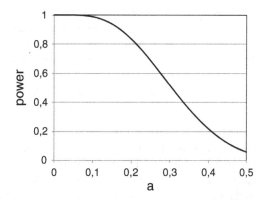

There are a number of factors affecting the power of a test. First, the test itself can be more or less effective. Second, the sample size affects the power. A larger sample size means higher power. Another aspect that affects the power is the choice of a one sided or two sided alternative hypothesis. A one sided hypothesis gives a higher power than a two sided hypothesis.

Power in software engineering experimentation is assessed and further discussed by Dybå et al. [49].

10.3.2 Parametric and Non-parametric Tests

Tests can be classified into parametric tests and non-parametric tests. Parametric tests are based on a model that involves a specific distribution. In most cases, it is assumed that some of the parameters, involved in a parametric test, are normally distributed. One test for normality is the Chi-2 test, which is further described below when discussing the different types of test. Parametric tests also require that parameters can be measured at least on an interval scale. If parameters cannot be measured on at least an interval scale this means generally that parametric tests cannot be used. In these cases there are a wide range of non-parametric tests available.

Non-parametric tests do not make the same type of assumptions concerning the distribution of parameters as parametric tests do. Only very general assumptions are made to derive non-parametric tests. The binomial test, described in the previous subsection is an example of a non-parametric test. Non-parametric tests are more general than parametric tests. This means that non-parametric tests, if they are available, can be used instead of parametric tests, but parametric tests cannot generally be used when non-parametric tests can be used. With respect to the choice of parametric or non-parametric test, there are two factors to consider:

Applicability	What are the assumptions made by the different tests? It is important that assumptions regarding distributions of parameters and assumptions concerning scales are realistic.
Power	The power of parametric tests is generally higher than for non-parametric tests. Therefore, parametric tests require fewer data points, and therefore smaller experiments, than non-parametric test if the assumptions are true.

The choice between parametric and non-parametric statistical methods is also discussed by Briand et al. [27]. There it is described that even if it is a risk using parametric methods when the required conditions are not fulfilled, it is in some cases worth taking that risk. Simulations have shown that parametric methods, such as the t-test, described below, are fairly robust to deviations from the preconditions (interval scale) as long as the deviations are not too large.

10.3.3   Overview of Tests

In addition to the binomial test introduced above, the following tests are described in this section:

t-test	One of the most often used parametric tests. The test is used to compare two sample means. That is, the design is one factor with two treatments.
Mann-Whitney	This is a non-parametric alternative to the t-test.
F-test	This is a parametric test that can be used to compare two sample distributions.
Paired t-test	A t-test for a paired comparison design.
Wilcoxon	This is a non-parametric alternative to the paired t-test.
Sign test	This is a non-parametric alternative to the paired t-test. The sign test is a simpler alternative to the Wilcoxon test.
ANOVA	(ANalysis Of VAriance). A family of parametric tests that can be used for designs with more than two levels of a factor. ANOVA tests can, for example, be used in the following designs: One factor with more than two levels, one factor and blocking variable, factorial design, and nested design.
Kruskal-Wallis	This is a non-parametric alternative to ANOVA in the case of one factor with more than two treatments.
Chi-2	This is a family of non-parametric tests that can be used when data are in the form of frequencies.

The different tests can be sorted with respect to design type and with respect to whether they are parametric or non-parametric as in Table 10.3.

For all tests that are described, the following items are presented in separate tables for each test:

Table 10.3 Overview of parametric/non-parametric tests for different designs

Design	Parametric	Non-parametric
One factor, one treatment		Chi-2, Binomial test
One factor, two treatments, completely randomized design	t-test, F-test	Mann-Whitney, Chi-2
One factor, two treatments, paired comparison	Paired t-test	Wilcoxon, Sign test
One factor, more than two treatments	ANOVA	Kruskal-Wallis, Chi-2
More than one factor	ANOVA[a]	

[a] This test is not described in this book. Refer instead to, for example, Marascuilo and Serlin [119] and Montgomery [125]

Input	The type of measurements needed to make the test applicable describes the input to the test. That is, this describes what requirements there are on the experiment design if the test should be applicable.
Null hypothesis	A formulation of the null-hypothesis is provided.
Calculations	It describes what to calculate based on the measured data.
Criterion	The criterion for rejecting the null hypothesis. This often involves using statistical tables and it is described which table to use from Appendix B. In this book tables are only provided for one level of significance, but for many tests references are given to other sources where more comprehensive tables are provided.

All tests are not described completely here. For more information concerning the tests refer to the references given in the text. For example, the Mann-Whitney test, the Wilcoxon test, the sign test and the Kruskal-Wallis test are described for the most straightforward case with few samples. If there are many samples (for example, more than about 35 for the sign test) it is in many cases hard to do the calculations and decisions as described below. In these cases it is possible to do certain approximations because there are so many samples. How to do this is described by, for example, Siegel and Castellan [157]. They also described how to do when ties (two or more equal values) occur for those tests.

The objective of the descriptions of the tests is that it should be possible to use the tests based on the descriptions and the examples. The intention is not to provide all details behind the derivations of the formulas.

Using the type of description outlined above, our simple example test, see Sect. 10.3.1, is summarized in Table 10.4.

In the above table the Binomial test is described for the null hypothesis that the two events are equally probable. It is possible to state other null hypotheses, such as $P(\text{event } 1) = 0.3$ and $P(\text{event } 2) = 0.7$. For a description of how to perform the test in those cases, see for example Siegel and Castellan [157].

For most of the tests in this chapter, examples of usage are presented. The examples are based on fictitious data. Moreover, the tests are primarily presented for a significance level of 5% for which tables are provided in Appendix B.

Table 10.4 Binomial test

Item	Description
Input	Number of events counted for two different kind of events (event$_1$ and event$_2$)
H_0	$P(\text{event } 1) = P(\text{event } 2)$
Calculations	Calculate $p = \dfrac{1}{2^N} \sum_{i=0}^{n} \binom{N}{i}$ where N is the total number of events, and n is the number of the most rare event
Criterion	Two sided ($H_1 : P(\text{event } 1) \neq P(\text{event } 2)$): reject H_0 if $p < \alpha/2$ One sided ($H_1 : P(\text{event } 1) < P(\text{event } 2)$): reject H_0 if $p < \alpha$ and event 1 is the most rare event in the sample

Table 10.5 t-test

Item	Description
Input	Two independent samples: $x_1, x_2, \ldots x_n$ and $y_1, y_2, \ldots y_m$
H_0	$\mu_x = \mu_y$, i.e. the expected mean values are the same
Calculations	Calculate $t_0 = \dfrac{\bar{x} - \bar{y}}{S_p \sqrt{\frac{1}{n} + \frac{1}{m}}}$ where $S_p = \sqrt{\dfrac{(n-1)S_x^2 + (m-1)S_y^2}{n+m-2}}$ and, S_x^2 and S_y^2 are the individual sample variances
Criterion	Two sided ($H_1 : \mu_x \neq \mu_y$): reject H_0 if $|t_0| > t_{\alpha/2, n+m-2}$. Here, $t_{\alpha, f}$ is the upper α percentage point of the t distribution with f degrees of freedom, which is equal to $n+m-2$. The distribution is tabulated, for example, in Table B.1 and by Montgomery [125], and Marascuilo and Serlin [119] One sided ($H_1 : \mu_x > \mu_y$): reject H_0 if $t_0 > t_{\alpha, n+m-2}$

More comprehensive tables are available in books on statistics, for example, by Marascuilo and Serlin [119] and Montgomery [125].

10.3.4   t-Test

The t-test is a parametric test used to compare two independent samples. That is, the design should be one factor with two levels. The t-test can be performed based on a number of different assumptions, but here an often-used alternative is described. For more information, refer for example to Montgomery [125], Siegel and Castellan [157], and Marascuilo and Serlin [119]. The test is performed as presented in Table 10.5.

Example of t-test. The defect densities in different programs have been compared in two projects. In one of the projects the result is

$$x = 3.42, \, 2.71, \, 2.84, \, 1.85, \, 3.22, \, 3.48, \, 2.68, \, 4.30, \, 2.49, \, 1.54$$

Table 10.6 Mann-Whitney

Item	Description
Input	Two independent samples: $x_1, x_2, \ldots x_n$ and $y_1, y_2, \ldots y_m$
H_0	The two samples come from the same distribution
Calculations	Rank all samples and calculate $U = N_A N_B + \frac{N_A(N_A+1)}{2} - T$ and $U' = N_A N_B - U$, where $N_A = \min(n, m)$, $N_B = \max(n, m)$, and T is the sum of the ranks of the smallest sample
Criterion	Tables providing criterion for rejection of the null hypothesis based on the calculations are provided, for example, in Table B.3 and by Marascuilo and Serlin [119]
	Reject H_0 if $\min(U, U')$ is less than or equal to the value in Table B.3

and in the other project the result is

$$y = 3.44,\ 4.97,\ 4.76,\ 4.96,\ 4.10,\ 3.05,\ 4.09,\ 3.69,\ 4.21,\ 4.40,\ 3.49$$

The null hypothesis is that the defect density is the same in both projects, and the alternative hypothesis that it is not. Based on the data it can be seen that $n = 10$ and $m = 11$. The mean values are $\bar{x} = 2.853$ and $\bar{y} = 4.1055$.

It can be found that $S_x^2 = 0.6506$, $S_y^2 = 0.4112$, $S_p = 0.7243$ and $t_0 = -3.96$.

The number of degrees of freedom is $f = n + m - 2 = 10 + 11 - 2 = 19$. In Table B.1, it can be seen that $t_{0.025,19} = 2.093$. Since $|t_0| > t_{0.025,19}$ it is possible to reject the null hypothesis with a two tailed test at the 0.05 level.

10.3.5 Mann-Whitney

The Mann-Whitney test is a non-parametric alternative to the t-test. It is always possible to use this test instead of the t-test if the assumptions made by the t-test seem uncertain. The test, which is based on ranks, is not described completely here. More details are presented by, for example, Siegel and Castellan [157][1], and Marascuilo and Serlin [119]. The test is summarized in Table 10.6.

Example of Mann-Whitney. When the same data is used, as in the example with the t-test, it can be seen that $N_A = \min(10, 11) = 10$ and $N_B = \max(10, 11) = 11$. The ranks of the smallest sample (x) are 9, 5, 6, 2, 8, 11, 4, 17, 3, 1 and the ranks of the largest sample (y) are 10, 21, 19, 20, 15, 7, 14, 13, 16, 18, 12. Based on the ranks it can be found that $T = 66$, $U = 99$ and $U' = 11$. Since the smallest of U and U' is smaller than 26, see Table B.3, it is possible to reject the null hypothesis with a two tailed test at the 0.05 level.

---

[1]Siegel and Castellan [157] describe the Wilcoxon-Mann-Whitney test instead of the Mann-Whitney test. The two tests are, however, essentially the same.

Table 10.7 F-test

Item	Description
Input	Two independent samples: $x_1, x_2, \ldots x_n$ and $y_1, y_2, \ldots y_m$
H_0	$\sigma_x^2 = \sigma_y^2$, i.e. the variances are equal
Calculations	Calculate $F_0 = \dfrac{\max(S_x^2, S_y^2)}{\min(S_x^2, S_y^2)}$, where S_x^2 and S_y^2 are the individual sample variances
Criterion	Two sided ($H_1 : \sigma_x^2 \neq \sigma_y^2$): reject H_0 if $F_0 > F_{\alpha/2, n_{max}-1, n_{min}-1}$, where n_{max} is the number of scores in the sample with maximum sample variance and n_{min} is the number of scores in the sample with minimum sample variance. $F_{\alpha/2, f_1, f_2}$ is the upper α percentage point of the F distribution with f_1 and f_2 degrees of freedom, which is tabulated, for example, in Table B.5 and by Montgomery [125], and Marascuilo and Serlin [119]
	One sided ($H_1 : \sigma_x^2 > \sigma_y^2$): reject H_0 if $F_0 > F_{\alpha, n_{max}-1, n_{min}-1}$, and $S_x^2 > S_y^2$

10.3.6 F-Test

The F-test is a parametric test that can be used to compare the variance of two independent samples. More details about the test are presented by, for example, Montgomery [125], Robson [144], and Marascuilo and Serlin [119]. The test is performed as presented in Table 10.7.

Example of F-test. When the same data is used, as in the example with the t-test, it can be found that $S_x = 0.6506$ and $S_y = 0.4112$, which means that $F_0 = 1.58$. It can also be seen that $n_{max} = 10$ and $n_{min} = 11$.

From Table B.5 it can be seen that $F_{0.025, 9, 10} = 3.78$. Since $F_0 < F_{0.025, 9, 10}$ it is impossible to reject the null hypothesis with a two tailed test at the 0.05 level. That is, the test does not reject that the two samples have the same variance.

10.3.7 Paired t-Test

The paired t-test is used when two samples resulting from repeated measures are compared. This means that measurements are made with respect to, for example, a subject more than once. An example of this is if two tools are compared. If two groups independently use the two different tools, the result would be two independent samples and the ordinary t-test could be applied. If instead only one group would be used and every person used both tools, we would have repeated measures. In this case the test examines the difference in performance for every person with the different tools.

The test, which is described in more detail by, for example, Montgomery [125], and Marascuilo and Serlin [119], is performed as presented in Table 10.8:

Example of paired t-test. Ten programmers have independently developed two different programs. They have measured the effort that was required and the result is displayed in Table 10.9.

Table 10.8 Paired t-test

Item	Description
Input	Paired samples: $(x_1, y_1), (x_2, y_2) \ldots (x_n, y_n)$
H_0	$\mu_d = 0$, where $d_i = x_i - y_i$, i.e. the expected mean of the differences is 0
Calculations	Calculate $t_0 = \dfrac{\bar{d}}{S_d/(\sqrt{n})}$, where $S_d = \sqrt{\dfrac{\sum_{i=1}^{n}(d_i - \bar{d})^2}{n-1}}$
Criterion	Two sided ($H_1 : \mu_d \neq 0$): reject H_0 if $|t_0| > t_{\alpha/2, n-1}$. Here, $t_{\alpha,f}$ is the upper α percentage point of the t distribution with f degrees of freedom. The distribution is tabulated, for example, in Table B.1 and by Montgomery [125], and Marascuilo and Serlin [119]. One sided ($H_1 : \mu_d > 0$): reject H_0 if $|t_0| > t_{\alpha, n-1}$

Table 10.9 Required effort

Programmer	1	2	3	4	5	6	7	8	9	10
Program 1	105	137	124	111	151	150	168	159	104	102
Program 2	86.1	115	175	94.9	174	120	153	178	71.3	110

The null hypothesis is that the required effort to develop program 1 is the same as the required effort to develop program 2. The alternative hypothesis is that it is not. In order to carry out the test the following are calculated:

$d = \{18.9, \ 22, \ -51, \ 16.1, \ 23, \ 30, 15, \ 19, \ 32.7, \ 9\}$

$S_d = 27.358$

$t_0 = 0.39$

The number of degrees of freedom is $f = n - 1 = 10 - 1 = 9$. In Table B.1, it can be seen that $t_{0.025,9} = 2.262$.

Since $t_0 < t_{0.025,9}$ it is impossible to reject the null hypothesis with a two sided test at the 0.05 level.

10.3.8 Wilcoxon

The Wilcoxon test is a non-parametric alternative to the paired t-test. The only requirements are that it is possible to determine which of the measures in a pair is the greatest and that it is possible to rank the differences. The test, which is based on ranks, is not described in detail here. A more detailed description is presented by, for example, Siegel and Castellan [157], and Marascuilo and Serlin [119]. The test is summarized in Table 10.10.

Example of Wilcoxon. When the same data is used, as in the example with the paired t-test, it is found that the ranks of the absolute values of the difference (d) are 4, 6, 10, 3, 7, 8, 2, 5, 9, 1. Based on this T^+ and T^- can be calculated to be 32 and 23.

Since the smallest of T^+ and T^- is larger than 8 (see Table B.4) it is impossible to reject the null hypothesis with a two-tailed test at the 0.05 level.

Table 10.10 Wilcoxon

Item	Description
Input	Paired samples: $(x_1, y_1), (x_2, y_2) \ldots (x_n, y_n)$
H_0	If all differences ($d_i = x_i - y_i$) are ranked $(1, 2, 3 \ldots)$ without considering the sign, then the sum of the ranks of the positive differences equals the sum of the ranks of the negative differences
Calculations	Calculate T^+ as the sum of the ranks of the positive d_i:s and T^- as the sum of the ranks of the negative d_i:s
Criterion	Tables that can be used to determine if H_0 can be rejected based on T^+, T^- and the number of pairs, n, are available. See for example Table B.4 or Siegel and Castellan [157], and Marascuilo and Serlin [119] Reject H_0 if $\min(T^+, T^-)$ is less than or equal to the value in Table B.4

Table 10.11 Sign test

Item	Description
Input	Paired samples: $(x_1, y_1), (x_2, y_2) \ldots (x_N, y_N)$
H_0	$P(+) = P(-)$, where $+$ and $-$ represent the two events that $x_i > y_i$ and $x_i < y_i$
Calculations	Represent every positive differences ($d_i = x_i - y_i$) by a $+$ and every negative difference by a $-$. Calculate $p = \dfrac{1}{2^N} \sum\limits_{i=0}^{n} \binom{N}{i}$, where N is the total number of signs, and n is number of signs of the most rare signs
Criterion	Two sided ($H_1 : P(+) \neq P(-)$): reject H_0 if $p < \alpha/2$ One sided ($H_1 : P(+) < P(-)$): reject H_0 if $p < \alpha$ and the $+$ event is the most rare event in the sample

10.3.9   Sign Test

The sign test is, as the Wilcoxon test, a non-parametric alternative to the paired t-test. The sign test can be used instead of the Wilcoxon test when it is not possible or necessary to rank the differences, since it is only based on the sign of the difference of the values in each pair. For example, it is not necessary to use Wilcoxon when it is possible to show significance with the sign test. This is due to that the sign test has a lower power. Moreover, the sign test is easier to perform.

The test is further described by, for example, Siegel and Castellan [157] and Robson [144], and is summarized in Table 10.11.

The reader may recognize that this test is a binomial test where the two events are $+$ and $-$ respectively.

Example of sign test. When the same data is used, as in the example with the paired t-test, it is found that there are 6 positive differences and 4 negative. This means that

$$p = \frac{1}{2^{10}} \sum_{i=0}^{4} \binom{10}{i} = \frac{193}{512} \approx 0.3770$$

Since $p > 0.025$ it is impossible to reject the null hypothesis with a two tailed test at the 0.05 level.

Table 10.12 ANOVA, one factor, more than two treatments

Item	Description
Input	a samples: $x_{11}, x_{12}, \ldots x_{1n_1}; x_{21}, x_{22}, \ldots x_{2n_2}; \ldots; x_{a1}, x_{a2}, \ldots x_{an_a}$
H_0	$\mu_{x_1} = \mu_{x_2} = \ldots = \mu_{x_a}$, i.e. all expected means are equal
Calculations	$SS_T = \sum_{i=1}^{a} \sum_{j=1}^{n_i} x_{ij}^2 - \dfrac{x_{..}^2}{N}$
	$SS_{Treatment} = \sum_{i=1}^{a} \dfrac{x_{i.}^2}{n_i} - \dfrac{x_{..}^2}{N}$
	$SS_{Error} = SS_T - SS_{Treatment}$
	$MS_{Treatment} = SS_{Treatment}/(a-1)$
	$MS_{Error} = SS_{Error}/(N-a)$
	$F_0 = MS_{Treatment}/MS_{Error}$
	where N is the total number of measurements and a dot index denotes a summation over the dotted index, e.g. $x_{i.} = \sum_j x_{ij}$
Criterion	Reject H_0 if $F_0 > F_{\alpha, a-1, N-a}$. Here, F_{α, f_1, f_2} is the upper α percentage point of the F distribution with f_1 and f_2 degrees of freedom, which is tabulated, for example, in Table B.5 and by Montgomery [125] and Marascuilo and Serlin [119]

Table 10.13 ANOVA table for the ANOVA test described above

Source of variation	Sum of squares	Degrees of freedom	Mean square	F_0
Between treatments	$SS_{Treatment}$	$a-1$	$MS_{Treatment}$	$F_0 = \dfrac{MS_{Treatment}}{MS_{Error}}$
Error[a]	SS_{Error}	$N-a$	MS_{Error}	
Total	SS_T	$N-1$		

[a] This is sometimes denoted within treatments

10.3.10 ANOVA (ANalysis Of VAriance)

Analysis of variance can be used to analyze experiments from a number of different designs. The name, analysis of variance, is used because the method is based on looking at the total variability of the data and the variability partition according to different components. In its simplest form the test compares the variability due to treatment and the variability due to random error.

In this section, it is described how to use ANOVA in its simplest form. The test can be used to compare if a number of samples has the same mean value. That is, the design is one factor with more than two treatments. The test is summarized in Table 10.12.

The results of an ANOVA test are often summarized in an ANOVA table. The results of a test for one factor with multiple levels can, for example, be summarized as in Table 10.13.

Notice that the described ANOVA test is just one variant of ANOVA tests. ANOVA tests can be used for a number of different designs, involving many

Table 10.14 ANOVA table

Source of variation	Sum of squares	Degrees of freedom	Mean square	F_0
Between treatments	579.0515	2	289.5258	0.24
Error	36,151	30	1,205	
Total	36,730	32		

Table 10.15 Kruskal-Wallis

Item	Description
Input	a samples: $x_{11}, x_{12}, \ldots x_{1n_1} ; x_{21}, x_{22}, \ldots x_{2n_2}; \ldots ; x_{a1}, x_{a2}, \ldots x_{an_a}$
H_0	The population medians of the a samples are equal.
Calculations	All measures are ranked in one series $(1, 2, \ldots n_1 + n_2 + \ldots + n_a)$, and the calculations are based on these ranks. See for example [119, 157].
Criterion	See, for example, Siegel and Castellan [157] and Marascuilo and Serlin [119]

different factors, blocking variables, etc. It would lead too far to describe these tests in detail here. Refer instead to, for example, Montgomery [125], and Marascuilo and Serling [119].

Example of ANOVA. The module sizes in three different programs have been measured. The result is:

Program 1: 221, 159, 191, 194, 156, 238, 220, 197, 197, 194
Program 2: 173, 171, 168, 286, 206, 140, 226, 248, 189, 208, 213
Program 3: 234, 188, 181, 207, 266, 153, 190, 195, 181, 238, 191, 260

The null hypothesis is that the mean module size is the same in all three programs. The alternative hypothesis is that it is not. Based on the data above the ANOVA table in Table 10.14 can be calculated.

The number of degrees of freedom are $f_1 = a - 1 = 3 - 1 = 2$ and $f_2 = N - a = 33 - 3 = 30$. In Table B.5, it can be seen that $F_{0.025,2,30} = 4.18$. Since $F_0 < F_{0.025,2,30}$ it is impossible to reject the null hypothesis at the 0.025 level.

10.3.11 Kruskal-Wallis

The Kruskal-Wallis one way analysis of variance by ranks is a non-parametric alternative to the parametric one factor analysis of variance described above. This test can always be used instead of the parametric ANOVA if it is not sure that the assumptions of ANOVA are met. The test, which is based on ranks, is not described in detail here. More details are presented by, for example, Siegel and Castellan [157] and Marascuilo and Serlin [119].

The test is summarized in Table 10.15.

Table 10.16 Frequency table for module size (variables) of two systems (groups)

Module size	System 1	System 2
small	15	10
medium	20	19
large	25	28

10.3.12 Chi-2

Chi-2 (sometimes denoted χ^2) tests can be performed in a number of different ways. All Chi-2 tests are, however, based on that data is in the form of frequencies. An example of frequencies for two systems with a number of modules can be that for system 1 there are 15 small modules, 20 medium modules and 25 large modules, while for system 2 there are 10 small modules, 19 medium modules and 28 large modules. This is summarized in Table 10.16.

In this case a Chi-2 test could be performed to investigate if the distribution of small, medium and large modules are the same for the two systems.

Chi-2 tests can also be performed with one group of data, in order to see, if one measured frequency distribution is the same as a theoretical distribution. This test can, for example, be performed in order to check if samples can be seen as normally distributed.

In Table 10.17, a Chi-2 test is summarized, which can be used to compare if measurements from two or more groups come from the same distribution.

Example of Chi-2 test. If a Chi-2 test is performed on the data in Table 10.16 then Table 10.18 can be constructed.

The null hypothesis is that the size distribution is the same in both systems, and the alternative hypothesis is that the distributions are different. Based on the data the test statistic can be calculated to $X_2 = 1.12$. The number of degrees of freedom is $(r-1)(k-1) = 2*1 = 2$. In Table B.2, it can be seen that $\chi^2_{0.05,2} = 5.99$. Since $X^2 < \chi^2_{0.05,2}$ it is impossible to reject the null hypothesis at the 0.05 level.

Chi-2 Goodness of fit test. A Chi-2 test can also be carried out in order to check if measurements are taken from a certain distribution, e.g., the normal distribution. In this case a goodness of fit test is performed according to Table 10.19

If the goodness of fit test is performed for a continuous distribution, the possible values that can be measured must be divided into intervals so that each interval can represent one value. This must, for example, be done for the normal distribution.

If the distribution of H_0 is completely specified (for example, $P(X = 1) = 2/3, P(X = 2) = 1/3$) then no parameters must be estimated from the measured data (i.e. $e = 0$). On the other hand, for example, if the null hypothesis only specifies that the values comply with a normal distribution, two parameters must be estimated. Both the mean value and the standard deviation of the normal distribution must be estimated, otherwise it is not possible to determine the values of the different expected values, E_i, for the intervals. Therefore, in this case, $e = 2$.

Table 10.17 Chi-2, k independent samples (groups)

Item	Description
Input	Data as frequencies for k groups
H_0	Measurements from the k groups are from the same distribution
Calculations	Create a contingency table. An example of a contingency table for two groups and three variables (i.e., the same dimensions as the data in Table 10.16) can be constructed as:

Variable	Group1	Group2	Combined
1	n_{11}	n_{12}	R_1
2	n_{21}	n_{22}	R_2
3	n_{31}	n_{32}	R_3
Total	C_1	C_2	N

In this table n_{ij} denotes the frequency for variable i and group j, C_i denotes the sum of the frequencies for group i and R_i denotes the sum for variable i. N is the sum of all frequencies

Compute $X^2 = \sum_{i=1}^{r} \sum_{j=1}^{k} \frac{(n_{ij} - E_{ij})^2}{E_{ij}}$ where $E_{ij} = \frac{R_i C_j}{N}$ (the expected frequency

if H_0 is true), r is the number of variables and k is the number of groups

Criterion	Reject H_0 if $X^2 > \chi^2_{\alpha,f}$, where f is the number of degrees of freedom determined as $f = (r-1)(k-1)$. $\chi^2_{\alpha,f}$ is the upper α percentage point of the Chi-2 distribution with f degrees of freedom, which is tabulated, for example, in Table B.2 and by Siegel and Castellan [157]

Table 10.18 Calculations for Chi-2 test (Expected values, E_{ij}, are displayed in parenthesis)

Module size	System 1	System 2	Combined
small	15 (12.8205)	10 (12.1795)	$R_1 = 25$
medium	20 (20)	19 (19)	$R_2 = 39$
large	25 (27.1795)	28 (25.8205)	$R_3 = 53$
Total	$C_1 = 60$	$C_2 = 57$	$N = 117$

Example: Chi-2 Goodness of fit test for normal distribution. 60 students have developed the same program and the measured size is displayed in Table 10.20.

The null hypothesis is that the data is normally distributed, and the alternative hypothesis that it is not. Based on the data, the mean and the standard deviation can be estimated: $x = 794.9833$, and $s = 83.9751$.

The range can be divided into segments which have the same probability of including a value if the data actually is normally distributed with mean x and standard deviation s. In this example the range is divided into ten segments. In order to find the upper limit (x) of the first segment the following equation should be solved:

$P(X < x) = 1/10$ where X is $N(\bar{x}, s)$, which in terms of the standard normal distribution corresponds to

$P(X_s < (x - \bar{x})/s) = 1/10$ where X_s is $N(0, 1)$, which is the same as

$P(X_s < z) = \int_{-\infty}^{\infty} \frac{1}{\sqrt{2/\pi}} e^{(-y^2)/2} dy = 1/10$ where X_s is $N(0, 1)$ and $x = sz + \bar{x}$.

Table 10.19 Chi-2, goodness of fit

Item	Description
Input	Data as frequencies for one group (i.e., $O_1, O_2, \ldots O_n$, where O_i represents the number of observations in category i). Compare with Table 10.2
H_0	Measurements are from a certain distribution
Calculations	Compute $X^2 = \sum_{i=1}^{n} \dfrac{(O_i - E_1)^2}{E_i}$, where E_i is the expected number of observations in category i if H_0 is true and n is the number of categories
Criterion	Reject H_0 if $X_2 > \chi^2_{\alpha,f}$, where f is the number of degrees of freedom determined as $f = n - e - 1$, and e is the number of parameters that must be estimated from the original data (see below). $\chi^2_{\alpha,f}$ is the upper α percentage point of the Chi-2 distribution with f degrees of freedom, which is tabulated, for example, in Table B.2 and by Siegel and Castellan [157]. This is a one sided test

Table 10.20 Measured size

757	758	892	734	800	979	938	866	690	877	773	778
679	888	799	811	657	750	891	724	775	810	940	854
784	843	867	743	816	813	618	715	706	906	679	845
708	855	777	660	870	843	790	741	766	677	801	850
821	877	713	680	667	752	875	811	999	808	771	832

Table 10.21 Segments

Segment	Lower boundary	Upper boundary	Number of values
1		687.3	8
2	687.3	724.3	6
3	724.3	750.9	4
4	750.9	773.7	6
5	773.7	795	5
6	795	816.3	9
7	816.3	839	2
8	839	865.7	6
9	865.7	902.6	9
10	902.6		5

These equations can be solved in a number of different ways. One way is to iterate and use a computer to help find z or x. Another way is to use a table of the standard normal distribution (which shows $P(X_s < z)$ for different values of z). This type of table is available in most books on statistics. It is also possible to use a specialized table that directly shows the limit values for the segments, i.e. the values of z. This type of table is presented by Humphrey [82].

The resulting segment boundaries and the number of values that fall into each segment are shown in Table 10.21.

The expected number of values (E_i) in each segment is $60/10 = 6$. This means that $X_2 = 7.3$. The number of degrees of freedom is $10 - 2 - 1 = 7$. In Table B.2, it can be seen that $\chi^2_{0.05,7} = 14.07$. Since $X^2 < \chi^2_{0.05,2}$ it is impossible to reject the null hypothesis at the 0.05 level. If we look at a histogram, see Fig. 10.10, of the data, we can see that it seems to be fairly normally distributed.

Fig. 10.10 Histogram

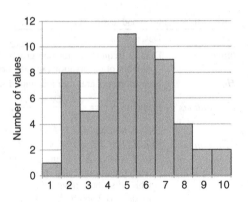

Chi-2 test final remarks. The Chi-2 test is based on certain assumptions, which are likely to be fulfilled if the expected values, E_i, are not too small. A rule of thumb is, if the number of degrees of freedom (f) is equal to 1, the Chi-2 test should not be used if any of the expected frequencies are less than 5. If $f > 1$ the Chi-2 test should not be used if more than 20% of the expected frequencies are less than 5 or any of them is less than 1. It should be observed that sometimes the test is used although the expected frequencies are not fulfilled. In these cases, this is a calculated risk.

One way to obtain larger expected frequencies is to combine related categories to new categories. However, the new categories must be meaningful. For more information concerning the Chi-2 test refer, for example, to Siegel and Castellan [157].

10.3.13 Model Adequacy Checking

Every statistical model is relying on specific assumption regarding, for example, distribution, independence and scales. If the assumptions are invalidated by the data set, the results of the hypothesis testing are invalid. Hence, it is crucial to check that all assumptions are fulfilled.

The checking of model adequacy is made depending on the assumptions. Below we describe three cases:

Normality   If a test assumes that the data is normally distributed, a Chi-2 test can be made to assess to which degree the assumption is fulfilled. The Chi-2 test is described above.

Independence   If the test assumes that the data is a sample from several independent stochastic variables, it is necessary to check that there is no correlation between the sample sets. This may be checked with scatter plots and by calculating correlation coefficients as discussed in the beginning of this section.

Residuals   In many statistical models, there is a term that represents the residuals (statistical error). It is often assumed that the residuals are normally distributed. A common way to check this property is to plot the residuals in a scatter plot and see that there is no specific trends in the data (the distribution looks random).

10.3.14 Drawing Conclusions

When the experiment data has been analyzed and interpreted, we need to draw conclusions regarding the outcome of the experiment. If the hypotheses are rejected we may draw conclusions regarding the influence of the independent variables on the dependent variables, given that the experiment is valid, see Chap. 8.

If, on the other hand, the experiment cannot reject the null hypothesis, we cannot draw any conclusions on the independent variables influence on the dependent variable. The only thing we have shown, in this case, is that there is no statistically significant difference between the treatments.

If we have found statistically significant differences, we want to make general conclusions about the relation between independent and dependent variables. Before this can be done we need to consider the external validity of the experiment, see Chap. 8. We can only generalize the result to environments that are similar to the experimental setting.

Although the result of the experiment may be statistically significant, it is not necessarily that the result is of any practical importance. Assume, for example, that method X was shown with a high statistical significance to be 2% more cost effective than method Y, although there is a high statistical significance, the improvement of changing from method Y to method X might not be cost effective. That is, it is necessary to study the observed effect size of different treatments and based on that draw conclusions and present recommendations. Kampenes et al. [92] give an overview of different effect size concepts and present a systematic review on how this is handled in published articles.

It may also be vice versa; although the experiment results may not be statistically significant or have a low statistical significance, the lessons learned from the experiment may still be of practical importance. The fact that a null hypothesis cannot be rejected with a certain level of significance does not mean that the null hypothesis is true. There may be problems with the design of the experiment, such as real threats to validity or too few data samples. Furthermore, depending on the situation and objective of the study, we may settle for a lower statistical significance since the results are of high practical importance. This issue is also related to the discussion regarding threats to the validity, see Sect. 8.9.

When finding a significant correlation between a variable A and a variable B, we cannot, in general, draw the conclusion that there is a *causal relation* between A and B. There may be a third factor C, that causes the measurable effects on A and B.

The conclusions drawn based on the outcome of the experiment, are input to a decision, e.g. that a new method will be applied in future projects, or that further experimentation is needed.

It should be noted that there are drawbacks of using hypothesis testing too. As Miller [122] points out, most null hypotheses are formulated in a way that they always will be rejected, if enough data points are provided, and it is not possible to actually obtain a sample that is representative of the whole population, for example, of all software engineers in the world. Care should always be taken when actions are taken based on the results of an experiment, and the experiment result should be seen as one factor in the decision process.

10.4   Example Analysis

The example is a continuation of the example in Sect. 9.4. Based on the experiment data from the execution, the first step is to apply descriptive statistics, i.e. to plot the data. Appropriate statistical methods should be used in relation to the measurement scales, as described in Sect. 10.1. A commonly used way to plot data is to use box plots. They provide an excellent opportunity to get an overview of the data and to identify outliers. If identifying an outlier, it is important to understand whether there is some underlying explanation. For example, it may be the case that one or a few subjects have a very different background than the others, and hence it must be ensured that their data is comparable to the data from the other subjects. It may be particularly critical if only one of the groups is affected. In general, we should be restrictive in removing data points, i.e. any removal of data should be well motivated and documented.

Once it is decided which data to include in the data analysis, it is time to take a look at the statistical analysis. The statistical analysis is always a challenge, and there are many different opinions about the use of different statistical methods and when to use parametric and non-parametric methods.

The first step is to check if the data is normally distributed, for example by plotting a histogram (Fig. 10.5) or by using the Chi-2 test as described in Sect. 10.3.12 or by using other alternative tests such as for example the so-called Kolmogorov–Smirnov test, the Shapiro–Wilks' W test, or the Anderson–Darling test. However with a small sample size, the data may look normally distributed without actually being normally distributed and normality tests may not detect it due to having few data points. Some parametric tests are more robust than others against deviations from normality. For example, the t-test is quite robust for non-normality, which is not the case for the ANOVA. Independently, it may be good to investigate whether the data is normally distributed.

Given the two-factor design (reading technique and requirements document) with two treatments each, there is a great need for the data to be normally distributed. If the data is normally distributed then it is possible to use an ANOVA. If the data is not normally distributed then there is a problem, since there is no non-parametric counterpart for this type of design as is illustrated in Table 10.3; if having only one factor with two treatments then there are non-parametric alternatives. Thus, even if there are simpler designs, the chosen design seemed quite straightforward and it is tempting to use it. However, it may not be a good choice to use this type of design.

It generates more data points, but it does result in some challenges when coming to the statistical analysis. Thus, it is important to be aware of the consequences in terms of analysis when selecting the experiment design. This type of design is sometimes referred to as being a crossover design, i.e. first subjects use or are exposed to one treatment and then they are exposed to a second treatment. Some of the challenges would be addressed if it was possible to only have one factor, i.e. the reading technique. However, it is not realistic to use the same requirements document for two inspections unless there is a long time between the two runs. Kitchenham et al. [99] present some statistical challenges related to crossover design. Having said that, crossover designs are not uncommon in software engineering since it is a trade-off between the statistical challenges and having (too) few subjects assigned to each treatment, although others argue that crossover designs cannot be recommended in software engineering [99].

If assuming that the data is normally distributed, then an ANOVA test can be applied. However, a challenge is that if the ANOVA shows a significant result, it is still not known which difference is significant. To do this some additional test has to be used after the ANOVA, for example, Fisher's Protected Least Significant Difference (PLSD) test [125]. The test requires a significant ANOVA to be used, i.e. it is protected by a significant ANOVA. Fisher's PLSD is used to make a pairwise comparison of the means. Once again it illustrates some of the statistical challenges that comes as a direct consequence of the experiment design. Thus, there is a need to have quite simple experiment designs to be able to make a correct statistical analysis.

If we would have chosen to divide the subjects into two groups and then assigned them to use either PBR or CBR on one and the same requirements document, we would only have one factor with two treatments. This means that a t-test or Mann-Whitney test could have been used depending on the outcome of the test for normality. On the other hand, we would have no indication of the interaction between subject and treatment. Whether this is better or worse than other alternative designs has to be decided in each individual case depending on the number of subjects and the validity threats identified.

10.5 Exercises

10.1. What is descriptive statistics and what is it used for?

10.2. What is a parametric and non-parametric test respectively, and when can they be applied?

10.3. What is the power of a test?

10.4. What is a paired comparison?

10.5. Explain the ANOVA test briefly.

Chapter 11
Presentation and Package

When an experiment is completed, the findings may be presented for different audiences, as defined in Fig. 11.1. This could, for example, be done in a paper for a conference or a journal, a report for decision-makers, a package for replication of the experiment, or as educational material. The packaging could also be done within companies to improve and understand different processes. In this case, it is appropriate to store the experiences in an experience base according to the concepts discussed by Basili et al. [16]. However, here we focus on the academic reporting in journals and conferences. If space limitations prevent complete reporting of all details, we encourage a technical report be published in parallel.

Jedlitschka and Pfahl propose a scheme for the academic reporting of experiments [86] which was later evaluated by Kitchenham et al. [101]. Jedlitschka and Pfahl's proposal is summarized in Table 11.1 and briefly elaborated in Sect. 11.1.

11.1 Experiment Report Structure

Structured abstract. The abstract should give the reader a quick summary of the key characteristics of the experiment. Structured abstracts are empirically demonstrated to be efficient tools to aid extraction of data [30] as well as writing good abstracts [31]. The elements of a structured abstract are:

- Background or Context,
- Objectives or Aims,
- Method,
- Results, and
- Conclusions

Example. An example of a structured abstract is presented to illustrate the items. In this case, the length of the structured abstract is limited to 300 words:

Context: Throughout an organization, people have different responsibilities and work tasks, hence, it is probable that different roles have different priorities when

C. Wohlin et al., *Experimentation in Software Engineering*,
DOI 10.1007/978-3-642-29044-2_11, © Springer-Verlag Berlin Heidelberg 2012

Table 11.1 Proposed reporting structure for experiment reports, by Jedlitschka and Pfahl [86]

Sections/subsections	Contents
Title, authorship	
Structured abstract	Summarizes the paper under headings of background or context, objectives or aims, method, results, and conclusions
Motivation	Sets the scope of the work and encourages readers to read the rest of the paper
Problem statement	Reports what the problem is; where it occurs, and who observes it
Research objectives	Defines the experiment using the formalized style used in GQM
Context	Reports environmental factors such as settings and locations
Related work	How current study relates to other research
Experimental design	Describes the outcome of the experimental planning stage
Goals, hypotheses and variables	Presents the refined research objectives
Design	Define the type of experimental design
Subjects	Defines the methods used for subject sampling and group allocation
Objects	Defines what experimental objects were used
Instrumentation	Defines any guidelines and measurement instruments used
Data collection procedure	Defines the experimental schedule, timing and data collection procedures
Analysis procedure	Specifies the mathematical analysis model to be used
Evaluation of validity	Describes the validity of materials, procedures to ensure participants keep to the experimental method, and methods to ensure the reliability and validity of data collection methods and tools
Execution	Describes how the experimental plan was implemented
Sample	Description of the sample characteristics
Preparation	How the experimental groups were formed and trained
Data collection performed	How data collection took place and any deviations from plan
Validity procedure	How the validity process was followed and any deviation from plan
Analysis	Summarizes the collected data and describes how it was analyzed
Descriptive statistics	Presentation of the data using descriptive statistics
Data set reduction	Describes any reduction of the data set e.g. removal of outliers
Hypothesis testing	Describes how the data was evaluated and how the analysis model was validated
Interpretation	Interprets the findings from the Analysis section
Evaluation of results and implications	Explains the results
Limitations of study	Discusses threats to validity
Inferences	How the results generalize given the findings and limitations
Lesson learnt	Descriptions of what went well and what did not during the course of the experiment
Conclusions and future work	Presents a summary of the study
Relation to existing evidence	Describes the contribution of the study in the context of earlier experiments
Impact	Identifies the most important findings
Limitations	Identifies main limitations of approach i.e. circumstances when the expected benefits will not be delivered
Future work	Suggestions for other experiments to further investigate
Acknowledgements	Identifies any contributors who do not fulfill authorship criteria
References	Lists all cited literature
Appendices	Includes raw data and/or detailed analyses which might help others to use the results

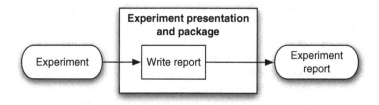

Fig. 11.1 Overview of presentation and package

it comes to what should be improved within a company. This has been found in previous studies in marketing, but is this true for software improvement as well? *Objective:* This paper evaluates how different roles in a software development organization view different issues in software process improvement and if such differences could be used in order to provide more tailor-made process improvements within an organization and uses this as a working hypothesis. *Method:* A quantitative questionnaire containing five different weighted questions related to software process improvement was developed. Eighty-four employees from all levels of a Swedish telecommunication company were then approached, of which 63 responded. *Results:* The different roles disagreed in three of the questions while they agreed in two of the questions. The disagreement was related to issues about importance of improvement, urgency of problems, and threat against successful process management, while the questions where the roles agreed focused on communication of the processes (documentation and teaching). *Conclusion:* It is concluded that it is important to be aware and take into account the different needs of different roles. This will make it possible to provide improvements tailored to specific roles which will probably help to overcome resistance to process improvements. It is also important to look into other areas and companies (for example, marketing) where it could be beneficial when conducting process improvements.

Motivation. The motivation or introduction set the scope and defines the objective of the research, hence it primarily reports the outcome of the scoping phase (see Chap. 7). Information about the intent of the work can also be included to clarify and capture the readers' interest. This provides the reader with an understanding of why the research has been carried out and why there is a need for it. The context in which the experiment is conducted should be briefly presented here.

Related work. Related work is important to provide a picture of how the current experiment is related to work conducted previously. Every experiment report does not need a complete systematic literature review (see Chap. 4), although being systematic in searching for literature is mostly beneficial. In particular, in the case of replication studies, all previous studies should be reported.

Experimental design. Here, the outcome of the planning phase is reported, see Chap. 8. The hypotheses, which are derived from the problem statement, are described in detail. The experimental design is presented, including the design type, variables measured, both the independent and the dependent, as well as the instrumentation.

A description of how the data will be collected and analyzed should be included. A characterization of the subjects should be provided. The discussion about the experiment's conclusion, internal, construct and external validity should be provided here together with the possible threats against the plans.

The purpose for describing these items is to enable other persons to both understand the design so that it is visible to the reader that the results are trustworthy and to enable replication of the study. In short, it should help the reader to get deeper a understanding of what has been done.

Execution. The first part to describe is how the operation is prepared, see Chap. 9. It is important to include descriptions of aspects that will ease replication of the experiment and to give insight into how activities have been carried out. The preparation of the subjects has to be presented. Information such as whether they attended some lessons or not is important to provide. The execution of the experiment should also be presented and how data was collected during the experiment.

Validation procedures of the data collection are another issue that has to be stressed and it has to be reported if sidesteps have been taken from the plans. All information is aimed to provide a case for the validity of the data and to highlight problems.

Analysis. A presentation of the data analysis, where the calculations are described together with the assumptions for using some specific analysis model, should be provided. Information about sample sizes, significance levels and application of tests must also be included so that the reader will know the prerequisites for the analysis. The reasons for the actions taken, for example outlier removal, should be described to avoid misunderstandings in the interpretation of the results. For more information see Chap. 10.

Interpretation. Raw results from the analysis are not enough to provide an understanding of the results and conclusions from the experiment. An interpretation must also be provided, see Chap. 10. It includes the rejection of the hypothesis or the inability to reject the null hypothesis. The interpretation summarizes how the results from the experiment may be used.

The interpretation should be done with references to validity, see Chap. 8. Factors that might have had an impact on the results should be described.

Conclusions and further work. Finally, the discussions about the findings and the conclusions are presented as a summary of the whole experiment together with the outcomes, problems, deviations from the plans and so forth. The results should also be related to work reported previously. It is important to address similarities and differences in the findings.

Ideas for future work might also be included in this section and information about where more information can be found to get a deeper insight to the experiment and to ease replication of the experiment.

Appendices. Information that is not vital for the presentation could be included in appendices. This could, for example, be the collected data and more information about the subjects and objects. If the intention is to produce a lab package, the material used in the experiment could be provided here.

11.2 Exercises

11.1. Why is it important to document an experiment thoroughly?

11.2. What is a lab package? Can you find any lab packages on the Internet?

11.3. Why is it important to report related work?

11.4. Why is it not enough just to provide the results from the analysis? In other words, why is a special interpretation of the results important?

11.5. Which in information in the report is most important when conducting a systematic literature review? When replicating an experiment?

Part III
Example Experiments

Chapter 12
Experiment Process Illustration

The primary objective of the presentation of this experiment is to illustrate experimentation and the steps in the experiment process introduced in the previous chapters. The presentation of the experiment in this chapter is focused on the experiment process rather than following the proposed report structure in Chap. 11.

The objective of the presented experiment is to investigate the performance in using the Personal Software Process (PSP) [82, 83] based on the individual background of the people taking the PSP course. The experiment, as reported here, is part of a larger investigation of the individual differences in performance within the PSP. Since "individual background" cannot be randomly assigned to subjects, the experiment is in fact a quasi-experiment.

The PSP is an individual process for a systematic approach to software development. The process includes, for example, measurement, estimation, planning and tracking. Furthermore, reuse is a key issue, and in particular the reuse of individual experiences and data. The PSP course introduces the process in seven incremental steps adding new features to the process using templates, forms and process scripts.

For the sake of simplicity, only two hypotheses are evaluated here. The data set for the larger study can be found in Appendix A.1.2. The experiment presented in this chapter uses a subset of the data.

12.1 Scoping

12.1.1 Goal Definition

The first step is to decide whether an experiment is a suitable way to analyze the problem at hand. In this particular case, the objective of the empirical study is to determine the differences in individual performance for people using the PSP given their background.

C. Wohlin et al., *Experimentation in Software Engineering*,
DOI 10.1007/978-3-642-29044-2_12, © Springer-Verlag Berlin Heidelberg 2012

The experiment is motivated by a need to understand the differences in individual performance within the PSP. It is well known, and accepted, that software engineers perform differently. One objective of introducing a personal process is to provide support for the individuals to improve their performance. In order to support improvement in the best possible way, it is important to understand what differences still can be expected within the PSP and if it is possible to explain and thus understand the individual differences.

Object of study. The object of study is the participants in the Personal Software Process (PSP) course and their ability in terms of performance based on their background and experience. Humphrey defines the Personal Software Process in his two books on the subject [82, 83].

Purpose. The purpose of the experiment is to evaluate the individual performance based on the background of the people taking the PSP course. The experiment provides insight in to what can be expect in terms of individual performance when using the PSP.

Perspective. The perspective is from the point of view of the researchers and teachers, i.e. the researcher or teacher would like to know if there is any systematic differences in the performance in the course based on the background of the individuals entering the PSP course. This also includes people who may want to take the course in the future or to introduce the PSP in industry.

Quality focus. The main effect studied in the experiment is the individual performance in the PSP course. Here, two specific aspects are emphasized. The choice is to focus on Productivity (KLOC/development time) and Defect density (faults/KLOC), where KLOC stands for thousands of lines of code.

Context. The experiment is run within the context of the PSP. Moreover, the experiment is conducted within a PSP course given at the Department of Communication Systems, Lund University in Sweden. This study is from the course given in 1996–1997, and the main difference from the PSP as presented by Humphrey [82] is that it was decided to use a coding standard and a line counting standard. Moreover, the course was run with C as a mandatory programming language independently of the background of the students. The experimental context characterization is "multi-test within object study", see Table 7.1. The study is focused on the PSP or more specifically the ten programs in Humphrey's book [82] denoted 1A–10A. The PSP course is taken by a large number of individuals (this particular year, 65 students finished the course). Thus, 65 subjects are included in the study, see Sect. 7.1. Thus, from this definition the study can be judged as being a controlled experiment. The lack of randomization of students, i.e. the students signed up for the course, means however that the study still lacks one important ingredient to make it fully into a controlled experiment. This is hence classified as a quasi-experiment, see Sect. 7.1.

12.1.2 Summary of Scoping

The summary is made according to Sect. 7.2.

Analyze *the outcome of the PSP*
for the purpose *of evaluation*
with respect to *the background of the individuals*
from the point of view of the *researchers and teachers*
in the context of *the PSP course.*

12.2 Planning

12.2.1 Context Selection

The context of the experiment is a PSP course at the university, and hence the experiment is run off-line (not in an industrial software development), it is conducted by graduate students (normally students in their fourth year at the university), and the experiment is specific since it is focused on the PSP in an educational environment. The ability to generalize from this specific context is further elaborated below when discussing threats to the validity in the experiment. The experiment addresses a real problem, i.e. the differences in individual performance and the understanding of the differences.

The use of the PSP as an experimental context provides other researchers with excellent opportunities to replicate the experiment as it is well defined. Furthermore, it means that there is no need to spend much effort in setting up the experiment in terms of defining and creating the environment in which the experiment is run. Humphrey [82] defines the experimental context, and hence there is no need to prepare forms for data collection and so forth.

12.2.2 Hypothesis Formulation

An important aspect of experiments is to know and to formally state clearly what is going to be evaluated in the experiment. This leads to the formulation of a hypothesis (or several hypotheses). Here, it has been chosen to focus on two hypotheses. Informally, they are:

1. Students both from the Computer Science and Engineering program and the Electrical Engineering program have taken the course. The students from the Computer Science and Engineering program normally have taken more courses in computer science and software engineering, and hence it is expected that

they have a higher productivity than students from the Electrical Engineering program.
2. As part of the first lecture, the students were asked to fill out a survey regarding their background in terms of experiences from issues related to the course, see Table A.1. This can be exemplified with, for example, knowledge in C. The students were required to use C in the course independently of their prior experience of the language. Thus, it was not required that the students had taken a C-course prior to entering the PSP course, which meant that some students learned C within the PSP course. This is not according to the recommendation by Humphrey [82]. The hypothesis based on the C experience is that students with more experience in C make fewer faults per lines of code.

Based on this informal statement of the hypotheses, it is now possible to state them formally and also to define what measures that are needed to evaluate the hypotheses.

1. Null hypothesis, H_0: There is no difference in productivity (measured as lines of code per total development time) between students from the Computer Science and Engineering program (CSE) and the Electrical Engineering program (EE).
   H_0: Prod(CSE) = Prod(EE)
   Alternative hypothesis, H_1: Prod(CSE) $\neq$ Prod(EE)
   Measures needed: student program (CSE or EE) and productivity (LOC/hour).
2. Null hypothesis, H_0: There is no difference between the students in terms of number of faults per KLOC (1,000 lines of code) based on the prior knowledge in C.
   H_0: Number of faults per KLOC is independent of C experience.
   Alternative hypothesis, H_1: Number of faults per KLOC changes with C experience.
   Measures needed: C experience and Faults/KLOC.

The hypotheses mean that the following data needs to be collected:

- Student program: measured by CSE or EE (nominal scale)
- Productivity is measured as LOC/Development time. Thus, program size has to be measured (lines of code according to the coding standard and the counting standard) and development time (minutes spent developing the program). The development time is translated to hours when the productivity is calculated. It should be noted that it was chosen to study the total program size (the sum of the ten programming assignments) and the development time for all ten programs. Thus, the individual assignments are not studied.
  Lines of code are measured by counting the lines of code using a line counter program (ratio scale). The lines counted are new and changed lines of code.
  Development time is measured in minutes (ratio scale).
  Productivity is hence measured on a ratio scale.
- C experience is measured by introducing a classification into four classes based on prior experience of C (ordinal scale). The classes are:

1. No prior experience.
2. Read a book or followed a course.
3. Some industrial experience (less than 6 months).
4. Industrial experience (more than 6 months).

The experience in C is hence measured on an ordinal scale.
- Faults/KLOC is measured as of the number of faults divided by the number of lines of code.

The hypotheses and measures put constraints on the type of statistical test to use, at least formally. The measurement scales formally determine the application of specific statistical methods, but we may want to relax these requirements for other reasons. This issue is further discussed below, when discussing the actual type of design in the experiment.

12.2.3 Variables Selection

The independent variables are student program and experience in C. The dependent variables are productivity and faults/KLOC.

12.2.4 Selection of Subjects

The subjects are chosen based on convenience, i.e. the subjects are students taking the PSP course. The students are a sample from all students at the two programs, but not a random sample.

12.2.5 Experiment Design

The problem has been stated, and the independent and dependent variables have been chosen. Furthermore, the measurement scales have been decided for the variables. Thus, it is now possible to design the experiment. The first step is to address the general design principles:

Randomization. The object is not assigned randomly to the subjects. All students use the PSP and its ten assignments. The objective of the study is not to evaluate the PSP vs. something else. The subjects are, as stated above, not selected randomly; they are the students that have chosen to take the course. Moreover, the assignments are not made in random order. The order is, however, not important, since the measures used in the evaluation are the results of developing the ten programs.

Blocking. No systematic approach to blocking is applied. The decision to measure the ten programs and evaluate based on this, rather than looking at each individual program, can be viewed as providing blocking for differences between the ten programs. Thus, blocking the impact of the differences between individual programs.

Balancing. It would have been preferable to have a balanced data set, but the experimental study is based on a course where the participants have signed up for the course, and hence it is impossible to influence the background of people and consequently unable to balance the data set.

Standard design types. The information available is compared with the standard type of designs outlined in Chap. 8. Both designs can be found among the standard types, and the statistical tests are available in this book.

1. The definition, hypotheses and measures for the first evaluation means that the design is: one factor with two treatments. The factor is the program and the treatments are CSE or EE. The dependent variable is measured on a ratio scale, and hence a parametric test is suitable. In this particular case, the t-test will be used.
2. The second design is of the type "one factor with more than two treatments". The factor is the experience in C with four treatments, see the experience grading above. The dependent variable is measured on a ratio scale and it is possible to use a parametric test for this hypothesis too. The ANOVA test is hence suitable to use for evaluation.

12.2.6 Instrumentation

The background and experience of the individuals is found through a survey handed out at the first lecture, see Table A.1 in Appendix A. This data provides the input to the characterization of the students, and hence are the independent variables in the experiment. The objects are the programs developed within the PSP course. The guidelines and measurements are provided through the PSP [82].

12.2.7 Validity Evaluation

There are four levels of validity threats to consider. *Internal validity* is primarily focused on the validity of the actual study. *External validity* can be divided into PSP students at Lund University forthcoming years, students at Lund University (or more realistically to students at the CSE and EE programs), the PSP in general, and for software development in general. The *conclusion validity* is concerned with relationship between treatment and outcome, and the ability to draw conclusions. *Construct validity* is about generalizing the result to the theory behind the experiment.

The internal validity within the course is probably not a problem. The large number of tests (equal to the number of students) ensures the internal validity is good.

Concerning the external threats, it is highly probable that similar results should be obtained when running the course in a similar way at Lund University. It is more difficult to generalize the results to other students, i.e. students not taking the course. They are probably not as interested in software development and hence they come from a different population. The results from the analysis can probably be generalized to other PSP courses, where it is feasible to compare participants based on their background in terms of computer science or electrical engineering or experience of a particular programming language.

The major threat regarding the conclusion validity is the quality of the data collected during the PSP course. The students are expected to deliver a lot of data as part of their work with the course. Thus, there is a risk that the data is faked or simply not correct due to mistakes. The data inconsistencies are, however, not believed to be particularly related to any specific background, hence the problem is likely the same independent of the background of the individuals. The conclusion validity is hence not considered to be critical.

The construct validity includes two major threats. The first threat is that the measurements as defined may not be appropriate measures of the entities, for example, is "LOC/Development time" a good measure of productivity? The second major threat to the construct validity is that it is part of a course, where the students are graded. This implies that the students may bias their data, as they believe that it will give them a better grade. It was, however, in the beginning of the course emphasized that the grade did not depend on the actual data. The grade was based on timely and proper delivery, and the understanding expressed in the reports handed in during the course.

The results are found for the PSP, but they are likely to hold for software development in general. There is no reason that people coming from different study programs or having different background experience from a particular programming language perform differently between the PSP and software development in general. This is probably valid when talking about differences in background, although the actual size of the difference may vary. The important issue is that there is a difference, and the actual size of the difference is of minor importance.

12.3 Operation

12.3.1 Preparation

The subjects (students) were not aware of what aspects were going to be studied. They were informed that the researchers wanted to study the outcome of the PSP course in comparison with the background of the participants. They were, however, not aware of the actual hypotheses stated. The students, from their point of view, did not primarily participate in an experiment; they were taking a course. All students were guaranteed anonymity.

The survey material was prepared in advance. Most of the other material was, however, provided through the PSP book [82].

12.3.2 Execution

The experiment was executed over 14 weeks, during which the ten programming assignments were handed in regularly. The data was primarily collected through forms. Interviews were used at the end of the course, primarily to evaluate the course and the PSP as such.

The experiment was, as stated earlier, run within a PSP course and in a university environment. The experiment has not been allowed to affect the course objectives. The main differences between running the PSP solely as a course has been the initial survey of the students' background.

12.3.3 Data Validation

Data was collected for 65 students. After the course, the achievements of the students were discussed among the people involved in the course. Data from six students was removed, due to that the data was regarded as invalid or at least questionable. Students have not been removed (at this stage) from the evaluation based on the actual figures, but due to our trust in the delivered data and whether or not the data is believed to be representative. The six students were removed due to:

- Data from two students was not filled in properly.
- One student finished the course much later than the rest, and that student had a long period when no work was done with the PSP. This may have affected the data.
- Data from two students was removed based on that they delivered their assignments late and required considerably more support than the other students did, hence it was judged that the extra advice may have affected their data.
- Finally, one student was removed based on that the background was completely different than the others.

This means removing six students out of the 65, hence leaving 59 students for statistical analysis and interpretation of the results.

12.4 Analysis and Interpretation

12.4.1 Descriptive Statistics

As a first step in analyzing the data, descriptive statistics are used to visualize the data collected.

Study program vs. productivity. Figure 12.1 shows the productivity for the two study programs, when dividing the population into classes based on productivity. The first class includes those with a productivity between 5 and 10 lines of code per hour. Thus, the eighth class includes those with a productivity between 40 and 45 lines of code per hour. From Fig. 12.1, it is possible to see that students from the Electrical Engineering program (EE) seem to have a lower productivity. Moreover, it is noticeable to see that the variation of the distribution seems to be larger among the students from the Computer Science and Engineering program (CSE). In total, there are 32 CSE students and 27 EE students. The mean value for CSE students is 23.0 with a standard deviation of 8.7, and for the EE students the mean value is 16.4 with a standard deviation of 6.3. To gain an even better understanding of the data, a box plot is drawn, see Fig. 12.2.

The whiskers in the box plot are constructed as proposed by Frigge et al. [60] and discussed in Chap. 10. For the whiskers, a value that is the length of the box multiplied with 1.5 and added or subtracted from the upper and lower quartiles respectively. For example, for the CSE students (see Fig. 12.2): median = 22.7, box length = $29.4 - 17.6 = 11.8$, the upper tail becomes: $29.4 + 1.5 * 11.8 = 47.1$.

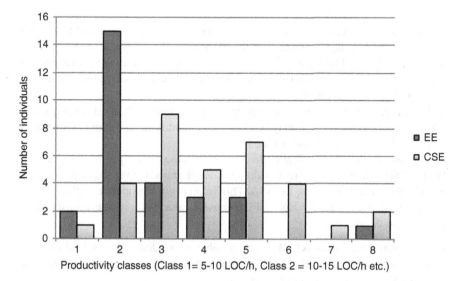

Fig. 12.1 Frequency distribution for the productivity (in classes)

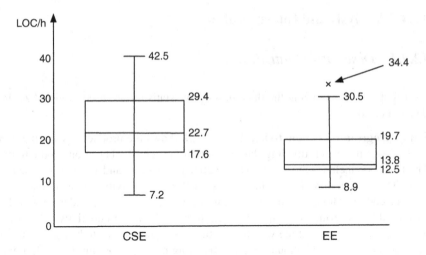

Fig. 12.2 Box plot of productivity for the two study programs

Table 12.1 Faults/KLOC for the different C experience classes

Class[a]	Number of students	Median value of faults/KLOC	Mean value of faults/KLOC	Standard deviation of faults/KLOC
1	32	66.8	82.9	64.2
2	19	69.7	68.0	22.9
3	6	63.6	67.6	20.6
4	2	63	63.0	17.3

[a] The different experience classes are explained in Sect. 12.2.2

There is, however, an exception to this rule, namely, that the upper and lower tails should never be higher or lower than the highest and lowest value in the data set, hence the upper tail becomes 42.5, which is the highest value. This exception is introduced to avoid negative values or other types of unrealistic values. The other values in Fig. 12.2 are found in a similar way.

From Fig. 12.2, it can be seen that there is a clear pattern that the EE students have a lower productivity. Thus, it may be possible to identify the difference statistically in a hypothesis test. The t-test is used below.

It is also important to look at outliers in comparison to the upper and lower tails. For the CSE-students, there are no values outside the tails. For the EE students, there is one value outside the tails, i.e. 34.4. This value is not consider an outlier since it is not judged as an extreme value. It is an unusual value, but it is determined to keep the value in the analysis.

C experience vs. faults/KLOC. The number of students for each class of C experience is shown in Table 12.1, together with the mean and median values, and standard deviation for respective class.

Fig. 12.3 Box plot for
faults/KLOC for class 1

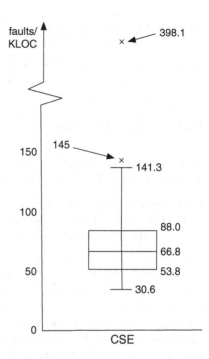

From Table 12.1, it can be seen that the distribution is skewed towards no
or little experience of C. If looking at the mean values of faults/KLOC, there
seems to be a tendency that the more experienced students create fewer faults. The
standard deviation is, however, extremely large, and the median varies unexpectedly
in comparison with the mean value and the underlying hypothesis. The standard
deviation for the first class is very high and a further investigation of the data is
recommended. Thus, box plot can be used for this data set too.

Box plots are constructed for all four experience classes. The plots for classes
2–4 reveal nothing, all values are within the boundaries of the whiskers, and hence
the upper and lower tails become equal to the highest and lowest value respectively.
The box plot for the first class is more interesting, and it is shown in Fig. 12.3.

From Fig. 12.3, it can be seen that the lower tail is equal to the lowest value of
faults/ KLOC. The upper tail on the other hand is not equal to the highest value, and
hence there is one or more unusual values. There are actually two unusual values,
namely 145 and 398.1. The latter value is an extreme one; it is more than ten times
higher than the lowest value. It is also almost three times as high as the second
highest value. Thus, it is possible to conclude that the high standard deviation can
be explained with the extreme value. For the second hypothesis, the ANOVA test is
used.

The descriptive statistics have provided a better insight into the data, both in
terms of what can be expected from the hypothesis testing and to potential problems
caused by outliers.

Table 12.2 Faults/KLOC for the different C experience class 1

Class	Number of students	Median value of faults/KLOC	Mean value of faults/KLOC	Standard deviation of faults/KLOC
1	31	66	72.7	29.0

12.4.2   Data Reduction

Data reduction can always be debated, since as soon as data points are removed information is lost. Two separate ways of reducing data can be identified:

- Single data points can be removed, for example, outliers, or
- The data can be analyzed and based on the analysis it may be concluded that due to high inter-correlation between some variables, some measures should be combined into some more abstract measure.

This means that it is possible to either remove data points or reduce the number of variables. In the case of removing data points, the main candidates are the outliers. It is by no means obvious that all outliers should be removed, but they are certainly candidates for removal. It is important to remember that data points should not just be removed because they do not fit with the belief or hypothesis. On the other hand, it is important to remove data points which may make a completely valid relationship invalid, due to that, for example, an extreme outlier is included, which is not expected if replicating the study.

To reduce the number of variables statistical methods for data reduction are needed. Some examples are principal component analysis and factor analysis [90, 91, 118]. These types of methods are not considered here, as the objective is not to reduce the number of variables.

It is probably better to be restrictive in reducing a data set, as there is always a risk that we aim for a certain result. Thus, for the data presented above, it was chosen to only remove the extreme outlier for the number of faults/KLOC. After removing the extreme outlier, the data for class 1 is summarized in Table 12.2.

The removal of the outlier decreased the mean value and standard deviation considerably. The mean number of faults/KLOC is still highest for class 1. However, the differences between the classes are not that large. After reducing the second data set with one data point, it is not possible to perform the statistical test. This is where the hypotheses are evaluated.

12.4.3   Hypothesis Testing

The first hypothesis regarding higher productivity for students following the Computer Science and Engineering program is evaluated using a t-test. An ANOVA test is applied to evaluate the hypothesis that more experience in C means fewer faults/KLOC.

Table 12.3 Results from the t-test

Factor	Mean diff.	Degrees of freedom (DF)	t-value	p-value
CSE vs. EE	6.1617	57	3.283	0.0018

Table 12.4 Results from the ANOVA-test

Factor: C vs. faults/KLOC	Degrees of freedom (DF)	Sum of squares	Mean square	F-value	p-value
Between treatments	3	3483	1160.9	0.442	0.7236
Error	55	144304	2623.7		

Study program vs. productivity. The results from the t-test (unpaired, two-tailed) are shown in Table 12.3.

From Table 12.3, it can be concluded that H_0 is rejected. There is a significant difference in productivity for students coming from different study programs. The p-value is very low so the results are highly significant. The actual reason for the difference has to be further evaluated.

C experience vs. faults/KLOC. This hypothesis is evaluated with an ANOVA test (factorial). The results of the analysis are shown in Table 12.4.

The results from the analysis are not significant, although some differences are observed in terms of mean value, see above, it is not possible to show that there is a significant difference in terms of number of faults/KLOC based on C experience.

Since the number of students in class 3 and 4 is very limited, class 2–4 are grouped together to study the difference between class 1 and the rest. A t-test was performed to evaluate if it was possible to differentiate between class 1 and the grouping of classes 2–4 into one class. No significant results were obtained.

12.5 Summary

We have investigated two hypotheses:

1. Study program vs. productivity
2. C experience vs. faults/KLOC

We are able to show that students from the Computer Science and Engineering program are more productive. This is in accordance with the expectation, although not formally stated in the hypothesis. The expectation was based on the knowledge that most students from CSE has taken more computer science and software engineering and courses than those from the Electrical Engineering program.

It is not possible to show with any statistical significance that experience in C influences the number of faults/KLOC. This is interesting in relation to that Humphrey [82] recommends that one should follow the PSP course with a well-known language in order to focus on the PSP and not the programming language as such. The results obtained may indicate one or several of the following results:

- The difference will become significant with more students.
- The number of faults introduced is not significantly affected by the prior experience. There may be a tendency to make a certain number of faults when developing software. The type of faults may vary, but the total number of faults introduced is about the same.
- The inexperienced students may write larger programs, which directly affects the number of faults/KLOC.

Other explanations can probably also be found, but they all have one thing in common that is the need for replication. Thus, replications is an important issue to enable us to understand, and hence control and improve the way software is developed. Furthermore, other factors must be studied as well.

From a validity point of view, it is reasonable to believe that students (in general) from a computer science program have higher productivity than students coming from other disciplines have. This is more or less inherent from the educational background and it is no surprise.

Since, it was not possible to show any statistically significant relation between experience in a programming language and the number of faults/KLOC; there are no conclusions to generalize. Further studies are needed, either through replication of the PSP experiment or similar studies in other environments.

12.6 Conclusion

The presented study is a quasi-experiment, since it compares factors which are not randomly assigned to subjects, but rather inherent properties of the subjects (i.e. educational background). It is conducted with students as subjects, which provides good internal validity at the expense of external validity of the results. Being conducted in the PSP context would help replication of the study, as the context is very well defined.

The study was conducted over several weeks, which mostly would have been a threat to the construct validity. However, since this is a quasi-experiment, that is less of a threat. There is no chance of cheating with the educational background. The students were informed about the future use of their collected data, but no explicit consent was obtained, which would have been preferred.

In the analysis, six data points were removed, since they did not consistently follow the experimentation process. Another three data point outside the tails of the box-plots were analyzed for being considered as outliers. Only an extreme value was removed, since it would have impacted highly on the standard deviation, and thus ruled the analysis outcome.

Chapter 13
Are the Perspectives Really Different?: Further Experimentation on Scenario-Based Reading of Requirements[1]

Background This chapter presents an experimental study as it was published, with the objective to show an example paper from an international journal. Furthermore, the intention is that it should work as a suitable study to practice reviewing skills on. It is important to notice that the paper has been reviewed and revised based on the feedback before being published in the Empirical Software Engineering journal. This means that the quality is higher than the average submitted experimental paper, although paper standards also have raised over time since its original publication. Reviewing scientific papers is further elaborated in Appendix A.2.

Abstract Perspective-Based Reading (PBR) is a scenario-based inspection technique where several reviewers read a document from different perspectives (e.g. user, designer, tester). The reading is made according to a special scenario, specific for each perspective. The basic assumption behind PBR is that the perspectives find different defects and a combination of several perspectives detects more defects compared to the same amount of reading with a single perspective. This paper presents a study which analyses the differences in the perspectives. The study is a partial replication of previous studies. It is conducted in an academic environment using graduate students as subjects. Each perspective applies a specific modelling technique: use case modelling for the user perspective, equivalence partitioning for the tester perspective and structured analysis for the design perspective. A total of 30 subjects were divided into 3 groups, giving 10 subjects per perspective. The analysis results show that (1) there is no significant difference among the three perspectives in terms of defect detection rate and number of defects found per hour, (2) there is no significant difference in the defect coverage of the three perspectives, and (3) a simulation study shows that 30 subjects is enough to detect relatively small perspective differences with the chosen statistical test. The results suggest that a combination of multiple perspectives may not give higher coverage of the defects

---

[1]This chapter was originally published in Empirical Software Engineering: An International Journal, Vol. 5, No. 4, pp. 331–356 (2000).

C. Wohlin et al., *Experimentation in Software Engineering*,
DOI 10.1007/978-3-642-29044-2_13, © 2001 Springer science+business media
(successor in interest of Kluwer Academic Publishers, Boston)

compared to single-perspective reading, but further studies are needed to increase the understanding of perspective difference.

13.1 Introduction

The validation of requirements documents is often done manually, as requirements documents normally include informal representations of what is required of an intended software system. A commonly used technique for manual validation of software documents is inspections, proposed by Fagan [54]. Inspections can be carried out in different ways and used throughout the software development process for (1) understanding, (2) finding defects, and (3) as a basis for making decisions. Inspections are used to find defects early in the development process, and have shown to be cost effective (e.g. by Doolan [45]).

A central part of the inspection process is the *defect detection* carried out by an individual reviewer reading the document and recording defects (a part of preparation, see Humphrey [81]). Three common techniques for defect detection are Ad Hoc, Checklist and Scenario-based reading [137]. Ad Hoc detection denotes an unstructured technique which provides no guidance, implying that reviewers detect defects based on their personal knowledge and experience. The checklist detection technique provides a list of issues and questions, capturing the knowledge of previous inspections, helping the reviewers to focus their reading. In the scenario-based approach, different reviewers have different responsibilities and are guided in their reading by specific scenarios which aim at constructing a model, instead of just passive reading.

A scenario[2] here denotes a script or procedure that the reviewer should follow. Two variants of scenario-based reading have been proposed: Defect-Based Reading [137] and Perspective-Based Reading [18]. The former (subsequently denoted DBR) concentrates on specific defect classes, while the latter (subsequently denoted PBR) focuses on the points of view of the users of a document.

Another part of the inspection process is the *compilation of defects* into a consolidated defect list where all individual reviewers' defect lists are combined. This step may include the removal of false positives (reported defects that were not considered to be actual defects) as well as the detection of new defects. This step is often done in a structured *inspection meeting* where a *team* of reviewers participate. The effectiveness of the team meeting has been questioned and studied empirically by Votta [175] and Johnson and Tjahjono [87].

---

[2]There is considerable risk for terminology confusion here, as the term *scenario* also is used within requirements engineering to denote a sequence of events involved in an envisaged usage situation of the system under development. A *use case* is often said to cover a set of related (system usage) scenarios. In scenario-based reading, however, the term scenario is a meta-level concept, denoting a procedure that a reader of a document should follow during inspection.

This paper describes research on scenario-based reading with a PBR approach. The research method is empirical and includes a formal factorial experiment in an academic environment. The presented experiment is a partial replication of previous experiments in the area and focuses on refined hypotheses regarding the differences among the perspectives in PBR. The paper concentrates on defect detection by *individual reviewers*, while the team meeting aspects are not included.

The structure of the paper is as follows. Section 13.2 gives an overview of related work by summarising results from previously conducted experiments in requirements inspections with a scenario-based approach. Section 13.3 includes the problem statement motivating the presented work. In Sect. 13.4, the experiment plan is described including a discussion on threats to the validity of the study, and Sect. 13.5 reports on the operation of the experiment. The results of the analysis is given in Sect. 13.6, and Sect. 13.7 includes an interpretation of the results. Section 13.8 provides a summary and conclusions.

13.2 Related Work

The existing literature on empirical software engineering includes a number of studies related to inspections, where formal experimentation has shown to be a relevant research strategy [178]. The experiment presented in this paper relates to previous experiments on inspections with a scenario-based approach. The findings of a number of experiments on scenario-based inspection of requirements documents are summarized below.

1. The *Maryland-95* study [137] compared DBR with Ad Hoc and Checklist in an academic environment. The experiment was run twice with 24 subjects in each run. The requirements documents used were a water level monitoring system (WLMS, 24 pages) and an automobile cruise control system (CRUISE, 31 pages).

   Result 1: DBR reviewers have significantly higher defect detection rates than either Ad Hoc or Checklist reviewers.

   Result 2: DBR reviewers have significantly higher detection rates for those defects that the scenarios were designed to uncover, while all three methods have similar detection rates for other defects.

   Result 3: Checklist reviewers do *not* have significantly higher detection rates than Ad Hoc reviewers.

   Result 4: Collection meetings produce *no* net improvement in the detection rate – meeting gains are offset by meeting losses.

2. The *NASA* study [18] compared PBR with Ad Hoc in an industrial environment. The experiment consisted of a pilot study with 12 subjects and a second main run with 13 subjects. There were two groups of requirements documents used; general requirements documents: an automatic teller machine (ATM, 17 pages),

a parking garage control system (PG, 16 pages); and two flight dynamics requirements documents (27 pages each).

Result 1:   Individuals applying PBR to general documents have significantly higher detection rates compared to Ad Hoc.

Result 2:   Individuals applying PBR to NASA-specific documents do not have significantly higher detection rates compared to Ad Hoc.

Result 3:   Simulated teams applying PBR to general documents have significantly higher detection rates compared to Ad Hoc.

Result 4:   Simulated teams applying PBR to NASA-specific documents have significantly higher detection rates compared to Ad Hoc.

Result 5:   Reviewers with more experience do *not* have higher detection rates.

3. The *Kaiserslautern* study [34] compared PBR with Ad Hoc in an academic environment using the ATM and PG documents from the NASA study. The experiment consisted of two runs with 25 and 26 subjects respectively.

Result 1:   Individuals applying PBR to general documents have significantly higher detection rates compared to Ad Hoc.

Result 2:   Simulated teams applying PBR to general documents have significantly higher detection rates compared to Ad Hoc.

Result 3:   The detection rates of five different defect classes are *not* significantly different among the perspectives.

4. The *Bari* study [61] compared DBR with Ad Hoc and Checklist in an academic environment using the WLMS and CRUISE documents from the Maryland-95 study. The experiment had one run with 30 subjects.

Result 1:   DBR did *not* have significantly higher defect detection rates than either Ad Hoc or Checklist.

Result 2:   DBR reviewers did *not* have significantly higher detection rates for those defects that the scenarios were designed to uncover, while all three methods had similar detection rates for other defects.

Result 3:   Checklist reviewers did *not* have significantly higher detection rates than Ad Hoc reviewers.

Result 4:   Collection meetings produced *no* net improvement in the detection rate – meeting gains where offset by meeting losses.

5. The *Trondheim* study [164] compared the NASA study version of PBR with a modified version of PBR (below denoted PBR2) where reviewers were given more instructions on how to apply perspective-based reading. The study was conducted in an academical environment using the ATM and PG documents from the NASA study. The experiment consisted of one run with 48 subjects.

Result 1:   PBR2 reviewers did *not* have significantly higher defect detection rates than PBR.]

Result 2:   Individuals applying PBR2 reviewed significantly longer time compared to those who applied PBR.

Result 3:   Individuals applying PBR2 suggested significantly fewer potential defects compared to those who applied PBR.

Result 4:   Individuals applying PBR2 had significantly lower productivity and efficiency than those who applied PBR.

6. The *Strathclyde* study [124] compared DBR with Checklist in an academic environment using the WLMS and CRUISE documents from the Maryland study. The experiment consisted of one run with 50 subjects.

Result 1:   In the WLMS document, DBR did *not* have significantly higher defect detection rates than Checklist.

Result 2:   In the CRUISE document, DBR had significantly higher defect detection rates than Checklist.

Result 3:   Collection meetings produced *no* net improvement in the detection rate – meeting gains were offset by meeting losses.

7. The *Linköping* study [147] compared DBR with Checklist in an academic environment using the WLMS and CRUISE documents from the Maryland study. More defects were added to the list of total defects. The experiment consisted of one run with 24 subjects.

Result 1:   DBR reviewers did *not* have significantly higher defect detection rates than Checklist reviewers.

Result 2:   DBR reviewers did *not* have significantly higher detection rates than Checklist reviewers.

8. The *Maryland-98* study [152] compared PBR with Ad Hoc in an academic environment using the ATM and PG documents from the Maryland study. The experiment consisted of one run with 66 subjects.

Result 1:   PBR reviewers had significantly higher defect detection rates than Ad Hoc reviewers.

Result 2:   Individuals with high experience applying PBR did *not* have significantly[3] higher defect detection rates compared to Ad Hoc.

Result 3:   Individuals with medium experience applying PBR had significantly higher defect detection rates compared to Ad Hoc.

Result 4:   Individuals with low experience applying PBR had significantly higher defect detection rates compared to Ad Hoc.

Result 5:   Individuals applying PBR had significantly lower productivity compared to those who applied Ad Hoc.

9. The *Lucent* study [138] replicated the Maryland-95 study in an industrial environment using 18 professional developers at Lucent Technologies. The

---

[3]Results 2–4 of the Maryland-98 study apply a significance level of 0.10, while 0.05 is the chosen significance level in all other results.

Table 13.1 Summary of studies

Study	Purpose	Environment	Subjects	Significant?
Maryland-95	DBR vs. AdHoc and checklist	Academic	24+24	YES
Bari	DBR vs. AdHoc and checklist	Academic	30	NO
Strathclyde	DBR vs. checklist	Academic	50	Inconclusive
Linköping	DBR vs. checklist	Academic	24	NO
Lucent	DBR vs. AdHoc and checklist	Industrial	18	YES
NASA	PBR vs. AdHoc	Industrial	12+13	YES
Kaiserslautern	PBR vs. AdHoc	Academic	25+26	YES
Trondheim	PBR vs. PBR2	Academic	48	NO
Maryland-98	PBR vs. AdHoc	Academic	66	YES

replication was successful and completely corroborated the results from the Maryland-95 study.

The results of the different studies vary substantially. An attempt to systematically address the combined knowledge, gained from experiments and replications is reported by Hayes [74], where meta-analysis is applied to the results of the Maryland-95, Bari, Strathclyde, Linköping and Lucent studies. It is concluded from the meta-analysis that the effect sizes for the inspection methods are inhomogeneous across the experiments. The Maryland-95 and Lucent studies show most similar results, and an interpretation of the meta-analysis identifies characteristics which make them different from the other three studies: (1) they are conducted in a context where the subjects are more familiar with the notation used, (2) they are conducted in the US where cruise control are more common in cars than in Europe where the other three studies are performed. These hypotheses are, however, not possible to test with the given data, and thus more experimentation is needed.

Table 13.1 includes a summary of the presented studies. The Maryland-95, NASA, Kaiserslautern, Maryland-98, and Lucent studies indicate that a scenario-based approach gives higher detection rate. The Bari, Strathclyde, and Linköping studies could, however, not corroborate these results, which motivates further studies to increase the understanding of scenario-based reading.

Many of the studies concluded that real team meetings were ineffective in terms of defect detection. (There may of course be other good reasons for conducting team meetings apart from defect detection, such as consensus building, competence sharing, and decision making.)

The study presented here is subsequently denoted the *Lund* study. The Lund study is a partial replication of the NASA study, and is based on a lab package [19] provided by the University of Maryland in order to support empirical investigations of scenario-based reading. The problem statement motivating the Lund study is given in the subsequent section.

13.3 Research Questions

The previous studies, summarised in Sect. 13.2, have mainly concentrated on comparing scenario-based reading with checklist and Ad Hoc techniques in terms of defect detection rates. The objective of the Lund study is, however, to investigate the basic assumption behind scenario-based reading, that the different perspectives find different defects. Another interest is the efficiency of the different perspectives in terms of defects detected per hour. The following two questions are addressed:

1. Do the perspectives detect different defects?
2. Is one perspective superior to another?

There are two aspects of superiority that are addressed: *effectiveness*, i.e. how high fraction of the existing defects are found (detection rate), and *efficiency*, i.e. how many defects are found per time unit.

The perspectives proposed by Basili et al. [18] are designer, tester and user. The users are important stakeholders in the software development process, and especially when the requirements are elicited, analysed and documented. The user role in PBR is focused on detecting defects at a high abstraction level related to system usage, while the designer is focused on internal structures and the tester is focused on verification.

Previous studies have mainly concentrated on the effectiveness in terms of detection rate. From a software engineering viewpoint it is important also to assess the efficiency (e.g. in terms of detected defects per time unit), as this factor is important for a practitioner's decision to introduce a new reading technique. The specific project and application domain constraints then can, together with estimations of how much effort is needed, be a basis for a trade-off between quality and cost.

One main purpose of PBR is that the perspectives detect different kinds of defects in order to minimise the overlap among the reviewers. Hence, a natural question is whether reviewers do find different defects or not. If they detect the same defects, the overlap is not minimised and PBR does not work as it was meant to. If all perspectives find the same kinds of defects it may be a result of (1) that the scenario-based reading approach is inappropriate, (2) that the perspectives may be insufficiently supported by their accompanying scenarios, or (3) that other perspectives are needed to gain a greater coverage difference. The optimal solution is to use perspectives with no overlap and as high defect detection rate as possible, making PBR highly dependable and effective. The Lund study addresses the overlap by investigating whether the perspectives detect different defects.

Research question 1 is also interesting from a defect content estimation perspective. The capture-recapture approach to defect content estimation uses the overlap among the defects that the reviewers find to estimate the number of remaining defects in a software artifact [51, 120]. The robustness of capture–recapture using PBR is studied by Thelin and Runeson [167], with the aim of investigating capture–recapture estimators applied to PBR inspections under the hypothesis that PBR works according to its underlying assumption. In the Lund study it is investigated whether the assumptions of PBR are factual. Hence, the Lund study and the Thelin and Runeson [167] study complement each other in order to answer the question whether capture–recapture estimations can be used for PBR inspections.

13.4   Experiment Planning

This section describes the planning of the reading experiment. The planning includes the definition of dependent and independent variables, hypotheses to be tested in the experiment, experiment design, instrumentation and an analysis of threats to the validity of the experiment [178].

The reading experiment is conducted in an academical environment with close relations to industry. The subjects are fourth-year students at the Master's programmes in Computer Science and Engineering and Electrical Engineering at Lund University.

13.4.1   Variables

The independent variables determine the cases for which the dependent variables are sampled. The purpose is to investigate different reading perspectives and methods, applied to two objects (requirements documents). The inspection objects are the same as in the University of Maryland lab package [19], and the design and instrumentation are also based on this lab package. The variables in the study are summarized in Table 13.2 together with brief explanations.

13.4.2   Hypotheses

Perspective-Based Reading is assumed to provide more efficient inspections, as different reviewers take different perspectives making the defect overlap smaller [18]. The objective of the study is to empirically test whether these assumptions are true. In consequence, hypotheses related to performance of different perspectives are stated below. The three null hypotheses address efficiency, effectiveness and distribution over perspectives.

- $H_{0,EFF}$. The perspectives are assumed to have the same finding efficiency, i.e. the number of defects found per hour of inspection is not different for the various perspectives.

Table 13.2 Variables

	Name	Values	Description
Independent variables	PERSP	{U,T,D}	One of three perspectives is applied by each subject: User, Tester, and Designer.
	DOC	{ATM,PG}	The inspection objects are two requirements documents: one for an automatic teller machine (ATM) and one for a parking garage control system (PG). The ATM document is 17 pages and contains 29 defects. The PG document is 16 pages and contains 30 defects.
Controlled variable	EXPERIENCE	Ordinal	The experience with user, tester, design perspectives is measured on a five-level ordinal scale and used in the allocation of subjects to perspectives. (See Sects. 13.4.3 and 13.6.4)
Dependent variables	TIME	Integer	The time spent by each reviewer in individual preparation is recorded by all subjects. The time unit used is minutes.
	DEF	Integer	The number of defects found by each reviewer is recorded, excluding false positives. The false positives are removed by the experimenters, in order to ensure that all defect candidates are treated equally.
	EFF	60*DEF/TIME	The defect finding efficiency, i.e. the number of defects found per hour, is calculated as (DEF*60)/TIME.
	RATE	DEF/TOT	The defect finding effectiveness, i.e. the fraction of found defects by total number of defects (also called detection rate) is calculated as DEF divided by the total number of known defects contained in the inspected documents.
	FOUND	Integer	The number of reviewers belonging to a certain perspective, which have found a certain defect in a specific document is recorded. This variable is used for analysing defect finding distributions for different perspectives.

- $H_{0,RATE}$. The perspectives are assumed to have the same effectiveness or detection rates, i.e. the fraction of defects identified is not different for the various perspectives.
- $H_{0,FOUND}$. The perspectives are assumed to find the same defects, i.e. the distributions over defects found are the same for the different perspectives.

Table 13.3 Experiment design

		PERSP		
		User	Designer	Tester
DOC	ATM	5	5	5
	PG	5	5	5

13.4.3 Design

To test these hypotheses an experiment with a factorial design [125] is used with two factors (PERSP and DOC). The design is summarized in Table 13.3. The experiment varies the three perspectives over two documents.

    The assignment of an individual subject to one of the three PBR perspectives (U, D, T), was conducted based on their reported experience (see Sect. 13.6.4), similar to the NASA study [18]. The objective of experience-based perspective assignment is to ensure that each perspective gets a fair distribution of experienced subjects, so that the outcome of the experience is affected by perspective difference rather than experience difference. The experience questionnaire required the subjects to grade their experience with each perspective on a five level ordinal scale. The subjects were then sorted three times, giving a sorted list of subjects for each perspective with the most experienced first. Within the same experience level, the subjects were placed in random order. The subjects were then assigned to perspectives by selecting a subject on top of a perspective list and removing this subject in the other lists before continuing with the next perspective in a round robin fashion starting with a randomly selected perspective, until all subjects were assigned a perspective.

    The instruments of the reading experiment consist of two requirements documents and reporting templates for time and defects. These instruments are taken from the University of Maryland lab package [19] and are reused with minimal changes.

    The factorial design described above is analysed with descriptive statistics (bar plots and box plots) and analysis of variance (ANOVA) [125] for the hypotheses $H_{0,EFF}$, and $H_{0,RATE}$. For the $H_{0,FOUND}$ hypothesis a Chi-square test [157] is used together with a correlation analysis [144].

13.4.4 Threats to Validity

The validity of the results achieved in experiments depends on factors in the experiment settings. Different types of validity can be prioritized depending on the goal of the experiment. In this case, threats to four types of validity are analysed [37, 178]: conclusion validity, internal validity, construct validity and external validity.

Conclusion validity concerns the statistical analysis of results and the composition of subjects. In this experiment, well known statistical techniques are applied which are robust to violations of their assumptions. One general threat to conclusion validity is, however, the low number of samples, which may reduce the ability to reveal patterns in the data. In particular, there are few samples for the Chi-square test, which is further elaborated in Sect. 13.6.3.

Internal validity concerns matters that may affect the independent variable with respect to causality, without the researchers knowledge. There are two threats to internal validity in this experiment, selection and instrumentation. The experiment was a mandatory part of a software engineering course, thus the selection of subjects is not random, which involves a threat to the validity of the experiment. The requirements documents used may also affect the results. The documents are rather defect-prone and additional issues in the documents could be considered as defects. On the other hand, it is preferable to have the same definition of defects as in the previous studies for comparison reasons. Other threats to internal validity are considered small. Each subject was only allocated to a single object and a single treatment, hence there is no threat of maturation in the experiment. The subjects applied different perspectives during inspection, but the difference among perspectives are not large enough to suspect compensatory equalisation of treatments or compensatory rivalry. The subjects were also told that their grading in the course was not depending on their performance in the experiment, only on their serious attendance. There is of course a risk that the subjects lack motivation; they may, for example, consider their participation a waste of time or they may not be motivated to learn the techniques. The teacher in the course in which the experiment was per-formed has, however, made a strong effort in motivating the students. It was clearly stated that a serious participation was mandatory for passing the course. It is the teacher's opinion that the students made a very serious attempt in their inspection.

Construct validity concerns generalisation of the experiment result to concept or theory behind the experiment. A major threat to the construct validity is that the chosen perspectives or the reading techniques for the perspectives may not be representative or good for scenario-based reading. This limits the scope for the conclusions made to these particular perspectives and techniques. Other threats to the construct validity are considered small. The subjects did not know which hypotheses were stated, and were not involved in any discussion on advantages and disadvantages of PBR, thus they were not able to guess what the expected results were.

External validity concerns generalisation of the experiment result to other environments than the one in which the study is conducted. The largest threat to the external validity is the use of students as subjects. However, this threat is reduced by using fourth-year students which are close to finalise their education and start working in industry. The setting is intended to resemble a real inspection situation, but the process that the subjects participate in is not part of a real software development project. The assignments are also intended to be realistic, but the documents are rather short, and real software requirements documents may include many more pages. The threats to external validity regarding the settings and assignments are, however, considered limited, as both the inspection process and the documents resemble real cases to a reasonable extent.

It can be concluded that there are threats to the construct, internal and external validity. However, these are almost the same as in the original studies. Hence, as long as the conclusions from the experiment are not drawn outside the limitations of these threats, the results are valid.

13.5 Experiment Operation

The experiment was run during spring 1998. The students were all given a 2 h introductory lecture where an overview of the study was given together with a description of the defect classification. A questionnaire on experience was given and each subject was assigned to a perspective, as described in Sect. 13.4.3. The students were informed that the experiment was a compulsory part of the course, but the grading was only based on serious participation in the study and not on the individual performance of the students. The anonymity of the students was guaranteed.

A 2 h exercise was held, where the three PBR perspectives were described and illustrated using a requirements document for a video rental system (VRS). During the second hour of the exercise, the subjects were practising their own perspective reading technique for the VRS document, and had the opportunity to ask questions. The data collection forms were also explained and used during the exercise. The perspective-based reading of the VRS document was completed by the students on their own after the classroom hours.

The hand-outs for the experiment, which were handed out during the exercise, included the following instrumentation tools:

1. Defect Classification which describes defect classes to be used in the defect list.
2. Time Recording Log for recording the time spent on reading.
3. Defect List for recording the found defects.
4. Reading Instruction, specific for the user, designer, and tester perspectives respectively.
5. Modelling Forms, specific for the user, designer, and tester perspectives respectively.
6. The requirements document (either ATM or PG).

The students were instructed not to discuss the ATM or PG documents and the defects that they find. They were allowed to discuss the PBR perspectives in relation to the VRS document before they started with the actual data collection.

13.6   Data Analysis

This section presents the statistical analysis of the gathered data. The data were collected from the hand-ins from subjects. Each defect in each subject's defect log was compared with the original 'correct' defect list provided by the University of Maryland lab package. In a meeting, the authors discussed each defect and decided whether it corresponded to a 'correct' defect. If no corresponding 'correct' defect was found, the reported defect was considered a false positive.[4] The reported time spent was also collected and the EFF, RATE, and FOUND measures were calculated. The total data sets are given in Tables 13.6–13.8.

13.6.1   Individual Performance for Different Perspectives

Box-plots[5] of individual performance in terms of number of defects found per hour (EFF), and the fraction of found defects against the total number of defects (RATE), are shown in Fig. 13.1. The box-plots are split by document and perspective.

For EFF, the Tester perspective on the PG document has a higher mean than the User and Designer perspectives, while for the ATM document, the Designer perspective has a higher mean. For RATE the Designer means are higher compared to the User and Tester perspectives for both documents. There are, however, too few data points per group for any further interpretation of the box-plots, with respect to outliers and skewness.

When several dependent variables are measured, the multi-variate analysis of variance (MANOVA) can be used to assess if there exists any statistically significant difference in the total set of means. The results of MANOVA tests regarding the effect of PERSP reveal no significance and indicate absence of interaction effects. Furthermore, there are no significant differences in the means of EFF, RATE for the PERSP variable, as shown by the analysis of variance (ANOVA) in Tables 13.4 and 13.5. From this analysis it can be concluded that the null hypotheses for EFF and RATE can not be rejected for any of the three perspectives.

---

[4]Some of the defects that were decided to be false positives may in fact be true defects if the defect list from the Maryland lab package is incomplete. It was decided, however, that it is important from a replication viewpoint that the same list of 'correct' defects was used. This decision is not considered to have any significant impact on the result as there were only few false positives that were questionable.

[5]The box-plots are drawn with the box height corresponding to the 25th and 75th percentile, with the 50th percentile (the median) marked in the box. The whiskers correspond to the 10th and 90th percentile.

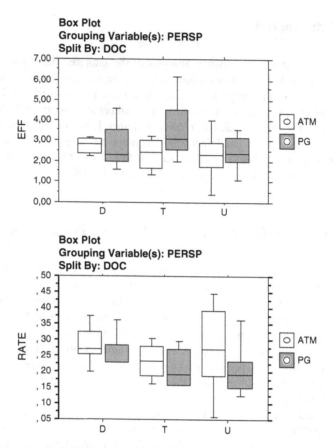

Fig. 13.1 Box plots for EFF and RATE split by DOC and PERSP

Table 13.4 ANOVA table for EFF

	DF	Sum of Sq	Mean Sq	F-Value	p-value	Lambda	Power
PERSP	2	1.751	0.875	0.737	0.4893	1.473	0.156
DOC	1	1.640	1.640	1.380	0.2516	1.380	0.193
PERSP * DOC	2	2.229	1.114	0.937	0.4055	1.875	0.187
Residual	24	28.527	1.189				

Table 13.5 ANOVA table for RATE

	DF	Sum of Sq	Mean Sq	F-Value	p-value	Lambda	Power
PERSP	2	0.012	0.006	0.802	0.4602	1.604	0.166
DOC	1	0.011	0.011	1.488	0.2344	1.488	0.205
PERSP * DOC	2	0.004	0.002	0.259	0.7739	0.518	0.085
Residual	24	0.172	0.007				

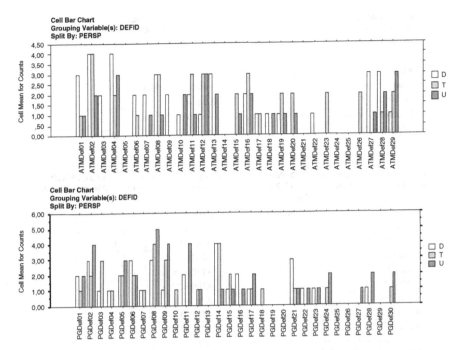

Fig. 13.2 Bar charts illustrating the distribution of number of reviewers that found each defect

13.6.2 Defects Found by Different Perspectives

The hypothesis $H_{0,FOUND}$ regarding the overlap of the found defects among the perspectives, is studied in this section. Descriptive statistics in the form of bar chart plots are shown in Fig. 13.2. For each document the distribution of number of found defects per perspective is shown. There do not seem to be any particular patterns in the different perspective distributions; the defect findings of each perspective seem similarly spread over the defect space. If there had been large differences in the perspective distributions, the bar plot would presumably have groups of defects where one perspective would have a high number of findings while the others would have a low number of findings.

In order to compare the distributions of found defects for each perspective and investigate if there is a significant difference among which defects the perspectives find, a contingency table is created for which a Chi Square test is made [157, pp. 191–194], as shown in Fig. 13.3. The defects that no perspective have found are excluded from the contingency tables (the "Inclusion criteria" in Fig. 13.3), as these cases do not contribute to the testing of differences.

The Chi Square p-values are far from significant, indicating that it is not possible with this test and this particular data set to show a difference in the perspectives? defect finding distributions. There are rules of thumb regarding when the Chi Square

Summary Table for DEFID, PERSP
Inclusion criteria: Counts>0 from PG.data

Num. Missing	0
DF	46
Chi Square	33,951
Chi Square P-Value	,9058
G-Squared	.
G-Squared P-Value	.
Contingency Coef.	,494
Cramer's V	,402

Summary Table for DEFID, PERSP
Inclusion criteria: Counts > 0 from ATM.data

Num. Missing	0
DF	46
Chi Square	41,676
Chi Square P-Value	,6538
G-Squared	.
G-Squared P-Value	.
Contingency Coef.	,535
Cramer's V	,448

Observed Frequencies for DEFID, PERSP
Inclusion criteria: Counts>0 from PG.data

	D	T	U	Totals
PGDef01	2	1	2	5
PGDef02	3	2	4	9
PGDef03	1	3	0	4
PGDef04	1	1	0	2
PGDef05	2	2	3	7
PGDef06	3	2	2	7
PGDef07	1	1	0	2
PGDef08	3	4	5	12
PGDef09	1	3	4	8
PGDef10	0	1	0	1
PGDef11	2	0	4	6
PGDef12	0	1	1	2
PGDef14	4	4	1	9
PGDef15	1	2	1	4
PGDef16	2	0	1	3
PGDef17	1	1	2	4
PGDef18	0	1	0	1
PGDef21	3	1	1	5
PGDef22	1	0	1	2
PGDef23	1	0	1	2
PGDef24	0	1	2	3
PGDef27	0	0	1	1
PGDef28	1	0	2	3
PGDef30	0	1	2	3
Totals	33	32	40	105

Observed Frequencies for DEFID, PERSP
Inclusion criteria: Counts > 0 from ATM.data

	D	T	U	Totals
ATMDef01	3	1	1	5
ATMDef02	4	4	2	10
ATMDef03	2	0	0	2
ATMDef04	4	2	3	9
ATMDef06	2	1	0	3
ATMDef07	2	0	1	3
ATMDef08	3	3	1	7
ATMDef09	2	0	0	2
ATMDef10	1	0	2	3
ATMDef11	2	3	1	6
ATMDef12	1	3	3	7
ATMDef13	3	0	2	5
ATMDef15	0	2	1	3
ATMDef16	2	3	2	7
ATMDef17	1	1	0	2
ATMDef18	1	0	1	2
ATMDef19	1	2	1	4
ATMDef20	0	2	1	3
ATMDef22	1	0	0	1
ATMDef23	0	2	0	2
ATMDef26	0	2	0	2
ATMDef27	3	0	1	4
ATMDef28	3	1	2	6
ATMDef29	1	2	3	6
Totals	42	34	28	104

Fig. 13.3 Chi Square tests and contingency tables for defects found by U, T, D per DOC

test can be used [157, pp. 199–200], saying that no more than 20% of the cells should have an expected frequency of less than 5, and no cell should have an expected frequency of less than 1. These rules of thumb are not fulfilled by the data set in this case, but it may be argued that the rules are too conservative and as the expected frequencies in our case are rather evenly distributed, the Chi Square test may still be valid (see further Sect. 13.6.3).

ATM Document

Correlation Analysis

	Correlation	p-Value	95% Lower	95% Upper
User, Tester	,480	,0076	,138	,720
User, Designer	,499	,0052	,162	,732
Tester, Designer	,258	,1789	-,120	,570

29 observations were used in this computation.

Correlation Analysis
Inclusion criteria: User > 0 OR Tester > 0 OR Designer > 0 from ATM-ctable.data

	Correlation	p-Value	95% Lower	95% Upper
User, Tester	,357	,0867	-,054	,665
User, Designer	,352	,0915	-,059	,662
Tester, Designer	,043	,8449	-,367	,439

24 observations were used in this computation.

PG Document

Correlation Analysis

	Correlation	p-Value	95% Lower	95% Upper
User, Tester	,463	,0092	,123	,706
User, Designer	,543	,0016	,228	,756
Tester, Designer	,601	,0003	,307	,790

30 observations were used in this computation.

Correlation Analysis
Inclusion criteria: User > 0 OR Tester > 0 OR Designer > 0 from PG-ctable.data

	Correlation	p-Value	95% Lower	95% Upper
User, Tester	,319	,1300	-,097	,640
User, Designer	,414	,0438	,012	,700
Tester, Designer	,493	,0134	,112	,748

24 observations were used in this computation.

Fig. 13.4 Correlation analysis of the perspectives for each document

The Chi Square test does not give a measure of the degree of difference. In order to analyse how different (or similar) the perspectives are, a correlation analysis is presented in Fig. 13.4, using the Pearson correlation coefficient [143, pp. 338–340].

Two different correlation analyses are provided for each document, one with all "correct" defects included and one where only those defects are included that were found by at least one reviewer. The latter may be advocated, as we are interested in the differences in the set of defects that are found by each perspective; the defects that no perspective find do not contribute to differences among perspectives.

The p-value indicates if the correlation coefficient is significant, and the confidence intervals presented indicate the range wherein the correlation coefficient is likely to be.

The correlation analysis indicates that there are significantly positive correlations among the perspectives, meaning that when one perspective finds a defect it is likely

Fig. 13.5 Defect coverage
for the PG and ATM
documents

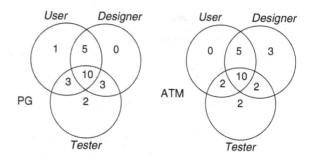

that others also find it. The only correlation coefficient that is far from significant is
the Designer-Tester correlation for the ATM document.

Another way of qualitatively analysing the overlap among the perspectives is
Venn-diagrams, as used in the NASA study [18, p. 151].

For the purpose of comparison we include such diagrams for the Lund study
data, as shown in Fig. 13.5. Each defect is categorised in one of seven classes
depending on which combinations of perspectives that have a FOUND measure
greater than zero. The numbers in the Venn-diagrams indicate how many defects
that belong to each class. For example, for the PG document, there are ten defects
which were found by all perspectives, while five defects were found by both the
user and designer perspectives and only one defect was found solely by the user
perspective.

This type of analysis is very sensitive to the number of subjects. It is enough that
only one reviewer finds a defect, for the classification to change. The probability
that a defect is found increases with the number of reviewers, and if we have a
large number of reviewers, the defects will be more likely to be included in the
class where all perspectives have found it. This means that this type of analysis
is not very robust, and does not provide meaningful interpretations in the general
case. In our case, we can at least say that the defect coverage analysis in Fig. 13.5
does not contradict our previous results that we cannot reject the hypothesis that the
perspectives are similar with respect the sets of defects that they find. The defects
found by all perspectives is by far the largest class.

13.6.3   Is the Sample Size Large Enough?

The outcome of the Lund study is that no significant difference among the perspectives can be detected. A question arises whether this is due to lack of differences
in the data, or that the statistical tests are not able to reveal the differences, for
example, due to the limited amount of data. In order to evaluate the Chi-square test
the perspective defect detection data sets are simulated with stochastic variations
among perspectives and the Chi-square test is applied to the simulated data.

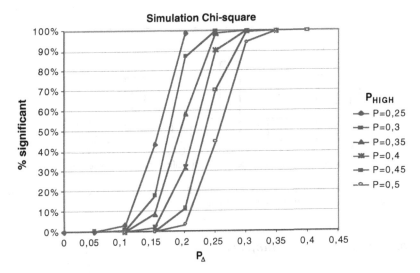

Fig. 13.6 Fraction of significant test results concerning $H_{0,FOUND}$

The simulation is designed to resemble the experiment presented in the previous section. The difference is that in the simulation case, the probability for detection of a specific defect by a perspective is an independent variable. Furthermore, only the FOUND dependent variable is applied, since the time aspect is not modelled. The simulation model is designed as follows:

- The number of defects in each simulated document is 30.
- For every simulated inspection, three perspectives are used with ten reviewers per perspective. It is assumed that a document contains three different types of defects, which have different probabilities of being detected. One perspective has high probability (P_{HIGH}) to detect one third of the defects and low probability (P_{LOW}) to detect the other two thirds of the defects. The difference between P_{HIGH} and P_{LOW} is denoted P_Δ. The probability levels are set to values between 0.05 and 0.5 in steps of 0.05, which are values around the measured mean in the Lund study.
- 1,000 runs of each inspection are simulated.

The $H_{0,FOUND}$ hypothesis is tested with the Chi-Square test and the results are presented in Fig. 13.6. Each simulated experiment is tested separately. The figure shows the fraction of tests that are rejected for each case. For all simulation cases with P_Δ larger than 0.3, the test can significantly show a difference among the simulated perspectives. For simulation cases with P_{HIGH} lower than 0.25, the differences can be shown if P_Δ is larger than 0.2. The tests are conducted with a significance level of 0.05. The simulation study shows that differences in FOUND are possible to detect with the Chi-Square test, even if the perspective differences are small and the sample size is small.

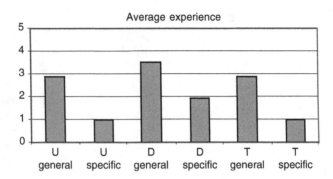

Fig. 13.7 Average experience of subjects regarding their general experience of their perspective and specific experience with their modelling technique

13.6.4   *Experience of Subjects*

The experience was measured through a questionnaire which covers each perspective in general, as well as experience with the specific modelling techniques of the three perspectives (use case modelling, equivalence partitioning, and structured analysis). The experience is measured for each general perspective and each specific modelling technique on a five level ordinal scale: 1 = none, 2 = studied in class or from book, 3 = practised in a class project, 4 = used on one project in industry, 5 = used on multiple projects in industry.

Figure 13.7 shows the average experience for each subject regarding the perspective to which the subject was assigned, both for the perspective in general and for the specific modelling technique.

It can be seen that the allocation of subjects (according to the algorithm explained in Sect. 13.4.3) has, as expected, resulted in a relatively balanced experience profile over the perspectives. It can also be noted that the students had very little industrial experience.

13.7   **Interpretations of Results**

In this section the data analysis is interpreted with respect to the hypotheses stated in Sect. 13.4.2. The first two hypotheses are tested using ANOVA and the third hypothesis is tested using a Chi-square test. The following three null-hypotheses can not be rejected:

- $H_{0,EFF}$ The perspectives are assumed to find the same number of defects per hour. This hypothesis can *not* be rejected.
- $H_{0,RATE}$ The perspectives are assumed to find the same number of defects. This hypothesis can *not* be rejected.

- $H_{0,FOUND}$ The perspectives are assumed to find the same defects. This hypothesis can *not* be rejected.

It can hence be concluded that there is no significant difference among the three perspectives, user, design and test. This is true for all the three hypotheses, i.e. there is no significant difference in terms of effectiveness or efficiency. Furthermore, there is no significant difference in time spent using the different perspectives, hence, the time spent does not bias in favour of any of the techniques. The lack of difference among the three perspectives does, if the result is possible to replicate and generalize, seriously affect the cornerstones of the PBR. The advantages of PBR are assumed to be that the different perspectives focus on different types of defects, and thus detect different defect sets. This study shows no statistically significant difference among the sets of defects found by the three perspectives, and thus the advantages of PBR can be questioned.

Threats to the conclusion validity of the results are that the number of samples is low, in particular for the Chi-square test. However, a simulation study reveals that the Chi-square test can with 30 subjects detect differences among perspectives for relatively small differences in detection probability. Furthermore, the bar charts over the defects found by different perspectives (see Fig. 13.2) do not indicate any clear pattern, which supports the non-significant results. The ANOVA statistics are applied within acceptable limits, and these do not show any difference among the perspectives. The specific perspectives and the reading techniques for the perspectives might also be a threat to the validity of the results, when trying to apply the results to scenario-based reading in general.

The validity threat regarding the motivation of subjects can be evaluated by comparing the detection rates of the Lund study with other studies. The individual PBR detection rate for the NASA study [18] was on average 0.249 for the pilot study and 0.321 for the main run, while the Lund study shows an average individual PBR detection rate of 0.252. The rates are comparable, supporting the assumption that the subjects in this study was as motivated as in the NASA study.

Other threats to the validity in Sect. 13.4.4 are not considered differently in the light of the result.

13.8 Summary and Conclusions

The study reported in this paper is focused on the evaluation of Perspective Based Reading (PBR) of requirements documents. The study is a partial replication of previous experiments in an academic environment based on the lab package from University of Maryland [19].

The objective of the presented study is twofold:

1. Investigate the differences in the performance of the perspectives in terms of effectiveness (defect detection rate) and efficiency (number of found defects per hour).

2. Investigate the differences in defect coverage of the different perspectives, and hence evaluate the basic assumptions behind PBR supposing that different perspectives find different defects.

The experiment setting includes two requirements documents and scenarios for three perspectives (*user* applying use case modelling, *designer* applying structured analysis, and *tester* applying equivalence partitioning). A total of 30 MSc students were divided into 3 groups, giving 10 subjects per perspective.

In summary the results from the data analysis show that:

1. There is no significant difference among the user, designer and tester perspectives in terms of defect detection rate and number of defects found per hour.
2. There is no significant difference in the defect coverage of the three perspectives.

The interpretation of these results suggests that a combination of multiple perspectives may not give higher defect coverage compared to reading with only one perspective.

The results contradict the main assumptions behind PBR. Some of the previous studies, summarized in Sect. 13.2, have shown significant advantages with Scenario-based Reading over Ad Hoc inspection, but no statistical analysis on the difference among perspective performance is made in any of the studies reported in Sect. 13.2. Furthermore, the previous studies in Sect. 13.2 have not taken the efficiency into account (number of defects found per hour), but concentrates on detection rate as the main dependent variable. From a software engineering perspective, where the cost and efficiency of a method are of central interest, it is very interesting to study not only the detection rate, but also if a method can perform well within limited effort.

There are a number of threats to the validity of the results, including:

1. The setting may not be realistic.
2. The perspectives may not be optimal.
3. The subjects may not be motivated or trained enough.
4. The number of subjects may be too small.

It can be argued that the threats to validity are under control, based on the following considerations: (1) The inspection objects are similar to industrial requirements documents; (2) The perspectives are motivated from a software engineering process view; (3) The subjects were fourth year students with a special interest in software engineering attending an optional course which they have chosen out of their own interest, and further, many companies have a large fraction of employees with fresh exams; (4) The presented simulation study shows that relatively small differences among the perspectives can be detected with the chosen analysis for the given number of data points.

A single study, like this, is no sufficient basis for changing the attitudes towards PBR. Conducting the same analyses on data from existing experiments as well as new replications with the purpose of evaluating differences among perspectives will bring more clarity into the advantages and disadvantages of PBR techniques, and also give a better control over the validity threats.

13.9 Data on Individual Performance

Table 13.6 Data for each subject

Id	Perspective	Document	Time	Defects	Efficiency	Rate
1	U	ATM	187	8	2.567	0.276
2	D	PG	150	8	3.200	0.267
3	T	ATM	165	9	3.273	0.310
4	U	PG	185	11	3.568	0.367
5	D	ATM	155	8	3.097	0.276
6	T	PG	121	8	3.967	0.267
7	U	ATM	190	7	2.211	0.241
8	D	PG	260	7	1.615	0.233
9	T	ATM	123	6	2.927	0.207
10	U	PG	155	6	2.323	0.200
11	D	ATM	210	11	3.143	0.379
12	T	PG	88	9	6.136	0.300
13	U	ATM	280	11	2.357	0.379
14	D	PG	145	11	4.552	0.367
15	T	ATM	170	5	1.765	0.172
16	U	PG	120	6	3.000	0.200
17	D	ATM	190	9	2.842	0.310
18	T	PG	97	5	3.093	0.167
19	U	ATM	295	2	0.407	0.069
20	D	PG	180	7	2.333	0.233
21	T	ATM	306	7	1.373	0.241
22	U	PG	223	4	1.076	0.133
23	D	ATM	157	6	2.293	0.207
24	T	PG	130	6	2.769	0.200
25	U	ATM	195	13	4.000	0.448
26	D	PG	200	7	2.100	0.233
27	T	ATM	195	8	2.462	0.276
28	U	PG	125	5	2.400	0.167
29	D	ATM	200	8	2.400	0.276
30	T	PG	150	5	2.000	0.167

13.10   Data on Defects Found by Perspectives

13.10.1   PG document

Table 13.7 Defects id D# found (1) or not found (0) by individuals reading the PG document

D#	Individuals user perspective						Tester perspective						Designer perspective					
	2	8	14	20	26	S	4	10	16	22	28	S	6	12	18	24	30	S
1	0	0	1	0	1	2	1	0	0	0	0	1	1	0	0	1	0	2
2	1	1	1	0	1	4	1	0	1	0	0	2	0	1	1	1	0	3
3	0	0	0	0	0	0	1	1	0	1	0	3	0	0	0	1	0	1
4	0	0	0	0	0	0	0	0	0	1	0	1	1	0	0	0	0	1
5	0	0	1	1	1	3	1	0	0	0	1	2	0	1	1	0	0	2
6	1	1	0	0	0	2	0	1	1	0	0	2	1	0	0	1	1	3
7	0	0	0	0	0	0	1	0	0	0	0	1	0	1	0	0	0	1
8	1	1	1	1	1	5	1	1	1	1	0	4	1	1	0	1	0	3
9	1	1	1	1	0	4	1	1	1	0	0	3	0	1	0	0	0	1
10	0	0	0	0	0	0	0	0	1	0	0	1	0	0	0	0	0	0
11	1	1	0	1	1	4	0	0	0	0	0	0	0	1	1	0	0	2
12	1	0	0	0	0	1	1	0	0	0	0	1	0	0	0	0	0	0
13	0	0	0	0	0	0	0	0	0	0	0	0	0	0	0	0	0	0
14	0	0	0	0	1	1	1	1	0	1	1	4	1	1	0	1	1	4
15	0	0	1	0	0	1	0	1	0	0	1	2	1	0	0	0	0	1
16	1	0	0	0	0	1	0	0	0	0	0	0	0	1	1	0	0	2
17	0	0	0	1	1	2	1	0	0	0	0	1	0	1	0	0	0	1
18	0	0	0	0	0	0	1	0	0	0	0	1	0	0	0	0	0	0
19	0	0	0	0	0	0	0	0	0	0	0	0	0	0	0	0	0	0
20	0	0	0	0	0	0	0	0	0	0	0	0	0	0	0	0	0	0
21	0	0	1	0	0	1	0	0	0	0	1	1	1	0	1	0	1	3
22	0	0	0	1	0	1	0	0	0	0	0	0	0	0	0	0	1	1
23	0	0	1	0	0	1	0	0	0	0	0	0	0	0	0	0	1	1
24	0	0	1	1	0	2	0	0	0	0	1	1	0	0	0	0	0	0
25	0	0	0	0	0	0	0	0	0	0	0	0	0	0	0	0	0	0
26	0	0	0	0	0	0	0	0	0	0	0	0	0	0	0	0	0	0
27	0	1	0	0	0	1	0	0	0	0	0	0	0	0	0	0	0	0
28	0	1	1	0	0	2	0	0	0	0	0	0	1	0	0	0	0	1
29	0	0	0	0	0	0	0	0	0	0	0	0	0	0	0	0	0	0
30	1	0	1	0	0	2	0	0	1	0	0	1	0	0	0	0	0	0
S	8	7	11	7	7	40	11	6	6	4	5	32	8	9	5	6	5	33

13.10.2 ATM document

Table 13.8 Defects if D# found (1) or not found (0) by individuals reading the ATM document

D#	Individuals user perspective						Tester perspective						Designer perspective					
	1	7	13	19	25	S	3	9	15	21	27	S	5	11	17	23	29	S
1	0	0	0	1	0	1	0	0	0	1	0	1	1	1	0	0	1	3
2	1	0	1	0	0	2	1	0	1	1	1	4	1	1	1	0	1	4
3	0	0	0	0	0	0	0	0	0	0	0	0	1	0	0	1	0	2
4	0	1	1	1	0	3	1	1	0	0	0	2	1	1	1	0	1	4
5	0	0	0	0	0	0	0	0	0	0	0	0	0	0	0	0	0	0
6	0	0	0	0	0	0	0	0	0	0	1	1	0	0	1	1	0	2
7	0	1	0	0	0	1	0	0	0	0	0	0	0	0	1	0	1	2
8	0	0	1	0	0	1	0	1	0	1	1	3	1	1	0	0	1	3
9	0	0	0	0	0	0	0	0	0	0	0	0	0	1	1	0	0	2
10	0	1	1	0	0	2	0	0	0	0	0	0	0	1	0	0	0	1
11	1	0	0	0	0	1	0	1	0	1	1	3	1	0	1	0	0	2
12	1	1	1	0	0	3	0	0	1	1	1	3	0	1	0	0	0	1
13	1	0	1	0	0	2	0	0	0	0	0	0	0	1	1	1	0	3
14	0	0	0	0	0	0	0	0	0	0	0	0	0	0	0	0	0	0
15	0	1	0	0	0	1	1	0	0	0	1	2	0	0	0	0	0	0
16	0	1	1	0	0	2	1	1	1	0	0	3	0	1	1	0	0	2
17	0	0	0	0	0	0	1	0	0	0	0	1	0	0	0	1	0	1
18	0	0	1	0	0	1	0	0	0	0	0	0	0	1	0	0	0	1
19	1	0	0	0	0	1	1	1	0	0	0	2	0	0	0	1	0	1
20	0	0	1	0	0	1	0	0	1	1	0	2	0	0	0	0	0	0
21	0	0	0	0	0	0	0	0	0	0	0	0	0	0	0	0	0	0
22	0	0	0	0	0	0	0	0	0	0	0	0	0	0	0	0	1	1
23	0	0	0	0	0	0	0	0	1	0	1	2	0	0	0	0	0	0
24	0	0	0	0	0	0	0	0	0	0	0	0	0	0	0	0	0	0
25	0	0	0	0	0	0	0	0	0	0	0	0	0	0	0	0	0	0
26	0	0	0	0	0	0	0	1	0	1	0	2	0	0	0	0	0	0
27	1	0	0	0	0	1	0	0	0	0	0	0	1	1	0	0	1	3
28	1	0	1	0	0	2	1	0	0	0	0	1	1	0	1	0	1	3
29	1	1	1	0	0	3	1	0	0	0	1	2	0	0	0	1	0	1
S	8	7	11	2	0	28	8	6	5	7	8	34	8	11	9	6	8	42

Acknowledgements First of all, the authors would like to thank the students who participated as subjects in the experiment. We would also like to give a special acknowledgement to Forrest Shull at University of Maryland who provided support on the UMD lab-package and gave many good comments on a draft version of this paper. We are also grateful for all constructive comments made by the anonymous reviewers. Thanks also to Claes Wohlin, Martin Höst and Håkan Petersson at Dept. of Communication Systems, Lund University, who have carefully reviewed this paper. Special thanks to Anders Holtsberg at Centre for Mathematical Sciences, Lund University, for his expert help on statistical analysis. This work is partly funded by the National Board of Industrial and Technical Development (NUTEK), Sweden, grant 1K1P-97-09690.

Appendices

Appendix A
Exercises

Explanations of the different types of exercises can be found in the Preface. In summary, the objective is to provide four types of exercises:

Understanding	These exercises aim at highlighting the most important issues from each chapter. Exercises are available in Chaps. 1–11.
Training	The objective of these exercises is to encourage practicing experimentation. This includes setting up hypotheses and performing the statistical analysis.
Reviewing	Chapters 12 and 13 include examples of experiments. The intention of this part is to provide help in reviewing and reading published experiments.
Assignments	These exercises are formulated to promote an understanding of how experiments can be used in software engineering to evaluate methods and techniques.

The understanding type questions can be found at the end of each chapter, while the three other types of exercises can be found in this appendix.

A.1 Training

The exercises are preferably solved either using a statistical program package or tables from books in statistics. The tables in Appendix B may be used, but the tables provided are only for the 5% significance level, so if other significance levels are used then other sources must be used. It should be remembered that Appendix B has primarily been provided to explain the examples in Chap. 10.

C. Wohlin et al., *Experimentation in Software Engineering*,
DOI 10.1007/978-3-642-29044-2, © Springer-Verlag Berlin Heidelberg 2012

A.1.1   Normally Distributed Data

The probably most complicated example of the statistical methods in Chap. 10 is the goodness of fit test for the normal distribution, see Sect. 10.2.12. Thus, it is appropriate to ensure a good understanding of that test.

1. Carry out the goodness of fit test, on the same data, see Table 10.20, using 12 segments instead.

A.1.2   Experience

In Chap. 12, the outcome of the Personal Software Process course is compared with the background of the students taking the course. The analysis conducted in Chap. 12 is only partial. The full data set is provided in Tables A.2 and A.3. In Table A.1, the survey material handed out at the first lecture is presented. The outcome of the survey is presented in Table A.2. The outcome of the PSP course is presented in Table A.3, where the following seven measures have been used to measure the outcome of the course:

Size	The number of new and changed lines of code for the ten programs.
Time	The total development time for the ten programs.
Prod.	The productivity measured as number of lines of code per development hour.
Faults	The number of faults logged for the ten programs. This includes all faults found, for example, including compilation faults.
Faults/KLOC	The number of faults for each 1,000 lines of code.
Pred. Size	The absolute relative error in predicting program size. The figures show the error in absolute percentages, for example, both over- and underestimates with 20% are shown as 20% without any sign indicating the direction of the estimation error.
Pred. Time	The absolute relative error in predicting the development time.

Based on the presentation in Chap. 12 and the data in Tables A.2 and A.3 answer the following questions.

1. How can the survey be improved? Think about what constitutes good measures of background, experience and ability.
2. Define hypotheses, additional to those in Chap. 12, based on the available data. Motivate why these hypotheses are interesting.
3. What type of sampling has been used?
4. Analyze the hypotheses you have stated. What are the results?
5. Discuss the external validity of your findings. Can the results be generalized outside the PSP? Can the results be generalized to industrial software engineers?

Table A.1 Student characterization

Area	Description	Answer
Study program (denoted Line)	Answer: Computer Science and Engineering or Electrical Engineering	
General knowledge in computer science and software engineering (denoted SE)	1. Little, but curious about the new course 2. Not my speciality (focus on other subjects) 3. Rather good, but not my main focus (one of a couple of areas) 4. Main focus of my studies	
General knowledge in programming (denoted Prog.)	1. Only 1–2 courses 2. 3 or more courses, no industrial experience 3. A few courses and some industrial experience 4. More than three courses and more than 1 year industrial experience	
Knowledge about the PSP (denoted PSP)	1. What is it? 2. I have heard about it 3. A general understanding of what it is 4. I have read some material	
Knowledge in C (denoted C)	1. No prior knowledge 2. Read a book or followed a course 3. Some industrial experience (less than 6 months) 4. Industrial experience	
Knowledge in C++ (denoted C++)	1. No prior knowledge 2. Read a book or followed a course 3. Some industrial experience (less than 6 months) 4. Industrial experience	
Number of courses (denoted Courses)	A list of courses was provided and the students were asked to put down a yes or no whether they had taken the course or not. Moreover, they were asked to complement the list of courses if they had read something else they thought was a particularly relevant course	

A.1.3 Programming

In an experiment, 20 programmers have developed the same program, where 10 of them have used programming language A and 10 have used language B. Language A is newer and the company is planning to change to language A if it is better than language B. During the development, the size of the program, the development time, the total number of removed defects and the number of defects removed in test have been measured.

Table A.2 Information from background survey

Subject	Line	SE	Prog.	PSP	C	C++	Courses
1	1	2	1	2	1	1	2
2	1	3	2	1	2	1	4
3	2	3	2	2	2	2	7
4	1	3	2	3	2	1	3
5	1	3	2	3	2	1	5
6	2	4	3	2	1	1	7
7	2	3	2	2	1	2	7
8	1	3	2	2	1	1	4
9	2	4	3	2	1	1	9
10	2	4	2	1	1	1	7
11	1	2	2	1	2	1	3
12	2	4	3	2	1	1	9
13	2	4	3	2	3	3	8
14	2	3	2	2	1	1	6
15	1	3	2	2	1	1	5
16	2	4	2	1	1	1	10
17	1	3	3	1	1	1	5
18	2	4	3	2	1	3	6
19	2	4	3	3	3	3	8
20	1	1	1	1	1	1	2
21	2	3	3	2	2	2	10
22	2	3	2	3	1	1	5
23	1	3	2	2	1	1	4
24	1	2	1	1	1	1	3
25	2	4	3	1	2	2	7
26	1	3	2	2	1	1	5
27	2	4	3	2	3	2	7
28	1	3	2	3	1	1	2
29	2	4	2	3	1	1	7
30	2	3	3	1	2	3	6
31	1	3	2	2	2	2	5
32	2	3	3	1	2	2	10
33	2	4	3	1	1	1	5
34	1	2	2	1	2	2	3
35	1	2	1	1	1	1	2
36	1	2	1	2	1	1	2
37	1	2	2	2	2	2	2
38	2	4	2	2	2	1	6
39	1	2	1	2	1	1	2
40	2	4	3	1	4	4	7
41	2	3	3	2	2	2	8
41	2	4	3	2	2	2	9

(*continued*)

Table A.2 (continued)

Subject	Line	SE	Prog.	PSP	C	C++	Courses
43	1	3	2	1	1	1	3
44	1	4	3	2	3	2	7
45	2	4	2	2	2	1	6
46	2	2	4	2	4	4	7
47	2	4	3	2	3	2	7
48	1	2	2	2	1	1	2
49	1	3	3	1	1	1	3
50	2	3	2	3	1	1	8
51	2	4	2	4	2	2	8
52	2	4	3	3	3	2	8
53	2	4	3	3	2	2	10
54	1	2	1	2	1	1	2
55	1	2	2	2	1	1	4
56	2	3	2	1	1	1	8
57	1	2	3	1	1	1	4
58	2	4	3	3	1	1	6
59	1	2	2	2	2	1	4

The programmers have been randomly assigned a programming language and the objective of the experiment is to evaluate if the language has any effect on the four measured variables. The collected data can be found in Table A.4. The data is fictitious.

1. Which design has been used in the experiment?
2. Define the hypotheses for the evaluation.
3. Use box plots to investigate the differences between the languages in terms of central tendency and dispersion with respect to all four factors. Is there any outlier and if so should it be removed?
4. Assume that parametric tests can be used. Evaluate the effect of the programming language on the four measured variables. Which conclusions can be drawn from the results?
5. Evaluate the effect of the programming language on the four measured variables using a non-parametric test. Which conclusions can be drawn from the results? Compare the results to those achieved when using parametric tests.
6. Discuss the validity of the results and if it is appropriate to use a parametric test.
7. Assume that the participating programmers have chosen the programming language themselves. What consequences does this have on the validity of the results? Do the conclusions still hold?

Table A.3 Outcome from the PSP course

Subject	Size	Time	Prod.	Faults	Faults/KLOC	Pred. size	Pred. time
1	839	3,657	13.8	53	63.2	39.7	20.2
2	1,249	3,799	19.7	56	44.8	44.1	21.2
3	968	1,680	34.6	71	73.3	29.1	25.1
4	996	4,357	13.7	35	35.1	24.3	18.0
5	794	2,011	23.7	32	40.3	26.0	13.2
6	849	2,505	20.3	26	30.6	61.1	48.2
7	1,455	4,017	21.7	118	81.1	36.5	34.7
8	1,177	2,673	26.4	61	51.8	34.6	32.5
9	747	1,552	28.9	41	54.9	51.0	18.2
10	1,107	2,479	26.8	59	53.3	22.6	14.0
11	729	3,449	12.7	27	37.0	26.9	52.0
12	999	3,105	19.3	63	63.1	26.0	19.8
13	881	2,224	23.8	44	49.9	47.9	39.9
14	730	2,395	18.3	94	128.8	63.0	20.3
15	1,145	3,632	18.9	70	61.1	33.3	34.8
16	1,803	3,193	33.9	98	54.4	52.9	21.8
17	800	2,702	17.8	60	75.0	34.3	26.7
18	1,042	2,089	29.9	64	61.4	49.3	41.5
19	918	3,648	15.1	43	46.8	49.7	71.5
20	1,115	6,807	9.8	26	23.3	34.1	22.4
21	890	4,096	13.0	108	121.3	19.3	34.8
22	1,038	3,609	17.3	98	94.4	21.4	52.0
23	1,251	6,925	10.8	498	398.1	21.8	34.1
24	623	4,216	8.9	53	85.1	40.5	36.3
25	1,319	1,864	42.5	92	69.7	43.7	45.0
26	800	4,088	11.7	74	92.5	42.6	36.2
27	1,267	2,553	29.8	88	69.5	53.0	30.1
28	945	1,648	34.4	42	44.4	33.3	17.9
29	724	4,144	10.5	49	67.7	32.8	17.8
30	1,131	2,869	23.7	102	90.2	29.2	15.5
31	1,021	2,235	27.4	49	48.0	18.0	25.0
32	840	3,215	15.7	69	82.1	85.6	54.0
33	985	5,643	10.5	133	135.0	27.3	31.0
34	590	2,678	13.2	33	55.9	83.0	20.0
35	727	4,321	10.1	48	66.0	17.0	22.7
36	955	3,836	14.9	76	79.6	33.3	36.8
37	803	4,470	10.8	56	69.7	18.2	27.7
38	684	1,592	25.8	28	40.9	35.0	34.1
39	913	4,188	13.1	45	49.3	25.3	27.5
40	1,200	1,827	39.4	61	50.8	31.6	20.9
41	894	2,777	19.3	64	71.6	21.3	22.4
42	1,545	3,281	28.3	136	88.0	35.0	16.1

(continued)

Table A.3 (continued)

Subject	Size	Time	Prod.	Faults	Faults/KLOC	Pred. size	Pred. time
43	995	2,806	21.3	71	71.4	15.6	38.3
44	807	2,464	19.7	65	80.5	43.3	26.4
45	1,078	2,462	26.3	55	51.0	49.1	51.6
46	944	3,154	18.0	71	75.2	59.0	39.2
47	868	1,564	33.3	50	57.6	50.4	45.2
48	701	3,188	13.2	31	44.2	21.2	49.7
49	1,107	4,823	13.8	86	77.7	19.3	28.4
50	1,535	2,938	31.3	71	46.3	29.6	20.7
51	858	7,163	7.2	97	113.1	58.4	32.9
52	832	2,033	24.6	84	101.0	48.4	25.6
53	975	3,160	18.5	115	117.9	29.5	31.5
54	715	3,337	12.9	40	55.9	41.7	26.6
55	947	4,583	12.4	99	104.5	41.0	22.3
56	926	2,924	19.0	77	83.2	32.5	34.7
57	711	3,053	14.0	78	109.7	22.8	14.3
58	1,283	7,063	10.9	186	145.0	46.5	26.6
59	1,261	3,092	24.5	54	42.8	27.4	45.3

A.1.4 Design

This exercise is based on data obtained from an experiment carried out by Briand, Bunse and Daly. The experiment is further described by Briand et al. [28].

An experiment is designed in order to evaluate the impact of quality object-oriented design principles when intending to modify a given design. The quality design principles evaluated are the principles provided by Coad and Yourdon [35]. In the experiment two systems are used with one design for each system. One of the designs is a 'good' design made using the design principles and the other is a 'bad' design not using the principles. The two designs are documented in the same way in terms of layout and content and are of the same size, i.e. they are developed to be as similar as possible except for following or not following the design principles. The objective of the experiment is to evaluate if the quality design principles ease impact analysis when identifying changes in the design.

The task for each participant is to undertake two separate impact analyses, one for each system design. Marking all places in the design that have to be changed but not actually change them makes the impact analyses. The first impact analysis is for a changed customer requirement and the second is for an enhancement in the systems functionality. Four measures are collected during the task:

Mod_Time: Time spent on identifying places for modification.
Mod_Comp: Represents the completeness of the impact analysis and is defined
             as:

Table A.4 Data for programming exercise

Programming language	Program size (LOC)	Development time (min)	Total number of defects	Number of test defects
A	1, 408	3,949	89	23
A	1, 529	2,061	69	16
A	946	3,869	170	41
A	1, 141	5,562	271	55
A	696	5,028	103	39
A	775	2,296	75	29
A	1, 205	2,980	79	11
A	1, 159	2,991	194	28
A	862	2,701	67	27
A	1, 206	2,592	77	15
B	1, 316	3,986	68	20
B	1, 787	4,477	54	10
B	1, 105	3,789	130	23
B	1, 583	4,371	48	13
B	1, 381	3,325	133	29
B	944	5,234	80	25
B	1, 492	4,901	64	21
B	1, 217	3,897	89	29
B	936	3,825	57	20
B	1, 441	4,015	79	18

$$\text{Mod\_Comp} = \frac{\text{Number of correct places found}}{\text{Total number of places to be found}}$$

Mod_Corr: Represents the correctness of the impact analysis and is defined as:

$$\text{Mod\_Corr} = \frac{\text{Number of correct places found}}{\text{Total number of places indicated as found}}$$

Mod_Rate: The number of correct places found per time unit, that is:

$$\text{Mod\_Rate} = \frac{\text{Number of correct places found}}{\text{Time for identification}}$$

The experiment is conducted at two occasions, in order to let each participant work with both the good design and the bad design. The subjects were randomly assigned to one of two groups, A or B. Group A worked with the good design at the first occasion and the bad design in the second. Group B studied the bad design first and then the good design. The collected data can be found in Table A.5.

Table A.5 Data for design exercise

Participant	Group	Good object-oriented design				Bad object-oriented design			
		Mod_Time	Mod_Comp	Mod_Corr	Mod_Rate	Mod_Time	Mod_Comp	Mod_Corr	Mod_Rate
P01	B	–	0.545	0.75	–	–	0.238	0.714	–
P02	B	–	0.818	1	–	–	0.095	1	–
P03	A	20	0.409	1	0.45	25	0.19	1	0.16
P04	B	22	0.818	1	0.818	25	0.238	1	0.2
P05	B	30	0.909	1	0.667	35	0.476	0.909	0.286
P07	A	–	0	–	–	38	0.476	1	0.263
P09	A	–	0.455	1	–	–	0.476	1	–
P10	B	–	0.409	0.9	–	–	0.381	1	–
P11	A	45	0.545	0.923	0.267	50	0.714	1	0.3
P12	B	–	0.773	1	–	–	0.714	1	–
P13	A	40	0.773	1	0.425	40	0.762	1	0.4
P14	B	30	0.909	1	0.667	30	0.333	0.875	0.233
P15	B	–	0.864	1	–	40	0.238	1	0.125
P16	B	30	0.773	1	0.567	–	–	–	–
P17	B	–	0.955	1	–	–	0.286	0.75	–
P18	B	–	0	–	–	–	0.19	1	–
P19	A	29	0.818	1	0.621	27	0.667	1	0.519
P20	A	9	0.591	1	1.444	15	0.19	0.8	0.267
P21	B	20	0.591	1	0.65	35	0.19	1	0.114
P22	B	30	0.682	1	0.5	20	0.714	1	0.75
P23	B	–	0.818	1	–	–	0.476	1	–
P24	A	30	0.773	1	0.567	40	0.762	1	0.4
P25	A	–	0.955	1	–	–	0.667	0.875	–
P26	B	25	0	0	0	25	0.095	0.5	0.08
P27	A	27	0.773	0.944	0.63	36	0.389	0.7	0.194
P28	A	25	0.773	1	0.68	30	0.667	1	0.467
P29	B	44	0.773	1	0.386	23	0.762	1	0.696
P31	A	–	0.409	1	–	–	0.286	0.75	–
P32	A	30	0.909	1	0.667	–	0.5	1	–
P33	A	65	0.818	1	0.277	–	0.619	1	–
P34	A	50	0.636	0.933	0.28	30	0.4	0.889	0.267
P35	A	10	0.591	1	1.3	10	0.667	1	1.4
P36	A	13	1	1	1.692	–	0.619	1	–

1. Which design has been used in the experiment?
2. Define the hypotheses for the evaluation.
3. How should the missing values in Table A.5 be treated?
4. Assume that parametric tests can be used. Evaluate the effect of the quality design principles on the four measured variables. Which conclusions can be drawn from the results?
5. Evaluate the effect of the quality design principles on the four measured variables using non-parametric tests. Which conclusions can be drawn from the results? Compare the results to those achieved when using parametric tests.
6. Discuss the validity of the results and if it is appropriate to use parametric tests.
7. The participants in the experiment are students taking a software engineering course that have volunteered to be subjects. From which population is the sample taken from? Discuss how this type of sampling will affect the external validity of the experiment? How can the sampling be made differently?

A.1.5 Inspections

This exercise refers to the example experiment in Chap. 13.

1. Rewrite the abstract in Chap. 13 to be a structured abstract, as defined in Chap. 11.
2. Conduct the scoping and planning steps for an *exact* replication of the experiment. Especially, define how many subjects should be enrolled to achieve a given level of confidence in the analysis.
3. Conduct the scoping step for a *differentiated* replication of the experiment. Define three different goal templates for three alternative replications. Discuss pros and cons of each alternative with respect to costs, risks and gains (see also Fig. 2.1).

A.2 Reviewing

Below is a list of questions, which are important to consider when reading or reviewing an article presenting an experiment. Use the list and review the examples presented in Chaps. 12 and 13, and also some experiment presented in the literature.

The list below should be seen as a checklist in addition to normal questions when reading an article. An example of a normal question may be; is the abstract a good description of the content of the paper? Some specific aspects to consider when reading an experiment article are:

- Is the experiment understandable and interesting in general?
- Does the experiment have any practical value?
- Are other experiments addressing the problem summarized and referenced?

- What is the population in the experiment?
- Is the sample used representative of the population?
- Are the dependent and independent variables clearly defined?
- Are the hypotheses clearly formulated?
- Is the type of design clearly stated?
- Is the design correct?
- Is the instrumentation described properly?
- Is the validity of the experiment treated carefully and convincing?
- Are different types of validity threats addressed properly?
- Has the data been validated?
- Is the statistical power sufficient, are there enough subjects in the experiment?
- Are the appropriate statistical tests applied? Are Parametric or non-parametric tests used and are they used correctly?
- Is the significance level used appropriate?
- Is the data interpreted correctly?
- Are the conclusions correct?
- Are the results not overstated?
- Is it possible to replicate the study?
- Is data provided?
- Is it possible to use the results for performing a meta-analysis?
- Is further work and experimentation in the area outlined?

A.3   Assignments

These assignments are based on the following general scenario. A company would like to improve their way of working by changing the software process. You are consulted as an expert in evaluating new techniques and methods in relation to the existing process. The company would like to know whether or not to change their software process.

You are expected to search for appropriate literature, review the existing literature on the subject, apply the experiment process and write a report containing a recommendation for the company. The recommendation should discuss both the results of the experiment and other relevant issues for taking the decision whether or not to change the process. Other relevant issues include costs and benefits for making the change. If you are unable to find the correct costs, you are expected to make estimates. The latter may be in terms of relative costs.

The assignments are intentionally fairly open-ended to allow for interpretation and discussion. Each assignment is described in terms of prerequisites needed to perform the assignment and then the actual task is briefly described. It should be noted that the assignments below are examples of possible experiments that can be conducted. The important issue to hold in mind is that the main objective is that the assignments should provide practice in using experiments as part of an evaluation procedure.

Finally, it should be noted that some organizations provide what is called lab packages that can be used to replicate experiments. Lab packages are important as they allow us to build upon work by others and hence hopefully come to more generally valid results by replication. Some lab packages can be found by a search on the Internet. It may also be beneficial to contact the original experimenter to get support and maybe also a non-published lab package.

A.3.1   Unit Test and Code Reviews

The company wants to evaluate if it is cost-effective to introduce code reviews. Unit testing is done today, although on non-reviewed code. Is this the best way to do it?

Prerequisites

- Suitable programs with defects that can be found during either reviews or testing.
- A review method, which may be ad hoc, but preferable it should be something more realistic, for example, a checklist-based approach. In this case, a checklist is needed.
- A testing method, which also may be ad hoc, but preferably it is based on, for example, usage or equivalence partitioning.

Task

- Evaluate if it is cost-effective to introduce code reviews.

A.3.2   Inspection Methods

Several different ways of conducting reviews are available. The company intends to introduce the best inspection method out of two possible choices. Which of the two methods is the best to introduce for the company?

Prerequisites

- Suitable software artifacts to review should be available.
- Two review methods with appropriate support in terms of, for example, checklists or description of different reading perspectives, see also Appendix A.1.5.

Task

- Assume that the company intends to introduce reviews of the chosen software artifacts, which method should they introduce? Determine which of the inspection methods that is best in finding defects. Is the best method also cost effective?

A.3.3   Requirements Notation

It is important to write requirements specification so that all readers interpret them easily and in the same way. The company has several different notations to choose from. Which is the best way of representing requirements?

Prerequisites

- A requirements specification written in several different notations, for example, natural language and different graphical representations.

Task

- Evaluate if it is beneficial to change the company's notation for requirements specifications. Assume that the company uses natural language today.

Appendix B
Statistical Tables

This appendix contains statistical tables for a significance level of 5%. More elaborated tables can be found in most books on statistics, for example [119], and tables are also available on the Internet. The main objective here is to provide some information, so that the tests that are explained in Chap. 10 become understandable and so that the examples provided can be followed. This is important even if statistical packages are used for the calculations, since it is important to understand the underlying calculations before just applying the different statistical tests. It is also worth noting the tables are a shortcut, for example, the values for the t-test, F-test and Chi-2 can be calculated from the respective distributions.

The following statistical tables are included:

- t-test (see Sects. 10.3.4, 10.3.7, and Table B.1)
- Chi-2 (see Sect. 10.3.12 and Table B.2)
- Mann-Whitney (see Sect. 10.3.5 and Table B.3)
- Wilcoxon (see Sect. 10.3.8 and Table B.4)
- F-test (see Sects. 10.3.6, 10.3.10, Table B.5)

C. Wohlin et al., *Experimentation in Software Engineering*,
DOI 10.1007/978-3-642-29044-2, © Springer-Verlag Berlin Heidelberg 2012

Table B.1 Critical values
two-tailed t-test (5%), see
Sects. 10.3.4 and 10.3.7

Degrees of freedom	t-value
1	12.706
2	4.303
3	3.182
4	2.776
5	2.571
6	2.447
7	2.365
8	2.306
9	2.262
10	2.228
11	2.201
12	2.179
13	2.160
14	2.145
15	2.131
16	2.120
17	2.110
18	2.101
19	2.093
20	2.086
21	2.080
22	2.074
23	2.069
24	2.064
25	2.060
26	2.056
27	2.052
28	2.048
29	2.045
30	2.042
40	2.021
60	2.000
120	1.980
∞	1.960

Table B.2 Critical values
one-tailed Chi2-test (5%), see
Sect. 10.3.12

Degrees of freedom	χ^2
1	3.84
2	5.99
3	7.81
4	9.49
5	11.07
6	12.59
7	14.07
8	15.51
9	16.92
10	18.31
11	19.68
12	21.03
13	22.36
14	23.68
15	25.00
16	26.30
17	27.59
18	28.87
19	30.14
20	31.41
21	32.67
22	33.92
23	35.17
24	36.42
25	37.65
26	38.88
27	40.11
28	41.34
29	42.56
30	43.77
40	55.76
60	79.08
80	101.88
100	124.34

Table B.3 Critical values two-tailed Mann-Whitney (5%), see Sect. 10.3.5

N_B N_A	5	6	7	8	9	10	11	12
3	0	1	1	2	2	3	3	4
4	1	2	3	4	4	5	6	7
5	2	3	5	6	7	8	9	11
6		5	6	8	10	11	13	14
7			8	10	12	14	16	18
8				13	15	17	19	22
9					17	20	23	26
10						23	26	29
11							30	33
12								37

Table B.4 Critical values two-tailed matched-pair Wilcoxon test (5%), see Sect. 10.3.8

n	T
6	0
7	2
8	3
9	5
10	8
11	10
12	13
13	17
14	21
15	25
16	29
17	34
18	40
19	46
20	52
22	66
25	89

Please note that in Table B.3, N_A is for the smaller sample and N_B for the larger sample.

Please note that Table B.5 provides the upper 0.025% point of the F distribution with f_1 and f_2 being the degrees of freedom. This is equivalent to $F_{0.0025, f_1, f_2}$.

Table B.5 Critical values two-tailed F-test (5%), see Sect. 10.3.6. For ANOVA, this is equivalent to a significance level of 2.5%, see Sect. 10.3.10

f_2 \ f_1	1	2	3	4	5	6	7	8	9	10	12	15	20	30	40	60	120	∞
1	648	800	864	900	922	937	948	957	963	969	977	985	993	1,001	1,006	1,010	1,014	1,018
2	38.5	39.0	39.2	39.2	39.3	39.3	39.4	39.4	39.4	39.4	39.4	39.4	39.4	39.5	39.5	39.5	39.5	39.5
3	17.4	16.0	15.4	15.1	14.9	14.7	14.6	14.5	14.5	14.4	14.3	14.2	14.2	14.1	14.0	14.0	14.0	13.9
4	12.2	10.6	9.98	9.60	9.36	9.20	9.07	8.98	8.90	8.84	8.75	8.66	8.56	8.46	8.41	8.36	8.31	8.26
5	10.0	8.43	7.76	7.39	7.15	6.98	6.85	6.76	6.68	6.62	6.52	6.43	6.33	6.23	6.18	6.12	6.07	6.02
6	8.81	7.26	6.60	6.23	5.99	5.82	5.70	5.60	5.52	5.46	5.37	5.27	5.17	5.07	5.01	4.96	4.90	4.85
7	8.07	6.54	5.89	5.52	5.29	5.12	4.99	4.90	4.82	4.76	4.67	4.57	4.47	4.36	4.31	4.25	4.20	4.14
8	7.57	6.06	5.42	5.05	4.82	4.65	4.53	4.43	4.36	4.30	4.20	4.10	4.00	3.89	3.84	3.78	3.73	3.67
9	7.21	5.71	5.08	4.72	4.48	4.32	4.20	4.10	4.03	3.96	3.87	3.77	3.67	3.56	3.51	3.45	3.39	3.33
10	6.94	5.46	4.83	4.47	4.24	4.07	3.95	3.85	3.78	3.72	3.62	3.52	3.42	3.31	3.26	3.20	3.14	3.08
12	6.55	5.10	4.47	4.12	3.89	3.73	3.61	3.51	3.44	3.37	3.28	3.18	3.07	2.96	2.91	2.85	2.79	2.72
15	6.20	4.76	4.15	3.80	3.58	3.41	3.29	3.20	3.12	3.06	2.96	2.86	2.76	2.64	2.59	2.52	2.46	2.40
20	5.87	4.46	3.86	3.51	3.29	3.13	3.01	2.91	2.84	2.77	2.68	2.57	2.46	2.35	2.29	2.22	2.16	2.09
30	5.57	4.18	3.59	3.25	3.03	2.87	2.75	2.65	2.57	2.51	2.41	2.31	2.20	2.07	2.01	1.94	1.87	1.79
40	5.42	4.05	3.46	3.13	2.90	2.74	2.62	2.53	2.45	2.39	2.29	2.18	2.07	1.94	1.88	1.80	1.72	1.64
60	5.29	3.93	3.34	3.01	2.79	2.63	2.51	2.41	2.33	2.27	2.17	2.06	1.94	1.82	1.74	1.67	1.58	1.48
120	5.15	3.80	3.23	2.89	2.67	2.52	2.39	2.30	2.22	2.16	2.05	1.94	1.82	1.69	1.61	1.53	1.43	1.31
∞	5.02	3.69	3.12	2.79	2.57	2.41	2.29	2.19	2.11	2.05	1.94	1.83	1.71	1.57	1.48	1.39	1.27	1.00

References

1. Anastas, J.W., MacDonald, M.L.: Research Design for the Social Work and the Human Services, 2nd edn. Columbia University Press, New York (2000)
2. Andersson, C., Runeson, P.: A spiral process model for case studies on software quality monitoring – method and metrics. Softw. Process: Improv. Pract. **12**(2), 125–140 (2007). doi: 10.1002/spip.311
3. Andrews, A.A., Pradhan, A.S.: Ethical issues in empirical software engineering: the limits of policy. Empir. Softw. Eng. **6**(2), 105–110 (2001)
4. American Psychological Association: Ethical principles of psychologists and code of conduct. Am. Psychol. **47**, 1597–1611 (1992)
5. Avison, D., Baskerville, R., Myers, M.: Controlling action research projects. Inf. Technol. People **14**(1), 28–45 (2001). doi: 10.1108/09593840110384762. URL http://www.emeraldinsight.com/10.1108/09593840110384762
6. Babbie, E.R.: Survey Research Methods. Wadsworth, Belmont (1990)
7. Basili, V.R.: Quantitative evaluation of software engineering methodology. In: Proceedings of the First Pan Pacific Computer Conference, vol. 1, pp. 379–398. Australian Computer Society, Melbourne (1985)
8. Basili, V.R.: Software development: a paradigm for the future. In: Proceedings of the 13th Annual International Computer Software and Applications Conference, COMPSAC'89, Orlando, pp. 471–485. IEEE Computer Society Press, Washington (1989)
9. Basili, V.R.: The experimental paradigm in software engineering. In: H.D. Rombach, V.R. Basili, R.W. Selby (eds.) Experimental Software Engineering Issues: Critical Assessment and Future Directives. Lecture Notes in Computer Science, vol. 706. Springer, Berlin Heidelberg (1993)
10. Basili, V.R.: Evolving and packaging reading technologies. J. Syst. Softw. **38**(1), 3–12 (1997)
11. Basili, V.R., Weiss, D.M.: A methodology for collecting valid software engineering data. IEEE Trans. Softw. Eng. **10**(6), 728–737 (1984)
12. Basili, V.R., Selby, R.W.: Comparing the effectiveness of software testing strategies. IEEE Trans. Softw. Eng. **13**(12), 1278–1298 (1987)
13. Basili, V.R., Rombach, H.D.: The TAME project: towards improvement-oriented software environments. IEEE Trans. Softw. Eng. **14**(6), 758–773 (1988)
14. Basili, V.R., Green, S.: Software process evaluation at the SEL. IEEE Softw. **11**(4), pp. 58–66 (1994)
15. Basili, V.R., Selby, R.W., Hutchens, D.H.: Experimentation in software engineering. IEEE Trans. Softw. Eng. **12**(7), 733–743 (1986)
16. Basili, V.R., Caldiera, G., Rombach, H.D.: Experience factory. In: J.J. Marciniak (ed.) Encyclopedia of Software Engineering, pp. 469–476. Wiley, New York (1994)

C. Wohlin et al., *Experimentation in Software Engineering*,
DOI 10.1007/978-3-642-29044-2, © Springer-Verlag Berlin Heidelberg 2012

17. Basili, V.R., Caldiera, G., Rombach, H.D.: Goal Question Metrics paradigm. In: J.J. Marciniak (ed.) Encyclopedia of Software Engineering, pp. 528–532. Wiley (1994)
18. Basili, V.R., Green, S., Laitenberger, O., Lanubile, F., Shull, F., Sørumgård, S., Zelkowitz, M.V.: The empirical investigation of perspective-based reading. Empir. Soft. Eng. 1(2), 133–164 (1996)
19. Basili, V.R., Green, S., Laitenberger, O., Lanubile, F., Shull, F., Sørumgård, S., Zelkowitz, M.V.: Lab package for the empirical investigation of perspective-based reading. Technical report, Univeristy of Maryland (1998). URL http://www.cs.umd.edu/projects/SoftEng/ESEG/manual/pbr_package/manual.html
20. Basili, V.R., Shull, F., Lanubile, F.: Building knowledge through families of experiments. IEEE Trans. Softw. Eng. 25(4), 456–473 (1999)
21. Baskerville, R.L., Wood-Harper, A.T.: A critical perspective on action research as a method for information systems research. J. Inf. Technol. 11(3), 235–246 (1996). doi: 10.1080/026839696345289
22. Benbasat, I., Goldstein, D.K., Mead, M.: The case research strategy in studies of information systems. MIS Q. 11(3), 369 (1987). doi: 10.2307/248684
23. Bergman, B., Klefsjö, B.: Quality from Customer Needs to Customer Satisfaction. Studentlitteratur, Lund (2010)
24. Brereton, P., Kitchenham, B.A., Budgen, D., Turner, M., Khalil, M.: Lessons from applying the systematic literature review process within the software engineering domain. J. Syst. Softw. 80(4), 571–583 (2007). doi: 10.1016/j.jss.2006.07.009
25. Brereton, P., Kitchenham, B.A., Budgen, D.: Using a protocol template for case study planning. In: Proceedings of the 12th International Conference on Evaluation and Assessment in Software Engineering. University of Bari, Italy (2008)
26. Briand, L.C., Differding, C.M., Rombach, H.D.: Practical guidelines for measurement-based process improvement. Softw. Process: Improv. Pract. 2(4), 253–280 (1996)
27. Briand, L.C., El Emam, K., Morasca, S.: On the application of measurement theory in software engineering. Empir. Softw. Eng. 1(1), 61–88 (1996)
28. Briand, L.C., Bunse, C., Daly, J.W.: A controlled experiment for evaluating quality guidelines on the maintainability of object-oriented designs. IEEE Trans. Softw. Eng. 27(6), 513–530 (2001)
29. British Psychological Society: Ethical principles for conducting research with human participants. Psychologist 6(1), 33–35 (1993)
30. Budgen, D., Kitchenham, B.A., Charters, S., Turner, M., Brereton, P., Linkman, S.: Presenting software engineering results using structured abstracts: a randomised experiment. Empir. Softw. Eng. 13, 435–468 (2008). doi: 10.1007/s10664-008-9075-7
31. Budgen, D., Burn, A.J., Kitchenham, B.A.: Reporting computing projects through structured abstracts: a quasi-experiment. Empir. Softw. Eng. 16(2), 244–277 (2011). doi: 10.1007/s10664-010-9139-3
32. Campbell, D.T., Stanley, J.C.: Experimental and Quasi-experimental Designs for Research. Houghton Mifflin Company, Boston (1963)
33. Chrissis, M.B., Konrad, M., Shrum, S.: CMMI(R): Guidelines for process integration and product improvement. Technical report, SEI (2003)
34. Ciolkowski, M., Differding, C.M., Laitenberger, O., Münch, J.: Empirical investigation of perspective-based reading: A replicated experiment. Technical report, 97-13, ISERN (1997)
35. Coad, P., Yourdon, E.: Object-Oriented Design, 1st edn. Prentice-Hall, Englewood (1991)
36. Cohen, J.: Weighted kappa: nominal scale agreement with provision for scaled disagreement or partial credit. Psychol. Bull. 70, 213–220 (1968)
37. Cook, T.D., Campbell, D.T.: Quasi-experimentation – Design and Analysis Issues for Field Settings. Houghton Mifflin Company, Boston (1979)
38. Corbin, J., Strauss, A.: Basics of Qualitative Research, 3rd edn. SAGE, Los Angeles (2008)
39. Cruzes, D.S., Dybå, T.: Research synthesis in software engineering: a tertiary study. Inf. Softw. Technol. 53(5), 440–455 (2011). doi: 10.1016/j.infsof.2011.01.004

40. Dalkey, N., Helmer, O.: An experimental application of the delphi method to the use of experts. Manag. Sci. **9**(3), 458–467 (1963)
41. DeMarco, T.: Controlling Software Projects. Yourdon Press, New York (1982)
42. Demming, W.E.: Out of the Crisis. MIT Centre for Advanced Engineering Study, MIT Press, Cambridge, MA (1986)
43. Dieste, O., Grimán, A., Juristo, N.: Developing search strategies for detecting relevant experiments. Empir. Softw. Eng. **14**, 513–539 (2009). URL http://dx.doi.org/10.1007/s10664-008-9091-7
44. Dittrich, Y., Rönkkö, K., Eriksson, J., Hansson, C., Lindeberg, O.: Cooperative method development. Empir. Softw. Eng. **13**(3), 231–260 (2007). doi: 10.1007/s10664-007-9057-1
45. Doolan, E.P.: Experiences with Fagan's inspection method. Softw. Pract. Exp. **22**(2), 173–182 (1992)
46. Dybå, T., Dingsøyr, T.: Empirical studies of agile software development: a systematic review. Inf. Softw. Technol. **50**(9-10), 833–859 (2008). doi: DOI:10.1016/j.infsof.2008.01.006
47. Dybå, T., Dingsøyr, T.: Strength of evidence in systematic reviews in software engineering. In: Proceedings of the 2nd ACM-IEEE International Symposium on Empirical Software Engineering and Measurement, ESEM '08, Kaiserslautern, pp. 178–187. ACM, New York (2008). doi: http://doi.acm.org/10.1145/1414004.1414034
48. Dybå, T., Kitchenham, B.A., Jørgensen, M.: Evidence-based software engineering for practitioners. IEEE Softw. **22**, 58–65 (2005). doi: http://doi.ieeecomputersociety.org/10.1109/MS.2005.6
49. Dybå, T., Kampenes, V.B., Sjøberg, D.I.K.: A systematic review of statistical power in software engineering experiments. Inf. Softw. Technol. **48**(8), 745–755 (2006). doi: 10.1016/j.infsof.2005.08.009
50. Easterbrook, S., Singer, J., Storey, M.-A., Damian, D.: Selecting empirical methods for software engineering research. In: F. Shull, J. Singer, D.I. Sjøberg (eds.) Guide to Advanced Empirical Software Engineering. Springer, London (2008)
51. Eick, S.G., Loader, C.R., Long, M.D., Votta, L.G., Vander Wiel, S.A.: Estimating software fault content before coding. In: Proceedings of the 14th International Conference on Software Engineering, Melbourne, pp. 59–65. ACM Press, New York (1992)
52. Eisenhardt, K.M.: Building theories from case study research. Acad. Manag. Rev. **14**(4), 532 (1989). doi: 10.2307/258557
53. Endres, A., Rombach, H.D.: A Handbook of Software and Systems Engineering – Empirical Observations, Laws and Theories. Pearson Addison-Wesley, Harlow/New York (2003)
54. Fagan, M.E.: Design and code inspections to reduce errors in program development. IBM Syst. J. **15**(3), 182–211 (1976)
55. Fenton, N.: Software measurement: A necessary scientific basis. IEEE Trans. Softw. Eng. **3**(20), 199–206 (1994)
56. Fenton, N., Pfleeger, S.L.: Software Metrics: A Rigorous and Practical Approach, 2nd edn. International Thomson Computer Press, London (1996)
57. Fenton, N., Pfleeger, S.L., Glass, R.: Science and substance: A challenge to software engineers. IEEE Softw. **11**, 86–95 (1994)
58. Fink, A.: The Survey Handbook, 2nd edn. SAGE, Thousand Oaks/London (2003)
59. Flyvbjerg, B.: Five misunderstandings about case-study research. In: Qualitative Research Practice, concise paperback edn., pp. 390–404. SAGE, London (2007)
60. Frigge, M., Hoaglin, D.C., Iglewicz, B.: Some implementations of the boxplot. Am. Stat. **43**(1), 50–54 (1989)
61. Fusaro, P., Lanubile, F., Visaggio, G.: A replicated experiment to assess requirements inspection techniques. Empir. Softw. Eng. **2**(1), 39–57 (1997)
62. Glass, R.L.: The software research crisis. IEEE Softw. **11**, 42–47 (1994)
63. Glass, R.L., Vessey, I., Ramesh, V.: Research in software engineering: An analysis of the literature. Inf. Softw. Technol. **44**(8), 491–506 (2002). doi: 10.1016/S0950-5849(02)00049-6

64. Gómez, O.S., Juristo, N., Vegas, S.: Replication types in experimental disciplines. In: Proceedings of the 4th ACM-IEEE International Symposium on Empirical Software Engineering and Measurement, Bolzano-Bozen (2010)
65. Gorschek, T., Wohlin, C.: Requirements abstraction model. Requir. Eng. **11**, 79–101 (2006). doi: 10.1007/s00766-005-0020-7
66. Gorschek, T., Garre, P., Larsson, S., Wohlin, C.: A model for technology transfer in practice. IEEE Softw. **23**(6), 88–95 (2006)
67. Gorschek, T., Garre, P., Larsson, S., Wohlin, C.: Industry evaluation of the requirements abstraction model. Requir. Eng. **12**, 163–190 (2007). doi: 10.1007/s00766-007-0047-z
68. Grady, R.B., Caswell, D.L.: Software Metrics: Establishing a Company-Wide Program. Prentice-Hall, Englewood (1994)
69. Grant, E.E., Sackman, H.: An exploratory investigation of programmer performance under on-line and off-line conditions. IEEE Trans. Human Factor Electron. **HFE-8**(1), 33–48 (1967)
70. Gregor, S.: The nature of theory in information systems. MIS Q. **30**(3), 491–506 (2006)
71. Hall, T., Flynn, V.: Ethical issues in software engineering research: a survey of current practice. Empir. Softw. Eng. **6**, 305–317 (2001)
72. Hannay, J.E., Sjøberg, D.I.K., Dybå, T.: A systematic review of theory use in software engineering experiments. IEEE Trans. Softw. Eng. **33**(2), 87–107 (2007). doi: 10.1109/TSE.2007.12
73. Hannay, J.E., Dybå, T., Arisholm, E., Sjøberg, D.I.K.: The effectiveness of pair programming: a meta-analysis. Inf. Softw. Technol. **51**(7), 1110–1122 (2009). doi: 10.1016/j.infsof.2009.02.001
74. Hayes, W.: Research synthesis in software engineering: a case for meta-analysis. In: Proceedings of the 6th International Software Metrics Symposium, Boca Raton, pp. 143–151 (1999)
75. Hetzel, B.: Making Software Measurement Work: Building an Effective Measurement Program. Wiley, New York (1993)
76. Hevner, A.R., March, S.T., Park, J., Ram, S.: Design science in information systems research. MIS Q. **28**(1), 75–105 (2004)
77. Höst, M., Regnell, B., Wohlin, C.: Using students as subjects – a comparative study of students and professionals in lead-time impact assessment. Empir. Softw. Eng. **5**(3), 201–214 (2000)
78. Höst, M., Wohlin, C., Thelin, T.: Experimental context classification: Incentives and experience of subjects. In: Proceedings of the 27th International Conference on Software Engineering, St. Louis, pp. 470–478 (2005)
79. Höst, M., Runeson, P.: Checklists for software engineering case study research. In: Proceedings of the 1st International Symposium on Empirical Software Engineering and Measurement, Madrid, pp. 479–481 (2007)
80. Hove, S.E., Anda, B.: Experiences from conducting semi-structured interviews in empirical software engineering research. In: Proceedings of the 11th IEEE International Software Metrics Symposium, pp. 1–10. IEEE Computer Society Press, Los Alamitos (2005)
81. Humphrey, W.S.: Managing the Software Process. Addison-Wesley, Reading (1989)
82. Humphrey, W.S.: A Discipline for Software Engineering. Addison Wesley, Reading (1995)
83. Humphrey, W.S.: Introduction to the Personal Software Process. Addison Wesley, Reading (1997)
84. IEEE: IEEE standard glossary of software engineering terminology. Technical Report, IEEE Std 610.12-1990, IEEE (1990)
85. Iversen, J.H., Mathiassen, L., Nielsen, P.A.: Managing risk in software process improvement: an action research approach. MIS Q. **28**(3), 395–433 (2004)
86. Jedlitschka, A., Pfahl, D.: Reporting guidelines for controlled experiments in software engineering. In: Proceedings of the 4th International Symposium on Empirical Software Engineering, Noosa Heads, pp. 95–104 (2005)
87. Johnson, P.M., Tjahjono, D.: Does every inspection really need a meeting? Empir. Softw. Eng. **3**(1), 9–35 (1998)

88. Juristo, N., Moreno, A.M.: Basics of Software Engineering Experimentation. Springer, Kluwer Academic Publishers, Boston (2001)
89. Juristo, N., Vegas, S.: The role of non-exact replications in software engineering experiments. Empir. Softw. Eng. **16**, 295–324 (2011). doi: 10.1007/s10664-010-9141-9
90. Kachigan, S.K.: Statistical Analysis: An Interdisciplinary Introduction to Univariate and Multivariate Methods. Radius Press, New York (1986)
91. Kachigan, S.K.: Multivariate Statistical Analysis: A Conceptual Introduction, 2nd edn. Radius Press, New York (1991)
92. Kampenes, V.B., Dyba, T., Hannay, J.E., Sjø berg, D.I.K.: A systematic review of effect size in software engineering experiments. Inf. Softw. Technol. **49**(11–12), 1073–1086 (2007). doi: 10.1016/j.infsof.2007.02.015
93. Karahasanović, A., Anda, B., Arisholm, E., Hove, S.E., Jørgensen, M., Sjøberg, D., Welland, R.: Collecting feedback during software engineering experiments. Empir. Softw. Eng. **10**(2), 113–147 (2005). doi: 10.1007/s10664-004-6189-4. URL http://www.springerlink.com/index/10.1007/s10664-004-6189-4
94. Karlström, D., Runeson, P., Wohlin, C.: Aggregating viewpoints for strategic software process improvement. IEE Proc. Softw. **149**(5), 143–152 (2002). doi: 10.1049/ip-sen:20020696
95. Kitchenham, B.A.: The role of replications in empirical software engineering – a word of warning. Empir. Softw. Eng. **13**, 219–221 (2008). URL 10.1007/s10664-008-9061-0
96. Kitchenham, B.A., Charters, S.: Guidelines for performing systematic literature reviews in software engineering (version 2.3). Technical Report, EBSE Technical Report EBSE-2007-01, Keele University and Durham University (2007)
97. Kitchenham, B.A., Pickard, L.M., Pfleeger, S.L.: Case studies for method and tool evaluation. IEEE Softw. **12**(4), 52–62 (1995)
98. Kitchenham, B.A., Pfleeger, S.L., Pickard, L.M., Jones, P.W., Hoaglin, D.C., El Emam, K., Rosenberg, J.: Preliminary guidelines for empirical research in software engineering. IEEE Trans. Softw. Eng. **28**(8), 721–734 (2002). doi: 10.1109/TSE.2002.1027796. URL http://ieeexplore.ieee.org/lpdocs/epic03/wrapper.htm?arnumber=1027796
99. Kitchenham, B., Fry, J., Linkman, S.G.: The case against cross-over designs in software engineering. In: Proceedings of the 11th International Workshop on Software Technology and Engineering Practice, Amsterdam, pp. 65–67. IEEE Computer Society, Los Alamitos (2003)
100. Kitchenham, B.A., Dybå, T., Jørgensen, M.: Evidence-based software engineering. In: Proceedings of the 26th International Conference on Software Engineering, Edinburgh, pp. 273–281 (2004)
101. Kitchenham, B.A., Al-Khilidar, H., Babar, M.A., Berry, M., Cox, K., Keung, J., Kurniawati, F., Staples, M., Zhang, H., Zhu, L.: Evaluating guidelines for reporting empirical software engineering studies. Empir. Softw. Eng. **13**(1), 97–121 (2007). doi: 10.1007/s10664-007-9053-5. URL http://www.springerlink.com/index/10.1007/s10664-007-9053-5
102. Kitchenham, B.A., Jeffery, D.R., Connaughton, C.: Misleading metrics and unsound analyses. IEEE Softw. **24**, 73–78 (2007). doi: 10.1109/MS.2007.49
103. Kitchenham, B.A., Brereton, P., Budgen, D., Turner, M., Bailey, J., Linkman, S.G.: Systematic literature reviews in software engineering – a systematic literature review. Inf. Softw. Technol. **51**(1), 7–15 (2009). doi: 10.1016/j.infsof.2008.09.009. URL http://www.dx.doi.org/10.1016/j.infsof.2008.09.009
104. Kitchenham, B.A., Pretorius, R., Budgen, D., Brereton, P., Turner, M., Niazi, M., Linkman, S.: Systematic literature reviews in software engineering – a tertiary study. Inf. Softw. Technol. **52**(8), 792–805 (2010). doi: 10.1016/j.infsof.2010.03.006
105. Kitchenham, B.A., Sjøberg, D.I.K., Brereton, P., Budgen, D., Dybå, T., Höst, M., Pfahl, D., Runeson, P.: Can we evaluate the quality of software engineering experiments? In: Proceedings of the 4th ACM-IEEE International Symposium on Empirical Software Engineering and Measurement. ACM, Bolzano/Bozen (2010)
106. Kitchenham, B.A., Budgen, D., Brereton, P.: Using mapping studies as the basis for further research – a participant-observer case study. Inf. Softw. Technol. **53**(6), 638–651 (2011). doi: 10.1016/j.infsof.2010.12.011

107. Laitenberger, O., Atkinson, C., Schlich, M., El Emam, K.: An experimental comparison of reading techniques for defect detection in UML design documents. J. Syst. Softw. **53**(2), 183–204 (2000)
108. Larsson, R.: Case survey methodology: quantitative analysis of patterns across case studies. Acad. Manag. J. **36**(6), 1515–1546 (1993)
109. Lee, A.S.: A scientific methodology for MIS case studies. MIS Q. **13**(1), 33 (1989). doi: 10.2307/248698. URL http://www.jstor.org/stable/248698?origin=crossref
110. Lehman, M.M.: Program, life-cycles and the laws of software evolution. Proc. IEEE **68**(9), 1060–1076 (1980)
111. Lethbridge, T.C., Sim, S.E., Singer, J.: Studying software engineers: data collection techniques for software field studies. Empir. Softw. Eng. **10**, 311–341 (2005)
112. Linger, R.: Cleanroom process model. IEEE Softw. pp. 50–58 (1994)
113. Linkman, S., Rombach, H.D.: Experimentation as a vehicle for software technology transfer – a family of software reading techniques. Inf. Softw. Technol. **39**(11), 777–780 (1997)
114. Lucas, W.A.: The case survey method: aggregating case experience. Technical Report, R-1515-RC, The RAND Corporation, Santa Monica (1974)
115. Lucas, H.C., Kaplan, R.B.: A structured programming experiment. Comput. J. **19**(2), 136–138 (1976)
116. Lyu, M.R. (ed.): Handbook of Software Reliability Engineering. McGraw-Hill, New York (1996)
117. Maldonado, J.C., Carver, J., Shull, F., Fabbri, S., Dória, E., Martimiano, L., Mendonça, M., Basili, V.: Perspective-based reading: a replicated experiment focused on individual reviewer effectiveness. Empir. Softw. Eng. **11**, 119–142 (2006). doi: 10.1007/s10664-006-5967-6
118. Manly, B.F.J.: Multivariate Statistical Methods: A Primer, 2nd edn. Chapman and Hall, London (1994)
119. Marascuilo, L.A., Serlin, R.C.: Statistical Methods for the Social and Behavioral Sciences. W. H. Freeman and Company, New York (1988)
120. Miller, J.: Estimating the number of remaining defects after inspection. Softw. Test. Verif. Reliab. **9**(4), 167–189 (1999)
121. Miller, J.: Applying meta-analytical procedures to software engineering experiments. J. Syst. Softw. **54**(1), 29–39 (2000)
122. Miller, J.: Statistical significance testing: a panacea for software technology experiments? J. Syst. Softw. **73**, 183–192 (2004). doi: http://dx.doi.org/10.1016/j.jss.2003.12.019
123. Miller, J.: Replicating software engineering experiments: a poisoned chalice or the holy grail. Inf. Softw. Technol. **47**(4), 233–244 (2005)
124. Miller, J., Wood, M., Roper, M.: Further experiences with scenarios and checklists. Empir. Softw. Eng. **3**(1), 37–64 (1998)
125. Montgomery, D.C.: Design and Analysis of Experiments, 5th edn. Wiley, New York (2000)
126. Myers, G.J.: A controlled experiment in program testing and code walkthroughs/inspections. Commun. ACM **21**, 760–768 (1978). doi: http://doi.acm.org/10.1145/359588.359602
127. Noblit, G.W., Hare, R.D.: Meta-Ethnography: Synthesizing Qualitative Studies. Sage Publications, Newbury Park (1988)
128. Ohlsson, M.C., Wohlin, C.: A project effort estimation study. Inf. Softw. Technol. **40**(14), 831–839 (1998)
129. Owen, S., Brereton, P., Budgen, D.: Protocol analysis: a neglected practice. Commun. ACM **49**(2), 117–122 (2006). doi: 10.1145/1113034.1113039
130. Paulk, M.C., Curtis, B., Chrissis, M.B., Weber, C.V.: Capability maturity model for software. Technical Report, CMU/SEI-93-TR-24, Software Engineering Institute, Pittsburgh (1993)
131. Petersen, K., Feldt, R., Mujtaba, S., Mattsson, M.: Systematic mapping studies in software engineering. In: Proceedings of the 12th International Conference on Evaluation and Assessment in Software Engineering, Electronic Workshops in Computing (eWIC). BCS, University of Bari, Italy (2008)
132. Petersen, K., Wohlin, C.: Context in industrial software engineering research. In: Proceedings of the 3rd ACM-IEEE International Symposium on Empirical Software Engineering and Measurement, Lake Buena Vista, pp. 401–404 (2009)

133. Pfleeger, S.L.: Experimental design and analysis in software engineering part 1–5. ACM Sigsoft, Softw. Eng. Notes, **19**(4), 16–20; **20**(1), 22–26; **20**(2), 14–16; **20**(3), 13–15; **20**, (1994)
134. Pfleeger, S.L., Atlee, J.M.: Software Engineering: Theory and Practice, 4th edn. Pearson Prentice-Hall, Upper Saddle River (2009)
135. Pickard, L.M., Kitchenham, B.A., Jones, P.W.: Combining empirical results in software engineering. Inf. Softw. Technol. **40**(14), 811–821 (1998). doi: 10.1016/S0950-5849(98) 00101-3
136. Porter, A.A., Votta, L.G.: An experiment to assess different defect detection methods for software requirements inspections. In: Proceedings of the 16th International Conference on Software Engineering, Sorrento, pp. 103–112 (1994)
137. Porter, A.A., Votta, L.G.: Comparing detection methods for software requirements inspection: a replicated experiment. IEEE Trans. Softw. Eng. **21**(6), 563–575 (1995)
138. Porter, A.A., Votta, L.G.: Comparing detection methods for software requirements inspection: a replicated experimentation: a replication using professional subjects. Empir. Softw. Eng. **3**(4), 355–380 (1998)
139. Porter, A.A., Siy, H.P., Toman, C.A., Votta, L.G.: An experiment to assess the cost-benefits of code inspections in large scale software development. IEEE Trans. Softw. Eng. **23**(6), 329–346 (1997)
140. Potts, C.: Software engineering research revisited. IEEE Softw. pp. 19–28 (1993)
141. Rainer, A.W.: The longitudinal, chronological case study research strategy: a definition, and an example from IBM Hursley Park. Inf. Softw. Technol. **53**(7), 730–746 (2011)
142. Robinson, H., Segal, J., Sharp, H.: Ethnographically-informed empirical studies of software practice. Inf. Softw. Technol. **49**(6), 540–551 (2007). doi: 10.1016/j.infsof.2007.02.007
143. Robson, C.: Real World Research: A Resource for Social Scientists and Practitioners-Researchers, 1st edn. Blackwell, Oxford/Cambridge (1993)
144. Robson, C.: Real World Research: A Resource for Social Scientists and Practitioners-Researchers, 2nd edn. Blackwell, Oxford/Madden (2002)
145. Runeson, P., Skoglund, M.: Reference-based search strategies in systematic reviews. In: Proceedings of the 13th International Conference on Empirical Assessment and Evaluation in Software Engineering. Electronic Workshops in Computing (eWIC). BCS, Durham University, UK (2009)
146. Runeson, P., Höst, M., Rainer, A.W., Regnell, B.: Case Study Research in Software Engineering. Guidelines and Examples. Wiley, Hoboken (2012)
147. Sandahl, K., Blomkvist, O., Karlsson, J., Krysander, C., Lindvall, M., Ohlsson, N.: An extended replication of an experiment for assessing methods for software requirements. Empir. Softw. Eng. **3**(4), 381–406 (1998)
148. Seaman, C.B.: Qualitative methods in empirical studies of software engineering. IEEE Trans. Softw. Eng. **25**(4), 557–572 (1999)
149. Selby, R.W., Basili, V.R., Baker, F.T.: Cleanroom software development: An empirical evaluation. IEEE Trans. Softw. Eng. **13**(9), 1027–1037 (1987)
150. Shepperd, M.: Foundations of Software Measurement. Prentice-Hall, London/New York (1995)
151. Shneiderman, B., Mayer, R., McKay, D., Heller, P.: Experimental investigations of the utility of detailed flowcharts in programming. Commun. ACM **20**, 373–381 (1977). doi: 10.1145/ 359605.359610
152. Shull, F.: Developing techniques for using software documents: a series of empirical studies. Ph.D. thesis, Computer Science Department, University of Maryland, USA (1998)
153. Shull, F., Basili, V.R., Carver, J., Maldonado, J.C., Travassos, G.H., Mendonça, M.G., Fabbri, S.: Replicating software engineering experiments: addressing the tacit knowledge problem. In: Proceedings of the 1st International Symposium on Empirical Software Engineering, Nara, pp. 7–16 (2002)
154. Shull, F., Mendonçça, M.G., Basili, V.R., Carver, J., Maldonado, J.C., Fabbri, S., Travassos, G.H., Ferreira, M.C.: Knowledge-sharing issues in experimental software engineering. Empir. Softw. Eng. **9**, 111–137 (2004). doi: 10.1023/B:EMSE.0000013516.80487.33

155. Shull, F., Carver, J., Vegas, S., Juristo, N.: The role of replications in empirical software engineering. Empir. Softw. Eng. **13**, 211–218 (2008). doi: 10.1007/s10664-008-9060-1

156. Sieber, J.E.: Protecting research subjects, employees and researchers: implications for software engineering. Empir. Softw. Eng. **6**(4), 329–341 (2001)

157. Siegel, S., Castellan, J.: Nonparametric Statistics for the Behavioral Sciences, 2nd edn. McGraw-Hill International Editions, New York (1988)

158. Singer, J., Vinson, N.G.: Why and how research ethics matters to you. Yes, you! Empir. Softw. Eng. **6**, 287–290 (2001). doi: 10.1023/A:1011998412776

159. Singer, J., Vinson, N.G.: Ethical issues in empirical studies of software engineering. IEEE Trans. Softw. Eng. **28**(12), 1171–1180 (2002). doi: 10.1109/TSE.2002.1158289. URL http://ieeexplore.ieee.org/lpdocs/epic03/wrapper.htm?arnumber=1158289

160. Simon S.: Fermat's Last Theorem. Fourth Estate, London (1997)

161. Sjøberg, D.I.K., Hannay, J.E., Hansen, O., Kampenes, V.B., Karahasanovic, A., Liborg, N.-K., Rekdal, A.C.: A survey of controlled experiments in software engineering. IEEE Trans. Softw. Eng. **31**(9), 733–753 (2005). doi: 10.1109/TSE.2005.97. URL http://ieeexplore.ieee. org/lpdocs/epic03/wrapper.htm?arnumber=1514443

162. Sjøberg, D.I.K., Dybå, T., Anda, B., Hannay, J.E.: Building theories in software engineering. In: Shull, F., Singer, J., Sjøberg D. (eds.) Guide to Advanced Empirical Software Engineering. Springer, London (2008)

163. Sommerville, I.: Software Engineering, 9th edn. Addison-Wesley, Wokingham, England/ Reading (2010)

164. Sørumgård, S.: Verification of process conformance in empirical studies of software development. Ph.D. thesis, The Norwegian University of Science and Technology, Department of Computer and Information Science, Norway (1997)

165. Stake, R.E.: The Art of Case Study Research. SAGE Publications, Thousand Oaks (1995)

166. Staples, M., Niazi, M.: Experiences using systematic review guidelines. J. Syst. Softw. **80**(9), 1425–1437 (2007). doi: 10.1016/j.jss.2006.09.046

167. Thelin, T., Runeson, P.: Capture-recapture estimations for perspective-based reading – a simulated experiment. In: Proceedings of the 1st International Conference on Product Focused Software Process Improvement (PROFES), Oulu, pp. 182–200 (1999)

168. Thelin, T., Runeson, P., Wohlin, C.: An experimental comparison of usage-based and checklist-based reading. IEEE Trans. Softw. Eng. **29**(8), 687–704 (2003). doi: 10.1109/ TSE.2003.1223644

169. Tichy, W.F.: Should computer scientists experiment more? IEEE Comput. **31**(5), 32–39 (1998)

170. Tichy, W.F., Lukowicz, P., Prechelt, L., Heinz, E.A.: Experimental evaluation in computer science: a quantitative study. J. Syst. Softw. **28**(1), 9–18 (1995)

171. Trochim, W.M.K.: The Research Methods Knowledge Base, 2nd edn. Cornell Custom Publishing, Cornell University, Ithaca (1999)

172. van Solingen, R., Berghout, E.: The Goal/Question/Metric Method: A Practical Guide for Quality Improvement and Software Development. McGraw-Hill International, London/Chicago (1999)

173. Verner, J.M., Sampson, J., Tosic, V., Abu Bakar, N.A., Kitchenham, B.A.: Guidelines for industrially-based multiple case studies in software engineering. In: Third International Conference on Research Challenges in Information Science, Fez, pp. 313–324 (2009)

174. Vinson, N.G., Singer, J.: A practical guide to ethical research involving humans. In: Shull, F., Singer, J., Sjøberg, D. (eds.) Guide to Advanced Empirical Software Engineering. Springer, London (2008)

175. Votta, L.G.: Does every inspection need a meeting? In: Proceedings of the ACM SIGSOFT Symposium on Foundations of Software Engineering, ACM Software Engineering Notes, vol. 18, pp. 107–114. ACM Press, New York (1993)

176. Wallace, C., Cook, C., Summet, J., Burnett, M.: Human centric computing languages and environments. In: Proceedings of Symposia on Human Centric Computing Languages and Environments, Arlington, pp. 63–65 (2002)

177. Wohlin, C., Gustavsson, A., Höst, M., Mattsson, C.: A framework for technology introduction in software organizations. In: Proceedings of the Conference on Software Process Improvement, Brighton, pp. 167–176 (1996)
178. Wohlin, C., Runeson, P., Höst, M., Ohlsson, M.C., Regnell, B., Wesslén, A.: Experimentation in Software Engineering: An Introduction. Kluwer, Boston (2000)
179. Wohlin, C., Aurum, A., Angelis, L., Phillips, L., Dittrich, Y., Gorschek, T., Grahn, H., Henningsson, K., Kågström, S., Low, G., Rovegård, P., Tomaszewski, P., van Toorn, C., Winter, J.: Success factors powering industry-academia collaboration in software research. IEEE Softw. (PrePrints) (2011). doi: 10.1109/MS.2011.92
180. Yin, R.K.: Case Study Research Design and Methods, 4th edn. Sage Publications, Beverly Hills (2009)
181. Zelkowitz, M.V., Wallace, D.R.: Experimental models for validating technology. IEEE Comput. 31(5), 23–31 (1998)
182. Zendler, A.: A preliminary software engineering theory as investigated by published experiments. Empir. Softw. Eng. 6, 161–180 (2001). doi: http://dx.doi.org/10.1023/A:1011489321999

Index

Printed in the United States
by Baker & Taylor Publisher Services